LIQUID BREAD

THE ANTHROPOLOGY OF FOOD AND NUTRITION

General Editor: *Helen Macbeth*

LIQUID BREAD

Beer and Brewing in Cross-Cultural Perspective

Edited by

Wulf Schiefenhövel and Helen Macbeth

Berghahn Books

New York • Oxford

First published in 2011 by

Berghahn Books
www.BerghahnBooks.com

Library of Congress Cataloging-in-Publication Data

Liquid bread : beer and brewing in cross-cultural perspective / edited by
Wulf Schiefenhövel and Helen Macbeth.
    p. cm.
Includes bibliographical references and index.
ISBN 978-0-85745-215-3 (hardback : alk. paper) -- ISBN 978-0-85745-216-0
(ebook : alk. paper)
1. Drinking customs--Cross-cultural studies. 2. Drinking of alcoholic
beverages--Cross-cultural studies. 3. Beer--Social aspects. 4. Brewing--Social
aspects. I. Schiefenhövel, Wulf, 1943- II. Macbeth, Helen M.
GT2884.L57 2011   1006509136
394.1'2--dc22
                    2011006667

British Library Cataloguing in Publication Data

A catalogue record for this book is available from the British Library

Printed in the United States on acid-free paper

ISBN: 978-0-85745-215-3 (hardback)
E-ISBN: 978-0-85745-216-0

CONTENTS

LIST OF FIGURES

LIST OF TABLES

PREFACE

Five thousand years ago, in today's Iraq, groups of scribes were busy carefully indenting cuneiform symbols in tables of wet clay. The output of this early form of writing must have been enormous, as museums and other collections are filled with evidence of their sedulousness. These texts usually do not report on successful wars of kings or princes, of other heroic deeds or about the drama of human life, love and death; they are just dry pieces of bookkeeping. Moreover, and this is surprising, a lot of this material centres around the production of cereals, the area needed to grow them, the amount of grain which could be harvested and the transformation of this grain into bread and beer. There is a great deal of arithmetic in these records: e.g., how many vessels, of which size, for what kind of beer, etc., should be produced. Obviously this part of administration was very important to the people concerned (Nissen, Damerow and Englund 1993; Damerow 1996). A large number of workers needed to be fed and given drink. Beer seems to have served both of these purposes at the same time. It is likely that specific preparations of bread were used in the first steps of beer production. Bread and beer are thus, from the onset of brewing in Mesopotamia, sisters in kind.

The title of this book refers to this early connection of bread and beer, as well as to the fact that in Bavaria, beer is colloquially named 'liquid bread'; a term which tells of the close connection of beer to daily nutrition in this part of the world, home of an astoundingly large number of breweries and of some of the world's finest beers. 'Liquid Bread' was thus an appropriate term to use for the conference on beer from which this volume arises, as this was held in Bavaria as one of the annual multidisciplinary conferences of the International Commission on the Anthropology of Food and Nutrition (ICAF).

The editors are most grateful to the Bavarian Brewers' Association, the Bavarian State Ministery for Science, Research and Art Association for Public Relations of the German Brewing Industry, Andechs Monastery Brewery, the Max-Planck-Society and the private brewery, Erdinger Weissbier, for support of the conference. We were very fortunate to be allowed to enjoy the facilities of the Max Planck Institute, Seewiessen, for the conference. We wish to thank Sabine Eggebrecht for assistance with the conference, and Cristina Toma, Toni

Cândea, Martina Vlkova, Cecilia Busby and Mandy Archer for assistance in preparing the manuscript for this volume.

WS and HMM
(December 2010)

References

Damerow, P. (1996) Food Production and Social Status as Documented in Proto-Cuneiform Texts. In Wiessner P. and Schiefenhövel, W. (eds) *Food and the Status Quest*, Berghahn Books, Oxford: 149–69.

Nissen, H.J., Damerow, P. and Englund, R.K. (1993*) Archaic Bookkeeping: Early writing and techniques of economic administration*, Chicago University Press, Chicago.

LIST OF CONTRIBUTORS

Dr Dante Aquino
Department of Environmental Science
and Management, College of Forestry and
Environmental Management, Isabela State
University, Cabagan, Isabela, Philippines

Dr François Belliard
Laboratoire Ligérien de Linguistique,
University of Orleans, Orléans, France

Prof. Dr Martin Brüne
Research Department for Cognitive
Neuropsychiatry and Psychiatric Preventive
Medicine, LWL University Hospital, Bochum,
Germany

Dr Luis Cantarero
Department of Psychology and Sociology,
University of Zaragoza, Zaragoza, Spain

Dr Paul Collinson
Anthropology Department, Oxford Brookes
University, Oxford, UK

Dr med. Gerhard Dammann
Psychiatric Services, Canton of Thurgau,
Münsterlingen, Switzerland

Dr Berthold Einwag
Institute for Near-Eastern Archaeology,
Ludwig Maximilian University, Munich,
Germany

Dr Igor de Garine
UMR 7206 Eco-anthropology and
Ethnobiology, Centre Nationale de la
Recherche Scientifique, France

Dra. Isabel González Turmo
Department of Social Anthropology,
University of Seville, Seville, Spain

Dr Mabel Gracia Arnaiz
Department of Anthropology, Philosophy and
Social Work, University of Rovira and Virgili,
Tarragona, Spain

Dr Monica Janowski   Department of Anthropology and Sociology,
                                School of Oriental and African Studies,
                                University of London, London, UK

Dr Peter Kaiser   Day Clinic for Psychiatry and Psychotherapy,
                                Schwäbisch Gmünd, Baden-Württemberg,
                                Germany

Dr. Ruth Kutalek   Ethnomedicine and International Health,
                                Centre for Public Health, Medical University
                                of Vienna, Vienna, Austria

Dr Helen Macbeth   Anthropology Department, Oxford Brookes
                                University, Oxford, UK

Prof. William McGrew   Leverhulme Centre for Human Evolutionary
                                Studies, Department of Biological
                                Anthropology, University of Cambridge,
                                Cambridge, UK

Dr Gerhard Medicus   Psychiatric Clinic, Hall, Tyrol, Austria

Dr F. Xavier Medina   Department of Food Systems, Culture and
                                Society, Open University of Catalonia,
                                Barcelona, Spain

Prof. Dr Adelheid Otto   Institute for Egyptology and Ancient Oriental
                                Studies, Johannes Gutenberg University,
                                Mainz, Germany

Dr Jana Parizkova   Obesity Management Centre, Institute of
                                Endocrinology, Prague, Czech Republic

Prof. Dr Gerard Persoon   Faculty of Social Sciences, Institute of Cultural
                                Anthropology and Developmental Sociology,
                                University of Leiden, Leiden, Netherlands

Dr Nancy Pollock   Departments of Anthropology and
                                Development Studies, Victoria University,
                                Wellington, New Zealand

Prof. Dr Wulf Schiefenhövel Human Ethology Group, Max Planck Institute,
                                Andechs, Germany

Monica Stacconi   Official School of Languages, Alcalá de
                                Henares, Spain

Dr Hans-Peter Stika   Archaeobotany and History of Vegetation,
                                Institute of Botany, University of Hohenheim,
                                Stuttgart, Germany

Dr Keith Thomas   Brewlab, Faculty of Applied Sciences,
                                    University of Sunderland, Sunderland, UK

Prof. Dr Walter van Beek   Department of Religious Studies, University
                                    of Tilburg, Tilburg, Netherlands

Martina Vlkova   Institute of Tropics and Subtropics, Czech
                                    University of Life Sciences, Prague, Czech
                                    Republic

Dr Martin Zarnkow   Weihenstephan Science Centre for Nutrition,
                                    Land Use and Environment, Technical
                                    University of Munich, Munich, Germany

INTRODUCTION
ASSEMBLING PERSPECTIVES ON BEER

Wulf Schiefenhövel and *Helen Macbeth*

What made you pick up this book? Was it the thought of that foaming pint while you relaxed in a British pub, a German beer garden, a Czech restaurant, an American or 'Continental' bar, on a beach or ski slope or in front of the television at home? Wherever your beer was purchased, in much of the world you would have been offered choice. The choice might only have been between different brand names of bottled beer, or it might have been between a wide range of ales, lagers, wheat and other beers from a cask, a keg, cans or bottles. Even people who do not drink beer will be aware of this diversity. Advertising proclaims that diversity. The brand names might enhance your enjoyment with imagined scenes stimulated by the advertisers. However, how much do you know about the marketing strategies behind the brand names? About the technologies of producing the diversity? About beer and brewing in antiquity or in non-European cultures? About the beneficial biological effects, as well as the risks of beer drinking? About the beers in societies of simple technology? About the symbolism and social importance of beer in totally different societies? About the important social roles of the conviviality engendered by beer?

This volume highlights the fact that, despite almost global commercial marketing of modern beers, beer brewed according to traditional recipes in other parts of the world can be very different from what most of us are used to. This was also the case for the prehistoric types of beer and even for beer drunk until about the middle of the nineteenth century, since these early beers were often mixed with all kinds of ingredients. It was often quite weak, with alcohol contents similar to our modern low alcohol products. This was frequently desired because beer, partially sterilised by the carbonic acid and the alcohol in it, was often drunk instead of water which could be polluted and a risk to health. It was given to children, even to pupils in schools (Schiefenhövel personal notes, and see www.effilee.de/wissen/Bier.html).

The chapters of our book bring together in a novel way discussions of evolutionary, archaeological, biomedical, technical, commercial, ethnographic, social and psychological facets of the rich cosmos of beer. In its cross-cultural and cross-disciplinary approach, the volume reflects the interests of the members of the International Commission on the Anthropology of Food and Nutrition (ICAF) (http://www.icafood.eu, see also the Preface), but the editors believe that this collation of perspectives on beer will also intrigue many readers in the general public.

For many, thinking about beer may first suggest the quenching of thirst on a hot day, as well as happy scenes in a convivial setting. In this volume, a deeper understanding of its social role in promoting conviviality and enjoyment in company is stressed. For example, Pollock (chapter 12) writing on male beer-drinking customs in New Zealand, de Garine (chapter 13) on beer-enhanced conviviality in Northern Cameroon, and Dammann (chapter 11) on beer drinking in university fraternities, all discuss, among other topics, the social role of beer because it benefits communication. Beer is, of course, also enjoyed for its different and interesting tastes, and undoubtedly also for the effects of alcohol on the brain. McGrew (chapter 1) presents examples of little studied voluntary ethanol ingestion among nonhuman animals. It is most likely that alcohol is acting on 'dock-on' mechanisms in the brain, originally evolved to facilitate biopsychological rewards. Moderate doses of alcohol will generally make people feel well, be a bit more social, talkative and outgoing (Kaiser, Medicus and Brüne, chapter 2). This creates a group effect, a feeling of belonging, which is important for us humans as social animals. This aspect of drinking beer, because it enhances social interactions, is, in one form or another, present in almost all the contributions to this book, and a topic returned to below.

The ways in which beer is consumed, even its preferred temperature, can be very different in different societies. North Americans like it very cold, as do many people in warm and tropical countries. To achieve this, glasses may be taken from the freezer before they are filled with beer. Others, such as connoisseurs in England, prefer to get their beer served at room temperature. In Germany, the host may ask you: 'Do you want your beer from the fridge or from the cellar?' The chosen answer may be used to reflect the knowledge of a true local. Bavarians have an unusual custom: in winter or when a person is suffering from some stomach or other health trouble, he may ask for his beer to be heated.

Brewing beer is a sophisticated process of which even afficionados may not be fully aware. This book provides information about modern brewing methods and also about how beer was made in antiquity and is still made in some traditional societies today. Thomas (chapter 3) gives an introduction to the complex, sophisticated process of modern industrial beer production. Zarnkow, Otto and Einwag (chapter 4) have carried out novel experimental studies which shed light on how beer was brewed in antiquity, i.e., around the time when this important food technology was first developed in Mesopotamia.

Stika (personal communication) argues that while agriculture and growing cereals had spread to Europe from the Near East, it is likely that beer brewing may have emerged in Europe, as in different parts of the world, independently and during different periods. In Chapter 5, Stika reports on findings of archaeological research in several sites in Europe where vessels, in which 'beerstone' can be detected with modern chemical techniques, indicate that they are likely to have been used for repeated beer brewing. Furthermore, by presenting his findings of evidence of charred barley malt in early Celtic drying-kilns from the Hochdorf site in southern Germany, he tries to reconstruct the taste of the early Celtic beer of Hochdorf.

In many other parts of the world methods of making beer are known. In pre-European South America, *chicha* was a drink that had for centuries been made from fermented maize starch (http://en.wikipedia.org/wiki/Chicha) and must have been the result of independent discovery, rather than by cultural migration of brewing knowledge. Belliard (chapter 16) describes, illustrated by schematic sketches, the different steps of brewing sorghum beer in the African country, Burkina Faso.

The technical term 'beer' is used for any alcoholic drink which is produced by fermenting sugar-rich extracts derived from any of a variety of starchy plants. The link with bread has already been mentioned in the Preface and beers made from bread still exist in some parts of the world (Samuel 2000). The majority of beers are and have been brewed from cereal grains, e.g. wild Einkorn (*Triticum boeoticum*); domesticated Einkorn (*Triticum monococcum*, a species which is known to have been used in antiquity, e.g., in Mesopotamia); the related wheat cultivars (*Triticum* spp.) and barley (*Hordeum vulgare*) in Europe; maize (*Zea mays*) in the Americas; rice (*Oryza sativa*) and millet (various genera of grass plants, belonging to the *Poaceae* family) in China; or sorghum (various genera of *Poaceae*) in China, India and modern Africa (Hornsey 2003). Nevertheless, other starchy vegetable matter has also been used for making beer-like beverages: Lewin and Levin (1998) refer to chewed manioc being used in South America.

The beers brewed by the large multinational brewing companies, by traditional local breweries, or by small specialist microbreweries in Europe or North America today are mostly based on barley which has been malted (see Thomas, chapter 3). However, to get an alcoholic drink from grains and starchy plants is quite difficult. There is no readily available sugar in these grains, but the more complex compound, starch. The human and mammalian body has enzymes (e.g., amylase), essential in digestion, which break down the starch and turn it into glucose. Mammalian physiology can do this chemical transformation quite swiftly, but to do the same outside the body takes processing. The breaking down of the starch contained in grain is exemplified in several chapters, which describe brewing processes in different periods and in various parts of the world. Zarnkow, Otto and Einwag (chapter 4) discovered that a weak beer can be made through exposure to the sun without an additional heat source. It is thus very likely, and a new insight, that beer brewers in antiquity, in this case in northern Syria of the Late Bronze Age, could simply rely on the sun's energy. In prehistoric Europe, on the other hand, malting was achieved by using the heat of fire, as Stika (chapter 5) describes. In a traditional African society in Burkina Faso a rich array of linguistic terms serves to identify the complex stepwise process of brewing beer described by Belliard (chapter 16), who shows how this exemplifies the local ways of perceiving this ancient craft. The chapter also includes ethnographic descriptions of how beer is consumed and its social significance.

In our own modern society beer brewing has become a 'high-tech' process. Thomas (chapter 3) explains not only the basic principles of beer brewing but also how the differences in taste are brought about. This is an important aspect for the brewing industry because the consumption of classic beers is gradually declining while consumption of wine and non-alcoholic drinks is rising. The answer of the breweries is to diversify, to produce new types of beers, beer-containing drinks and beers with low alcohol. The traditional wheat beers, *Weizenbier*, also called *Weissbier*, of Bavaria and other regions of Europe are top-fermenting beers, as was the traditional method of brewing in earlier times. These have a slightly lower alcohol content than bottom-fermenting la-ger beers and have experienced a recent surge in popularity, especially among women in Germany, for whom unfiltered wheat beers with high yeast content are considered particularly healthy. On the other hand, the bottom-fermenta-tion technique requires a cooling space, cold caves in the past and refrigeration in modern times, but because of their stable quality, even after long storage, this type of lager beer (e.g., Pilsner or *Pils*) became popular internationally.

The result is that beer-making is a much more complex procedure than wine-making. It is the extraction of the sugars from grains or other starchy plants through sprouting, malting and mashing which provides the classifica-tory difference between those alcoholic drinks called 'beers' and those called 'wines'. The latter are derived from fermenting sugary fruits, a much simpler biochemical process which can happen even without human interference. Also technically a wine, the fermentation of a mixture of honey and water produces mead, which in pre-Roman times was very popular in Northern Europe and is currently experiencing a small renaissance. Then there are the wines made from saps such as bamboo wine and palm wine (Battcock and Azam-Ali 1998). A palm wine (*tuak*) is made and drunk in Indonesia and in New Guinea. As with all classifications, some marginal cases exist, for example parsnip wine and banana wine, as do cases where the nomenclature is misleading, such as rice wine and barley wine. Janowski (chapter 17) reports on a rice beer (*bo-rak*) in Sarawak. Drawing upon early post-Second World War reports by Tom Harrisson and her own later research based on reports from local informants, she describes the significant social role of *borak* drinking in the traditional life of that society. However, she goes on to give reasons why *borak* was aban-doned in association with religious, economic and social changes. Aquino and Persoon (chapter 18) describe a number of traditional drinks previously con-sumed in north east Luzon in the Philippines and go on to discuss their replacement by beer brewed by modern, multinational, commercial breweries and the significance of one large company in particular. What is striking in the above examples is that the drinking of alcohol of some sort is central to the social gathering and ceremonies of peoples in different societies.

Originally fermentation of wine, most likely the oldest alcoholic drink (McGovern 2003), was probably promoted by wild yeasts, such as *Sacchero-myces exiguus* or *Saccheromyces minor*. The genetic variation between and within the various species of the *Saccheromyces* genus has now been studied at the molecular level (http://www.yeastgenome.org) and different, carefully controlled variants, are today used industrially in the production of different types of beer and wine. Bakers' yeast, *Saccheromyces cerevisiae*, is most commonly used not only for bread but also for several types of fermentation for alcoholic beverages. It is used for most ales, while *Saccheromyces carlsbergensis* or *Saccheromyces pastorianus* tend to be used in lagers, but there are variants of this genus for further diversity in the fermentation process and taste (http://www.yeastgenome.org). It is interesting that in making the two most important alcoholic drinks worldwide, wine and beer, the same class of microorganism has been used since ancient times.

Alcohol was and is consumed in very many traditional societies, but where it is not, some alternative forms of mind-altering drugs will usually be found. The First Nations of North America, as well as the Melanesians, Micronesians and Polynesians of the South Pacific, are examples of peoples who did not develop an indigenous technology of beer brewing, nor did they make wine, even though either would have been environmentally possible, since there were starchy or sugary plants available as raw material. South Pacific islanders traditionally made and make *kava*, a non-alcoholic but mildly hallucinogenic drink, made from *Piper methysticum* (Mückler 1996), and in many countries of the West Pacific, as well as in southern India and Taiwan, chewing betel nut *(Areca catechu)* has been very popular since pre-European times (Farnworth 1976).

These examples, together with the multitude of other hallucinogenic drugs consumed now and in the past around the world, serve to demonstrate that humans, as a species, derive pleasure in escaping from the realities of everyday life through altered states of consciousness, regardless of how bad the consequences which may later plague the body. Douglas (1987: 11) suggests that alcohol can help a drinker gain the sensation of 'an intelligible, bearable world' closer to imagined ideals.

It can thus be argued that taking some form of mind-altering stimulant has a social role. In many cases this is connected to social and religious ceremonies. Alcohol is among those substances which create a special experience, generating, in the perception of those ingesting them, psychosocial interaction and communication with the supernatural. Beer fits this pattern of a catalyst to various social activities, as is apparent from three chapters regarding fieldwork in Africa. Regarding six ethnic groups in north-west Cameroon, de Garine (chapter 13) provides a broad-ranging and holistic ethnography with information on the brewing processes and timetable and on the nutritional and intoxicating effects, but what is relevant to this introduction are the local concepts with regard to mythology and religion and the social aspects, including value and the stimulation of pleasure. Van Beek (chapter 14) concentrates on beer symbolism, and with detailed fieldwork notes he compares two African societies, the Kapsiki/Higi in north Cameroon and the Dogon of Mali, with emphasis on gender roles. In chapter 15, Kutalek refers to several traditionally brewed alcoholic drinks in Tanzania, and describes in detail the ritual use of the local *pombe* beer of the Bena in South West Tanzania. She gives examples of her informants' ideas on beer production, consumption and social meaning.

In the specific context of university fraternities in USA and Germany, and in their fraternity ceremonies and rituals, Dammann (chapter 11) describes the often excessive student consumption of beer, but he also draws attention to some fraternity rules which perhaps contribute to a limitation of frequency of excessive drinking. He refers to data which suggest that a certain amount of binge drinking in youth, if not too frequent, may confer social advantages not only immediately but also later in life. The extensive range of social perspectives on why societies maintain beer-drinking cultures must remain limited in this volume, but readers should note an earlier volume in this series edited by Igor and Valerie de Garine (2001), *Drinking: Anthropological Approaches*.

Germany (in particular in Bavaria, but elsewhere too) and the Czech Republic are countries with rich traditions of beer brewing. The monasteries in these and neighbouring countries, which housed not only the academic but also the technological elites of their times, began to brew beer in the seventh century. As Meussdoerffer (chapter 6) recounts, the then newly emerging cities had their first breweries. Even though hops (a member of the *Cannabaceae* family) were known and grown for a long time, it was only in the twelfth century that the female flower of *Humulus lupulus* was routinely added to the mash. Hops made the beer more durable and tasty. This was a brewing innovation developed in monasteries such as Weihenstephan in Freising, one of the two oldest breweries still existing. Another is the brewery of Weltenburg Monastery on the banks of the Danube, not far from Regensburg (http://de.wikipedia.org/wiki/Bayerische_Staatsbrauerei_Weihenstephan). In Bavaria, the 'Purity Law' for beer was proclaimed in 1516 in the city of Ingolstadt by Count Wilhelm IV; it stated that only water, malt and hops were to be used in beer. For some reason yeast was not mentioned although it had always been an ingredient. The prices for beer were also regulated – and strictly controlled.

Meussdoerffer (chapter 6) takes an historical approach to the role of beer in German culture through the centuries, during which time it became the most popular beverage. He views it as unsurprising that Germans and foreigners perceive beer to be important in German national identity, but he also stresses the significance of the federal, rather than the unified, history of Germany and how that has led to a regional diversity in the beers for which Germany and its neighbours are famous. Parízková and Vlkova (chapter 10) write about beer in one of those neighbouring countries, the Czech Republic, where the reputation for its beer and beer drinking is also strongly linked to internal and external concepts of the nation. The Czech Republic is one of the cradles of the art of brewing beer. The Czech cities of Plzen (or Pilsen) and Ceske Budejovice (or Budweis) have given their names to two of the most famous beers in the world.

Medina (chapter 7) points out that it is not only in central Europe but also in the Mediterranean that beer is an ancient drink. Also interested in how drinks are used in concepts of region, Medina makes the point that beer has been excluded from the classic model of the 'Mediterranean diet'. His chapter provides a discussion of the separate images of the 'beer countries' of the north and the 'wine countries' of the south within Europe, despite the brewing and high levels of consumption of beer in countries such as Spain and Italy, and despite the production of wine wherever grapes will grow in the north, reminding the reader of the wide geographic spread of wine drinkers throughout northern latitudes. An interesting perspective to add to this subject is that while the Spanish, Portuguese and Catalans use a word for beer derived from the Latin word *cervisia*, (i.e. *cerveza*, *cerveja* and *cervesa* respectively), the Italians and French (both with 'Latin' languages) use the words, *birra* and *bière*, which like the English word *beer*, and German word *Bier*, derive from an old Germanic word.

The significance of image is similarly stressed in chapter 9 by Collinson and Macbeth with regard to Britain, where local and traditional brand names are retained for beers which are in fact brewed by very large and powerful international drink companies. Both where beer is drunk and the importance of brand names are themes in this chapter, written at a time when British pubs are closing all around the country. The pub is considered to be symbolic of something essentially British, a social centre of community life in each locality, a place of communal conviviality based on the consumption of beer. The authors show how reality has changed but an image is retained as pub owners do what they can to maintain the *image* of a traditional pub central to and enhancing a local community, because that image attracts the outsiders who enable the pub to survive.

Social conviviality, image and nationality, are also highlighted in Pollock's chapter (chapter 12), as well as a gender issue, when she describes the great significance of beer in the culture of New Zealand and its link to 'blokism' (from 'bloke', a colloquial term for 'man'), rugby and (horse) racing in a country with very high per capita consumption of beer. She includes a discussion of the strong gender differences in consumption in the past, both in image and in reality, but shows that this has been changing, although the 'beer belly' is still a visible testament to the role of beer in contemporary male culture in New Zealand.

In north European society, identity might also be flagged by our choices of wines or of beers. Demossier (2004) wrote, about wine selection, that it 'conveyed a real sense of prestige. Wine can be described as a food for hierarchy'; elsewhere (2005) she argued that by choosing which wine to buy and in what circumstances to drink it, people are 'identity building'. The truth of this can be exemplified wherever seeming knowledge of fine wines is flaunted as a form of sophistication. However, flaunting sophistication is seldom relevant to the

identity building that occurs with beer, where, in contrast to the wine connois-
seur, some individuals may wish to proclaim their 'common man' status by or-
dering beer, or they may wear their ethnicity with pride, as when a Bavarian or
Czech demonstrably chooses some local beer or an Englishman travels to find
a particular regional ale. In Denmark, Johansen *et al.* (2006) revealed symbols
of identity linked to an underlying socioeconomic effect and/or a difference
in educational level in their research on 3.5 million supermarket shopping
transactions. They found a significant correlation of purchases of wine with
purchases of generally more healthy foods (fruit, fresh vegetables, poultry, low
fat cheeses and milk, etc.), while purchases of beer correlated with less healthy
foods (chips, sausages, pork, lamb, ready-prepared meals, sugar, charcuterie,
etc.). This is interesting because it might relate not only to concepts of sophistication, but also to the fact that knowledge about the cardiovascular benefits
of red wine (Frankel *et al.* 1993) is more widespread than knowledge of the
similar benefits in beer (Wright *et al.* 2008; Kaiser *et al.*, chapter 2), especially
in those beers that include hops. On the other hand, it might just be related to
prices.

González Turmo's chapter (chapter 8) exemplifies beer drinking and brewing in one of the most southern cities in Europe, Seville, and how the conviviality of the drinking place has been adapted to the traditional patterns of
social life in Andalucia. As the historical components in this chapter date back
about 150 years, beer drinking is shown not to be just a contemporary, modern
habit in this region, with its very hot summers. The author also identifies the
significant use of local brand names, despite multinational changes in brewery
ownership, demonstrating that the image of locality given by brand names still
has an importance in marketing. This is an issue which is reiterated in several
chapters of this volume.

The brand names of beers are often carried over from the times when particular beers were produced by small, local breweries. Even though so many of
these breweries have now been bought by global companies, the brand names
are kept for marketing purposes, as already discussed. Chapters 19 (by Gracia
Arnaiz) and 20 (by Cantarero and Stacconi) in this volume are particularly
concerned with this issue of marketing and the kind of messages modern beer
advertisements present, often a mix between tradition and allusion to modern
life. Cantarero and Stacconi use two television advertisements for different
brands of beer as ethnographic data for their discussion of the efforts that
modern beer producers make in order to associate drinking their brand of
beer with relaxation and pleasure. Gracia Arnaiz pursues this theme, and identifies aspects that have been changing in the relationship between producers
and consumers and how those links are mediated through advertising.

However, this marketing pressure should also be reviewed for its negative
effects. From the biomedical perspective taken by Kaiser, Medicus and Brüne
(chapter 2), the positive physiological and psychological effects of moderate
alcohol consumption must be balanced by the severe dangers of excessive
drinking. The figures are quite alarming. In Germany, for instance, according to

Soyka (2001), 2.5 million people (approximately 3 per cent of the population, or 4.8 per cent of males and 1.3 per cent of females) have serious problems with alcohol. This group has their life expectancy reduced by about twelve years, and the problems create enormous costs for the country's health system. The situation can be disastrous in countries where alcohol was previously unknown or hardly known and very rarely consumed. In Papua New Guinea, alcohol (almost exclusively consumed as beer) is responsible for a variety of very severe consequences, such as poverty as wage earners spend their money on buying beer. Regularly, one sees trucks with men returning home for the weekend provisioned with large amounts of beer, bought in cartons and usually drunk before the home village is reached (Marshall 1982). This can be followed by irresponsible and outright illegal behaviour, and in particular by domestic violence against women and rape. So far, no remedy has been found.

Taking an overall view of the material presented in this volume, we are confronted with a question that parallels McGrew's opening sentence (chapter 1). Why would humans from so many cultures, so geographically dispersed, habitually ingest this potentially toxic beverage? Some of the answers are reflected in McGrew's hypotheses 3 to 7 (chapter 1) for nonhuman species, i.e., energy-seeking, health-enhancing, taste-rewarding and enhancement of pleasure or relief of pain through altered states of mind. Other chapters have extended our understanding of these hypotheses in relation to human societies. The economic dimension should never be omitted in such discussions, since a significant reason for the contemporary geographic spread of beer-drinking practices around the world is due, like the worldwide availability of Coca Cola, to the economic power of large multinational brewing companies to infiltrate every economic zone, with affordable, hygienically safe, bottled or canned beers. This is particularly demonstrated by Aquino and Persoon (chapter 18) on the Philippines. However, with humans it is essential that one should also consider far more complex sociocultural explanations along with the biological effects. What becomes clear from the contributions to this volume are the social and communal benefits of the conviviality and altered states of mind biologically engendered by beer. Beer is indeed a topic meriting cross-disciplinary insight.

Drawing this introductory chapter to a close we want to stress that beer is a truly international drink, which today is increasingly produced and marketed globally as well as still being brewed in small traditional ways. In trying to find reasons why beer-drinking cultures have been, since antiquity, and remain widespread, we found it essential to refer to perspectives from totally different academic disciplines. Yet despite the many books on beer and brewing, we know of no other volume that has brought these diverse and relevant perspectives together. The juxtaposition of these perspectives from different disciplines allows further deductions which have not so far been identified. So, we hope that the reader will discover in this volume a new range of information on brewing, marketing and drinking beer, appreciate the way in which beer is embedded into social and ritual cultures of so many societies around the world and perhaps one day illuminate a new dimension. As our volume has no chapter that can replace the taste-rewarding hedonism of drinking beer, we recommend that it is best for readers to carry out their own participant observation of beer-drinking in the surroundings they find most congenial.

In ancient Mesopotamia, beer brewing was so important that it was the only profession directly linked to a deity. So, it is appropriate to finish this chapter with some lines of arguably the most famous beer poem, the hymn to Ninkasi, a Mesopotamian goddess, in the version rendered into English by Hornsey (2003: 89):

> ... *You are the one who waters the malt set on the ground,*
> *The noble dogs keep away even the potentates,*
> *Ninkasi, you are the one who waters the malt set on the ground,*
> *The noble dogs keep away even the potentates,*
> *You are the one who soaks the malt in a jar,*
> *The waves rise, the waves fall,*
> *Ninkasi, you are the one who soaks the malt in a jar,*
> *The waves rise, the waves fall,*
> *You are the one who spreads the cooked mash on large reed mats,*
> *Coolness overcomes,*
> *Ninkasi, you are the one who spreads the cooked mash on large reed mats,*
> *Coolness overcomes,*
> *You are the one who holds with both hands the great sweet wort,*
> *Brewing [it] with honey [and] wine,*
> *(You the sweet wort to the vessel)*
> *Ninkasi*
> ...
> *(You the sweet wort to the vessel)*
> *The filtering vat, which makes a pleasant sound,*
> *You place appropriately on [top of] a large collector vat.*
> *Ninkasi, the filtering vat, which makes a pleasant sound,*
> *You place appropriately on [top of] a large collector vat.*
> *When you pour out the filtered beer of the collector vat,*
> *It is [like] the onrush of Tigris and Euphrates,*
> *Ninkasi, you are the one who pours out the filtered beer of the collector vat,*
> *It is [like] the onrush of Tigris and Euphrates.*

References

Battcock, M. and Azam-Ali, S. (1998) *Fermented Fruits and Vegetables: A global perspective*, F.A.O. Agricultural Services Bulletin No.134, Rome.
de Garine, I. and Garine, V. (eds) (2001) *Drinking: Anthropological approaches*,

Berghahn Books, Oxford.

Demossier, M. (2004) Contemporary lifestyles: the case of wine. In Sloan, D. (ed.) *Culinary Taste: Consumer behaviour in the international restaurant sector*, Elsevier Butterworth Heinemann, Oxford, 93–108.

Demossier, M. (2005) Consuming wine in France: the 'wandering' drinker and the 'vinanomie'. In Wilson, T.M. (ed.) *Drinking Cultures*, Berg, Oxford.

Douglas, M. (1987) A distinctive anthropological perspective. In Douglas, M. (ed.) *Constructive Drinking: Perspectives on drink from anthropology*, Cambridge University Press, Cambridge.

Farnworth, E.R. (1976) Betel nut – its composition, chemistry and uses, *Sciences in New Guinea*, 4: 85–90.

Frankel, E.N., Kanner, J., German, J.B, Parks, E. and Kinsella, J.E. (1993) Inhibition of oxidation of human low-density lipoprotein by phenolic substances in red wine, *Lancet*, 341(8843): 454–457.

Hornsey, I.S. (2003) *A History of Beer and Brewing*, The Royal Society of Chemistry, Cambridge. Also as: http://www.rsc.org/publishing/ebooks/2003/9780854046300.asp.

Johansen, D., Friis, K., Skovenburg, E. and Gronbaek, M. (2006) Food buying habits of people who buy *wine* or *beer*: cross-sectional study, *British Medical Journal*, 332(7540): 519–521.

Lewin, L. (1998) *Phantastica: A Classic Survey on the Use and Abuse of Mind-Altering Plants*, Park Street Press, Rochester, Vermont.

Marshall, M. (ed.) (1982) *Through a Glass Darkly: Beer and modernisation in Papua New Guinea*, Monograph 18, IASER Press, Boroko (Papua New Guinea).

McGovern, P.E. (2003) *Ancient Wine: The search for the origins of viniculture*, Princeton University Press, Princeton, New Jersey.

Mückler. H. (1996) Kava in Ozeanien: Neue Betrachtungen zu einer Kulturpflanze und deren Bedeutung im kulturellen Kontext, *Mitteilungen der Anthropologischen Gesellschaft Wien, Band CXXV*, Wien: 207–224.

Samuel, D. (2000) Brewing and baking. In Nicholson, P.T. and Shaw, I. (eds) *Ancient Egyptian materials and technology,* Cambridge University Press, Cambridge, 537–586.

Schiefenhövel, W. personal notes on the school for poor children and orphanage, founded by the theologian August Francke in Halle, Germany, in 1695.

Soyka, M. (2001) Psychische und soziale Folgen chronischen Alkoholismus, *Deutsches Ärzteblatt*, 98(42): 2732–2736.

Wright, C.A., Bruhn, C.M., Heymann, H. and Bamforth, C.W. (2008) Beer and wine consumers' perceptions of the nutritional value of alcoholic and non-alcoholic beverages, *Journal of Food Science*, 73(1): H8–11.

Websites

http://www.bonable.de
http://www.effilee.de/wissen/Bier.html
http://www.icafood.eu
http://de.wikipedia.org/wiki/Bayerische_Staatsbrauerei_Weihenstephan
http://en.wikipedia.org/wiki/Chicha
http://www.yeastgenome.org

CHAPTER 1
NATURAL INGESTION OF ETHANOL BY ANIMALS: WHY?

W.C. McGrew

Introduction

Why would any organism habitually ingest a toxic substance? If toxins decrease net fitness in terms of lifetime reproductive success, then natural selection should favour individuals that avoid consuming them, versus those that do. Ethanol is such a toxin, e.g. it directly kills nerve cells. Yet, it is naturally consumed by a variety of animal taxa, both invertebrate and vertebrate: Diptera, especially *Drosophila* spp.; Hymenoptera; Lepidoptera; among birds, Passeriformes, e.g. waxwings, *Bombycilla* spp.; among mammals, Bovidae, Proboscidae, Suidae (for review of references, see Dudley 2000; Eriksson and Nummi 1982). So, do the benefits outweigh the costs?

Ethanol is produced by fermentation of sugars by yeast (microscopic fungi). In nature, this most commonly involves the simple sugars found in ripe fruit, and so ingestion is associated with facultative or obligate frugivory. Toxicity is said to be an evolved strategy of micro-organisms that allows them to triumph over macro-organisms in competition for these calorific resources (Janzen 1977). Thus, there is an evolutionary '*arms race*' between yeasts and other fruit-eaters, whether these be other microbes or large-bodied vertebrates. The counter strategy of ethanol consumers is physiological, and is basically the same from butterfly to barfly. Ethanol is metabolised (detoxified) by a two-stage, enzymatic process: alcohol dehydrogenase (ADH) breaks down ethanol into acetaldehyde, then aldehyde dehydrogenase (ALDH) breaks that down into acetate, and acetate is then incorporated into the Krebs cycle.

The yeasts' strategy is not decisive, however, as ethanol ingestion is commonplace. In fruit flies *(Drosophila* spp.), all stages of the life cycle consume ethanol and the larvae develop in an alcoholic culture of rotting fruit pulp. Both in humans and nonhumans, ethanol ingestion goes beyond direct consumption of fruit to the liquid form, wine, garnered from monosaccharides in fruit, nectar, sap, honey, etc. For example, seven species of mammals, including three species of primates (pentailed treeshrew, *Pitlocercus lowii*; common treeshrew, *Tupaia glis*; slow loris, *Nycticebus coucang*) regularly consume the fermented nectar of the bertam palm, *Eugeissona tristis* (Wiens *et al.* 2008).

However, humans apply simple technology such as heat to complex carbohydrates, such as starch, to break down polysaccharides into simple sugars for fermentation, thus producing beer from cereals or tubers. Finally, humans apply even more impressive technology (distillation) to transform low-concentration alcoholic fluids to high-concentration ones (spirits). Production of ethanol for ingestion seems to be a human universal, found in all societies with access to apt raw materials (Brown, 1991).

Finally, one must explain not only the physiological aspects of ethanol ingestion, but also its behavioural and cognitive aspects. Ethanol-consuming organisms of all types sometimes ingest it to the point of intoxication (as measured by altered motor patterns) and show high appetitive motivation (as measured by response to deprivation or willingness to work for ethanol as a reward) (Fitzgerald 1972).

Hypotheses

Seven hypotheses seem to explain ethanol ingestion. These need not be mutually exclusive, but each can be tested individually, at least in principle. These are presented below in order of increasing complexity:

1. **accident**, ingestion may be an inadvertent by-product of frugivory
2. **pathology**, ingestion may be anomalous by nature or nurture, in individuals that knowingly or otherwise seek self-injury
3. **nutrition**, ingestion may be energy-seeking
4. **medicine**, ingestion may be health-enhancing
5. **gustation**, ingestion may be taste-rewarding
6. **hedonism**, ingestion may be psychologically disinhibiting, leading to enhanced pleasure or to relief of pain
7. **cognition**, ingestion may alter intellectual capacity, leading to risk-taking or altered states of consciousness

Below, each of these hypotheses will be examined in terms of what is known in the published literature on ethanol ingestion by nonhuman species.

Results

Accidental ingestion seems likely for ingestion of pulpy, succulent fruits that gradually ripen, especially since ethanol is always present in ripe fruits (Dudley

2002). Fruits need not be 'rotten' or overripe before fermentation starts; rather, it is only a matter of sufficient sugar content plus yeast spores, and the latter are ubiquitous. However, ethanol levels in ripe fruit are low, typically of the order of 0.1 per cent, so that their consumption is unlikely to have physiological or behavioural effects on fitness. Higher ethanol levels in rotting fruit are signalled by distinctive odour, taste, and even appearance, with the former often being detectable at a distance before the fruit is handled. This makes accidental ingestion of significant levels of ethanol unlikely.

More conclusive evidence of non-accidental ingestion comes from goal-directed selection of fermented fruit over non-fermented fruit. This is well-known in *Drosophila* life-history, e.g., egg-laying, but there seem to be no data for vertebrates, except as natural history anecdotes (e.g., Siegel 1989). In unnatural conditions in captivity, preference for ethanol can be developmentally induced in a wide range of vertebrates, but the procedures typically require extreme experimental manipulation (Siegel and Brodie 1984). Again, this suggests that habitual ingestion in nature is accidental.

Finally, when whole clades of insects normally ingest ethanol, it seems unlikely to be happenstance. The same applies to certain passerines, especially long-distance, migratory frugivores, but the situation for mammals remains unclear.

Pathological ingestion of ethanol may explain individual cases by analogy to alcoholism in humans. This explanation is strengthened by studies reporting successful experimental induction of ethanol addiction in nonhumans (e.g. Kornet *et al.* 1990) and naturalistic accounts (Marais 1969: 98–101, on wild baboons). Furthermore, genetically based variation in ADH and ALDH isozymes across human populations have been implicated in cross-cultural differences in alcohol abuse (see review in Dudley 2002).

However, for the reasons given above, pathology cannot account for obligate ingestion of ethanol in invertebrates and (apparently) birds. Again, the situation for mammals in natural circumstances remains unclear, as anecdotes (that is, accounts of rare or even unique events) may indicate only idiosyncrasy (that is, persistent individual patterns of behaviour, e.g., Carrington, 1959: 68) and may not generalise to widespread habits (Siegel 1989). Even if systematic, comprehensive data showed mammals to be regular consumers of ethanol, and even if short-term studies revealed no ill-effects, longer-term data are needed to test the hypothesis of lifespan pathology.

Nutritional ingestion of ethanol seems straight-forward: it is a better source of calories than unfermented carbohydrates, in terms of direct kcal/g yield. Furthermore, the odour plumes of ethanol may attract frugivores to indirect benefits of available calories from sugars present in patches of both ripe and overripe fruit (Dudley 2000).

However, a diet in which a high proportion of calories come from ethanol (and human alcoholism is sometimes defined accordingly) is malnutritional. Such '*empty*' calories may be deficient in other nutrients, although this varies from spirits to wine to beer, with the latter sometimes being labelled as '*liquid bread*' (see editors' Preface). Finally, the most sensible argument against nutritional ingestion of ethanol by frugivores is dietary selectivity. Why not just eat sugar-rich fruit at peak ripeness so as to get the caloric benefit and to avoid the toxic cost?

Medicinal ingestion of ethanol seemed an unlikely explanation until recently, but recent findings from epidemiological studies on humans (e.g. Cleophas 1999) and on medicinal plant use in non-humans (Huffman 1997) suggest otherwise. Moderate levels of alcohol consumption may lower cardiovascular risk in all vertebrates, although it is unlikely to account for invertebrate ingestion of ethanol, given the latter's very different circulatory systems. Studies of medicinal plant use by mammals, although burgeoning, focus mainly on secondary compounds (e.g. alkaloids) and not on ethanol, and none yet has linked ethanol to symptom relief or improved health. However, this hypothesis is virtually untested for non-humans, so little can be said.

Gustatory ingestion of ethanol is the simplest explanation of all: Like humans, other animals may consume alcohol because it tastes good. The gustatory sense of chimpanzees closely resembles that of humans (Kalmus 1970) and wild chimpanzees favour tastes that signal calories (Nishida *et al.* 2000). Natural history accounts (e.g., Sikes 1971: 242) suggest that wild animals such as elephants cannot resist overdoing their ingestion of fermented fruit, even to the point of inebriation. Anecdotes from home-reared apes suggest the same: a female chimpanzee used to mix herself martini cocktails (Temerlin 1975). These reports are suspect on grounds of anthropomorphism, but could be easily tested by taste tests on 'enculturated' apes who typically favour a diet of processed cultivars.

The real problem with the gustatory hypothesis, however, is its proximate nature. Even if it holds, it merely pushes back the question to the ultimate (i.e. fitness) level. Why would natural selection shape a sensory system that makes a toxin taste good? Why would evolution produce an appetitive drive for substance that would appear to reduce lifetime reproductive success?

Hedonic ingestion of ethanol is based on its psychoactive properties of disinhibition, assuming that disinhibition may increase pleasure or decrease pain. Such emotional-motivational processes in the central nervous system of vertebrates are complex but well-studied. In humans, ingestion of ethanol produces a short-term effect of enhanced well-being that is manifest in playfulness, or of analgesia. By homology, given similar cerebral functioning, one might expect similar processes in large-brained mammals, especially anthropoids. Again, natural history and companion animal anecdotes suggest such effects. But for an invertebrate, lacking even a brain, much less a complex cerebral cortex, it is hard to know how to test such an hypothesis. Even if butterflies or wasps appear to be tipsy in their actions (and who can know of their motives?), their behaviour is not attributed with the capacity for play.

The potential costs of hedonism are obvious, in terms of increased vulnerability to predation, competition, or other hazards, or of potentially greater injury incurred by ignoring painful stimuli. This would seem to be especially acute for arboreal or volant creatures, where a single instance of motor dysfunction could be fatal. Captive chimpanzees and orangutans who voluntarily consume large amounts of ethanol show all the symptoms of human drunkenness, from locomotor ataxia, to hyper-excitability, to stupor (Fitzgerald 1972). Even a hangover could be a handicap, in competition with a teetotalling rival. However, the potential benefits of disinhibition should not be ignored. If playfulness enhances inventiveness and inventiveness leads to behavioural adaptation, then ethanol ingestion may facilitate more efficient foraging or more creative social strategising. These are difficult ideas to test, as are all hypotheses related to play (Spinka *et al.* 2001).

The *cognitive* hypothesis for ethanol ingestion suggests that it may enhance or safeguard intellectual functioning. Being cortically based, this hypothesis may be inseparable from the hedonic hypothesis, but there may be a distinction between functioning neural modules for emotion and for cognition. Ruitenberg *et al.* (2002) recently showed for humans that light-to-moderate alcohol consumption is associated with a reduced risk of dementia.

Disinhibited brains may differently calculate probabilities or risks, or may even reconstitute their perceptual worlds, as in altered states of consciousness. One can imagine a socially subordinate individual emboldened by ethanol surprising its superiors and so improving its social status. Similarly, a normally shy individual may benefit socially by initiating new social affiliations. High risks may lead to high payoffs. However, when squirrel monkeys ingest ethanol, it is the dominant individuals who become more aggressive, not the subordinates (Winslow and Miczek 1988).

By the same token, high risks may lead to high, even fatal or disastrous costs. For every envisioned reward, there is an equally costly punishment. The key is relative probability of outcomes, as calculated by a strategising, rational brain. In the long run (for chronic as opposed to acute problems to be solved), it seems intuitively unlikely that an ethanol-disinhibited individual is likely to out-think a more temperate one. However, this is an empirical question, in which the effects of ethanol ingestion dosage on everything from reaction time to Machiavellian deception need to be tested, in a range of vertebrates. However, again, one assumes that this hypothesis will be of little use in understanding hard-wired invertebrates.

Discussion

It seems clear that no single hypothesis explains ethanol ingestion by all animal taxa, from fruit fly to elephant. For *Drosophila*, it seems likely that all but Hypothesis 3 are irrelevant, and not even worth trying to test. (For *Homo sapiens* it seems likely that none of them could be falsified, at least for all cases). Furthermore, it is clear that for none of the hypotheses are there adequate data, certainly not in print, and probably not even envisioned. Targeted testing of these ideas is underway, but it is sporadic (Eriksson and Nummi 1982; Dudley 2002). Most of what we think we know about mammalian ethanol ingestion is no more than natural history notes. This means that humans may be the only mammalian species to use alcohol in any real way, and if so, it can be added to the short list of derived traits that are both unique and universal to the species (Brown 1991). But the fact that many organisms have ADH and ALDH (Prinzinger and Hakimi 1996) suggests that there is more to the story than this.

Given all these caveats, what can be said however tentatively? Dudley's (2000) masterly treatment in principle supports Hypothesis 3 for normative cases. Animals ingest ethanol to get energy, and this works fine in environments of evolutionary adaptedness. That is, at the low levels of ethanol available in nature, the catabolisation of ethanol from fruits is straightforward. But what to make of over-indulgence, of drunken pachyderms or tipsy waxwings? It seems that non-humans in nature have access only to 'wine', but usually in solid, not liquid, form. Carrington's (1959) description of a wild African elephant addicted to fermented millet raided from a village seems to be the only case of non-human 'beer' consumption. Similarly, at various places in West Africa where villagers tap palm trees (e.g., *Elaeis guineensis*) for natural fermented palm wine, wild chimpanzees pilfer the containers and drink the contents (Carvalho, personal communication).

Dudley (2000) invokes the principle of *hormesis*, which entails a nutrient–toxin continuum. That is, chemical compounds that are beneficial in low dosages may be harmful at high dosages. In human beings, this may apply to ethanol and alcoholism, just as over-consumption of salt links to hypertension, sucrose to diabetes, and saturated fats to coronary disease. In all cases, a substance that is rare in nature has become readily accessible in unnatural conditions, usually as a by-product of the agricultural domestication of plants and animals, or of industrial technology. We humans over-indulge in ethanol ingestion because we have become brewers, vintners, and distillers. Thus, cultural evolution in hominids has taken us from wine to beer to spirits.

Acknowledgements

I thank Wulf Schiefenhövel for the invitation to take part in the sixteenth conference of the International Commission for the Anthropology of Food (ICAF) on 'Fluid Bread: Images and Usages of Beer in Cross-Cultural Perspective'; funding for attendance was provided by Miami University (Ohio); Linda Marchant and Lauren Sarringhaus provided critical comments on the manuscript, which was word processed by Diana Deaton.

References

Brown, D.E. (1991) *Human Universal,* McGraw-Hill: New York.
Carrington, R. (1959) *Elephants,* Penguin Books: Harmondsworth, UK.

Cleophas, T.J. (1999) Wine, beer and spirits and the risk of myocardial infarction: a systematic review, *Biomedicine and Pharmacology*, 53: 417–423.

Dudley, R. (2000) Evolutionary origins of human alcoholism in primate frugivory, *Quarterly Review of Biology*, 75: 3–15.

Dudley, R. (2002) Fermenting fruit and the historical ecology of ethanol ingestion: is alcoholism in modern humans an evolutionary hangover? *Addiction*, 9: 381–388.

Eriksson, K. and Nummi, H. (1982) Alcohol accumulation from ingested berries and alcohol metabolism in passerine birds, *Ornis Fennica*, 60: 2–9.

Fitzgerald, F.L. (1972) Voluntary alcohol consumption in apes. In, Kissin, B. and Begleiter, H. (eds) *The Biology of Alcoholism: Physiology and Behavior*, Plenum: New York: 169–192.

Huffman, M.A. (1997) Current evidence for self-medication in primates: a multidisciplinary perspective, *Yearbook of Physical Anthropology*, 40: 171–200.

Janzen, D.H. (1977) Why fruits rot, seeds mold, and meat spoils, *American Naturalist*, 111: 697–713.

Kalmus, H. (1970) The sense of taste of chimpanzees and other primates, *The Chimpanzee*, 2: 130–141.

Kornet, M., Gooseu, C. and von Ree, J.M. (1990) The effect of interrupted alcohol supply on spontaneous alcohol consumption by rhesus monkeys, *Alcohol and Addiction*, 25: 407–412.

Marais, E. (1969) *The Soul of the Ape*, Penguin Books: Harmondsworth, UK.

Nishida, T., Ohigashi, H. and Koshimizu, K. (2000) Tastes of chimpanzee plant foods, *Current Anthropology*, 41: 431–438.

Prinzinger, R. and Hakimi, G.A. (1996) Alcohol resorption and alcohol degradation in the European starling, *Sturnus vulgaris*. *Journal für Ornithologie* 137: 319–327.

Ruitenberg, A., van Swieten, J.C., Witteman, J.C., Mehta, K.M., van Duijn, C.M., Hofman, A. and Breteler, M.M. (2002) Alcohol consumption and risk of dementia: the Rotterdam Study, *The Lancet*, 359: 281–286.

Siegel R.K. and Brodie, M. (1984) Alcohol self-administration by elephants, *Bulletin of the Psychonomic Society*, 22: 49–52.

Siegel, R.K. (1989) *Intoxication*, E.P. Dutton: New York.

Sikes, S.K. (1971) *The Natural History of the African Elephant*, Elsevier: New York.

Spinka, M., Newberry, R.C. and Bekoff, M. (2001) Mammalian play: training for the unexpected, *Quarterly Review of Biology*, 76: 141–168.

Temerlin, M.K. (1975) *Lucy. Growing up human, a chimpanzee daughter in a psychotherapist's family*, Science and Behavior Books, Palo Alto: USA.

Wiens, F., Zitzmann, A., Lachance, M-A., Yegles, M., Pragst, F., Wurst, F.M., von Holst, D., Saw, L.G. and Spanagel, R. (2008), Chronic intake of fermented floral nectar by wild treeshrews, *Proceedings of the National Academy of Sciences (USA)*, 105: 10426–10431.

Winslow, J.T. and Miczek, K.A. (1988) Androgen dependency of alcohol effects of aggressive behavior: a seasonal rhythm in high-ranking squirrel monkeys, *Psychopharmacology*, 95: 92–98.

CHAPTER 2
HEALTHY OR DETRIMENTAL? PHYSIOLOGICAL, PSYCHIATRIC AND EVOLUTIONARY ASPECTS OF DRINKING BEER

Peter Kaiser, Gerhard Medicus and *Martin Brüne*

Beer as a Provider of Valuable Nutrients

Alcohol, in one of several aspects, is a valuable food source as it provides a high amount of energy per weight (see table 2.1); this was probably the reason for the large amounts of beer being given to workers in Mesopotamia (Damerow 1996) and throughout history. Beer, like wine, contains a large number of potentially health-promoting substances and had, in the past, an important role, since water was often contaminated with pathogens like *Escherichia coli*, *Salmonella typhimurium*, etc., whereas beer, due to its content of alcohol and carbonic acid, was, from this perspective, a much safer drink than the water available in the towns of the past.

Table 2.1 Nutritional value of beer
(Pilsner Beer) per 100ml:

Kcal/KJ	47/195
Water	92g
Ethanol	4g
Carbohydrates	3.2g
Proteins	0.5g
Minerals	0.2g
Organic acids, fat	minimal

Flavonoids and Phytoestrogens in Beer

More than 2,000 compounds are contained in beer, among them more than 50 polyphenols, stemming mainly from barley. These polyphenols are naturally occurring substances comprising flavonoids which are exclusively produced by plants, e.g., hops, and they are abundant in grapes and red wine, but exist only in traces in white wine (with the exception of champagne). Phytoestrogens and structurally related hop flavonoids are often confounded in the literature. Flavonoids from red wine are deemed responsible for the benefits of the 'Mediterranean diet', yet they are also present in beer.

The most abundant flavonoids in our diet are flavanols (catechins plus proanthocyanidins), anthocyanins and their oxidation products. The main polyphenol dietary sources are fruits and beverages like fruit juice, wine, tea, coffee, chocolate and beer. As several unique flavonoid compounds have recently been isolated from hops, they are present in beer. Their chemical structures are similar to other plant-derived compounds which are found in the normal human diet. They have been shown to possess chemopreventive properties against cancer due, in part, to inhibition of cytochrome P450 enzymes which activate carcinogens (Henderson, et al. 2000). The concentration of flavonoids in beer, and possibly their absence, depend on the selection of particular hop varieties, the hopping rate, or the type of hop products used in brewing. The efficiency of transfer of, for example, 8-prenylnaringenin from hops to beer is between 10 and 20 per cent (Tekel et al. 1999). Losses of flavonoids were due to incomplete extraction from the hops into the wort (13–25 per cent), adsorption to insoluble malt proteins (18–26 per cent), and adsorption to yeast cells (11–32 per cent) during fermentation (Stevens et al., 1999).

In the days when the monasteries were the spearhead of technological innovation, monks cultivated hops in their gardens in order to make a sleeping draught. Not surprisingly, as hops are a plant of the hemp family (*Cannabinaceae*), they were used as a mild sedative, to calm gastric upsets and to fight sexual arousal (Dörfler and Roselt 1990). Compounds like Hopein and Methylbutenol are thought to be responsible for these effects. In former centuries hops were smoked in England (Reinhardt 1911) in a similar way to opium.

The female flowers of the hop plant, *Humulus lupulus*, have a mild sterilising effect and act as a preservative and a flavouring agent in beer. Hops contain oils, bitter compounds and flavour compounds. It is often said that hops have a powerful estrogenic activity and that beer may also be estrogenic. A phytoestrogen stemming from hops can indeed be detected in beer, but the levels are low and should not pose any cause for concern (Milligan et al. 2000). Hops' phytoestrogens are able to induce menstruation in female hop pickers. This is a different physiological mechanism from that leading to the once well-known *Hopfenpflückerinnenkrankheit* (disease of female hop pickers), an allergic reaction with symptoms like dermatitis, vomiting, sweating and fever. Both phenomena have been observed in the days when the harvest was done by hand. Extracts of several estrogenic herbs, including hops, were shown *in vitro* to inhibit growth of T-47D cells, suggesting that certain herbs and phytoestrogens may have potential effects on the prevention of breast cancer (Dixon-Shanies and Shaikh 1999).

In the yeast *(Saccharomyces cerevisiae)* one can detect 17-ß-estradiol, an ovarian hormone, inducing the growing of the breast-glands in both sexes (in males called gynecomastia) (Kolata 1984; Feldman *et al.* 1984). Furthermore, the amount of the pituitarian gland hormone, prolactin, stimulating milk-production is doubled when lactating women consume beer, confirming the popular advice that breastfeeding mothers should drink a glass of beer a day (Grossmann 1988). Today, hops-extract has even been included in some herbal preparations sold for 'breast enhancement'.

Effects of Beer on Specific Organs or Organ-Systems

Table 2.2 summarises literature on the effects of beer, identifying risk factors and benefits.

Table 2.2　Risk factors versus prophylactic effects of alcohol consumption

Risk factor for	Postulated mechanism	Literature
Alcoholic liver disease	Food habits (beer consumption and pork)	Bode *et al.* 1998
Liver cirrhosis (Spirits > beer)	Drinking behaviours in beer-drinking countries	Kerr *et al.* 2000
Pancreatitis	Intraductal protein precipitation	Niebergall-Roth *et al.* 1998
Stimulation of gastric acid, stomach ulcer	Maleic acid and succinic acid in fermented beverages	Teyssen *et al.* 1999
Cancer of gastro-intestinal tract	Direct and indirect effects of ethanol	Groenbaek *et al.* 1998
Allergy	Hypersensitivity to barley protein	Figueredo *et al.* 1999

Beneficial for	Postulated mechanism	Literature
Reduced risk for development of kidney stones	Amount of fluid intake	Ottenjann 1999 Borghi *et al.* 1999 Hirvonen *et al.* 1999
Reduced risk for development of diabetes mellitus	No fast increase in both glucose and insulin concentration within a max. 1 hour after consumption (compared to soft drinks)	Janssens *et al.* 1999
Reduction of Helicobacter pylori-induced gastritis, ulcers of stomach and small intestine (wine > beer)	Direct effect of ethanol	Brenner *et al.* 1999

Kidney Stones

Beer consumption is inversely associated with risk of kidney stones (*nephro-lithiasis*); each bottle of beer consumed per day was estimated to reduce the risk by 40 per cent (RR[1] 0.60; 95 per cent CI[2] 0.47–0.76; Hirvonen *et al* 1999). Others emphasise that a sufficiently high intake of water, non-alcoholic apple cider and probably other fluids (coffee, tea), equally has a preventative effect on *nephro-lithiasis* and its recurrence without the disadvantages of beer or wine, and that the role of fruit juice is still to be defined (Ottenjann 1999; Borghi *et al.*1999).

Pancreatitis

Unlike pure ethanol solutions and distilled spirits, beer strongly stimulates pancreatic enzyme output, probably due to non-alcoholic fermentation products. During chronic alcoholism, the ethanol-induced inhibition is replaced by an enhanced enzyme output that causes intraductal protein precipitation. The occurrence of protein precipitates is considered to be crucial in the development of chronic alcoholic pancreatitis. Other ethanol-induced secretory alterations that may contribute to the development of alcoholic pancreatitis are decreased secretion of trypsin inhibitor, increased cholinergic tone, and changes in the concentration of lithostathine (Niebergall-Roth *et al.* 1998). In other words, moderate consumption of beer seems to protect against a disease of this organ whereas alcoholism can lead to the destruction of pancreas tissue.

Cancer

No association was found for light to moderate consumption of beer and the risk of prostate cancer (a positive association was suggested for wines) (Schuurman *et al.* 1999) or breast cancer (Zhang *et al.* 1999), whereas Groenbaek *et al.* (1998) found (in a large sample: 15,000 men, 13,000 women) a three times higher risk for cancer of the oropharynx, larynx, oesophagus, and liver in consumers of beer or spirits (7 to 23 beers a week) compared to wine drinkers with an equal amount of alcohol intake (Groenbaek *et al.* 1998).

A study from Denmark revealed an association between a high consumption of beer and spirits and an increased risk of lung cancer, whereas wine intake may provide some protection (Prescott *et al.* 1999). In contrast, Finnish researchers concluded that alcohol consumption is not a risk factor for lung cancer among male cigarette smokers (Woodson *et al.* 1999).

Healthy Effects of Alcohol

More than thirty international studies support the hypothesis that low to moderate doses of alcohol have a protective effect against cardiovascular diseases and thereby reduce the risk of heart attacks and cerebral strokes. Mechanisms examined and considered responsible for this risk reduction are shown in Table 2.3.

Table 2.3   Risk reductions identified

- Anti-arteriosclerotic:
  - Increase of HDL, decrease of LDL
  - Reduction of homocysteine, especially in beer
- Haemolytic: decreases the risks of coronary heart disease and ischaemic stroke but may increase risk of subarachnoid haemorrhage
- Antithrombotic: anti-fibrinogen effect through decreased platelets aggregation, as well as increased fibrinolysis (same general effects as the haemolytic properties)
- Vasodilatatoric: decrease of (especially diastolic) blood pressure

Alcohol has beneficial and harmful effects on coronary heart disease (CHD). A review summarises the state of knowledge on the relationship between myocardial infarction and alcohol consumption (following Cleophas, 1999):

1. Small doses of alcohol (1–4 drinks a day; wine, beer, and spirits) are associated with a slightly reduced risk of mortality and CHD.
1a. Apart from a direct beneficial effect of low doses of alcohol on mortality and CHD, some psychological factors may contribute to its beneficial effect.
2. High doses of alcohol (> or = 5 drinks a day) are not associated with a reduced risk of death and CHD.
2a. Apart from a direct harmful effect of high alcohol intake, confounding factors, particularly those of a psychological nature, may very well contribute to the loss of benefits for moderate drinkers.

Relationship between Alcohol Consumption and Mortality

In a longitudinal study, covering more than ten years, the mortality rate in 1,422 men was lower in men reporting moderate alcohol intake than in either non-drinkers or heavier drinkers (> 34 gr alcohol daily, equivalent to approximately 700 ml. of beer). Cardiovascular mortality was higher in non-drinkers and non-cardiovascular mortality was greater in the heavier drinkers. A multivariate analysis showed this relationship between reported alcohol consumption and subsequent mortality to be largely independent of differences in smoking, blood pressure, plasma cholesterol, and type of employment (Marmot *et al.* 1981).

In another study the lowest risk was observed at one to six alcoholic beverages a week. Abstainers had a relative risk of 1.37 (95 per cent CI 1.20–1.56) whereas those drinking more than 70 beverages a week had a relative risk of 2.29 (1.75–3.00). Among the drinkers, the risk was significantly increased only among those drinking more than 42 beverages a week. Sex, age, body mass index, and smoking did not significantly modify the risk function. The risk among heavy drinkers was slightly reduced when smoking was controlled for. The risk function was similar in the first and second period of six years of observation (Groenbaek *et al.* 1994).

Some studies suggest that moderate alcohol intake significantly reduces even the total cause of mortality and hypothesise that a generally healthier lifestyle in the group of light to moderate drinkers compared to teetotallers and heavy drinkers may be responsible for this. After an almost ten-year follow-up in an Australian survey elderly men taking any alcohol lived on average 7.6 months and women 2.7 months longer, compared with non-drinkers (Simons 2000). Especially for beer, the favourable biochemical changes in blood could be demonstrated in CHD-patients (Gorinstein *et al.* 1997). Several researchers (e.g., Renaud and Lorgeril 1992; Criqui and Ringel 1994; Jepson *et al.* 1995; Groenbaek *et al.* 1999) found an inverse relationship between incidence of ischaemic heart disease and wine consumption in different countries, but no such relation or only a poor one for the other types of beverages.

The High-density Lipoprotein (HDL)

HDL (sometimes called 'good' cholesterol) levels are significantly higher in drinkers than in non-drinkers, indicating that regular consumption of small to moderate amounts of alcoholic beverages, regardless of the type, reduces the risk of arteriosclerosis and myocardial infarct compared with non-drinkers (Rimm *et al.* 1991; Gaziano *et al.* 1999). Other research groups confirm this analysis, finding no differences between the effects of beer, wine and spirits regarding serum HDL, especially in the group of consumers who are light (1–20 g/day) or moderate (21–40 g/day) drinkers (Koppes *et al.* 2000). Others hypothesise that alcohol increases serum paraoxonase activity, an HDL-associated enzyme which protects against LDL (low density lioprotein, the 'bad' cholesterol) oxidation (van der Gaag *et al.* 1999).

Over 80 per cent of men and 55 per cent of women in Germany drink alcohol on a regular basis. The majority of the consumers (65 per cent of men, 87 per cent of women) are light (1–20 g/day) or moderate (21–40 g/day) drinkers. The impact of drinking habits on cardiovascular and all-cause mortality as well as cardiovascular risk factors and liver disease parameters was estimated by an analysis of independent representative samples of the German population (15,400 persons), and regional samples of the Berlin-Spandau population (2,370 in total), aged 25–69 years. A mortality follow-up seven years later was conducted for this population. Higher serum HDL-cholesterol (having protective effects against cardiovascular disease) and higher Gamma GT levels (indicating damaged liver functions) were observed with increasing alcohol intake. In light and moderate drinkers no significant relationship was seen with non-HDL-cholesterol, triglycerides, blood pressure and body mass index, compared to teetotallers. Men who consumed 1–20 g alcohol/day had a significantly lower all-cause and cardiovascular mortality. Compared to non-drinkers, the risk was almost 50 per cent lower. These results suggest that light (and possibly moderate) alcohol consumption reduces the risk of cardiovascular and total mortality risk and has a favourable effect on HDL-cholesterol (Hoffmeister *et al.* 1999).

To find out whether the protective effect of small to moderate amounts of alcohol could be confirmed in areas where much of the alcohol consumed is taken in the form of beer, a prospective cohort study spanning the years from 1984 to 1992 was conducted among 2000 men and women, aged 45–64, in a population of southern Germany (Augsburg region; Keil *et al.* 1997, see Table 2.4).

Table 2.4   Alcohol Study in the Augsburg Area, Germany

Alcohol consumption % of total population	Average alcohol intake/d	Average alcohol intake/d from beer	8-years of follow-up: occurred deaths/ incident CHD (fatal/ nonfatal)	Hazard rate ratio (CHD events): drinker/non-drinkers	Hazard rate ratio (total mortality): drinker/non-drinkers
Male 87%	42g	33g	96 (all causes) /62	0.51 (0.1–19.9g/d) (95%CI, 0.27–0.95)	0.59 (0.1–19.9g/d) (95% CI, 0.36–0.97)
				does not change much with higher intake.	0.46 (20–39.9g/d) (95% CI, 0.20–0.80)
					1.04 (>or = 80g/d) (95% CI, 0.54–2.00)
Female 56%	16g	8g	45 (all causes)		0.46 (0.1–19.9g/d) (95% CI, 0.22–0.96)

(source: Keil *et al.* 1997)

During the eight years of follow-up, 96 deaths (all causes) and 62 incident CHD events (nonfatal and fatal) occurred in men, and 45 deaths (all causes) occurred in women.

Alcohol and Lifestyle

Most researchers attribute the U-shaped curve of low health risks among moderate drinkers versus higher risks in abstainers and heavy drinkers to a combination of beneficial and harmful effects of ethanol itself. Perhaps a large part, but not all, of the greater benefit seen in wine drinkers vis-à-vis drinkers of other alcohol can be attributed to an advantageous lifestyle, like low rates of smoking and obesity in the former (Wannamethee and Shaper 1999).

Generally speaking, it is the accepted interpretation of the U-shaped curve described above that the lowest point on the curve (light/moderate drinking) represents an optimum exposure to alcohol and that the increased risk in non-drinkers reflects the consequence of sub-optimum exposure. Non-drinkers, both ex-drinkers and lifelong teetotallers, consistently show an increased prevalence of conditions likely to increase morbidity and mortality compared with occasional or light drinkers. In addition, regular light drinkers tend to have lifestyles very advantageous for health.

Negative Effects on Health due to Alcohol Consumption

The detrimental influence of alcohol drinking on other organs and organ systems, e.g., the brain, or on the functioning of the liver, especially on the protein metabolism, has been examined thoroughly and is beyond the scope of this article. A historical overview is found in Klatsky (1998).

Most studies examining the role of alcohol consumption in arteriosclerosis and cardiovascular disease have overlooked the possible effect of drinking patterns. An investigation of the association between the habit of heavy acute intake of beer and spirits (binging) and the four-year progression of carotid atherosclerosis in middle-aged Finnish men showed, after adjustment for age, baseline carotid atherosclerosis and average weekly alcohol consumption level, the highest atherosclerosis progression was in men who usually consumed a whole bottle of vodka or more in one session (Kauhanen *et al.* 1999). This form of alcohol intake is clearly risky for one's health.

Psychiatric Diseases Caused by Alcohol Misuse

Generally, high and chronic intake of alcohol, a potentially toxic substance, has bad effects not only on the liver and other organs involved in breaking down and digesting alcohol, but also on the brain and its cognitive and regulatory functions, necessary for leading a normal, socially adjusted life. The potentially toxic effects of alcohol have been well-known since antiquity. Yet alcohol consumption and alcohol-related disorders became a major socio-political problem only from mediaeval times, and especially after the industrial revolution, associated with poverty in large parts of the population (Zernig *et al.* 2000; Schott 2001). It is understandable that psychiatrists like Emil Kraepelin, who waged a fight against alcoholism (1899, 1923), were deeply worried about the socially disruptive effects of alcohol misuse and strongly recommended total abstinence. Cultural alcohol drinking traditions in the West, however, have withstood these and many other attempts (e.g., prohibitionist church groups), whereas Islam has been more successful in banning alcohol.

Clinical Aspects

It is useful to distinguish between the misuse of a substance and the development of an addiction to it. Misuse can be drinking, for example, in order to attain 'Dutch courage' for an act of bravery or using alcohol as an anti-depressant or as a sleeping drug. Alcohol consumption leading to 0.2–0.4 ppm (representing approximately half a litre to one litre of normal beer drunk by a man of 70 kg bodyweight within 1 hour; in women, the same amount of alcohol leads to higher alcohol concentrations in the blood) has measurable effects on performance. Behavioural effects begin with a loss of inhibition (excitative stage), which is followed, when more alcohol is consumed, by uncoordinated speech and movement. In the hypnotic stage, increased levels of alcohol lead to sleepiness, unconsciousness, a lack of reflexes and breathing difficulties (life-threatening from 4 ppm onwards).

Frequent misuse of alcohol can lead to addiction. The following forms can be distinguished (after Jellinek 1960): *type* α: conflict drinkers (alcohol consumption to 'solve' emotionally stressful situations); *type* β: occasional drinkers, e.g., during social occasions; *type* γ: addictive drinkers with dose increases until, in some cases, lack of control; *type* δ: habitual drinkers / level drinkers, (e.g., wine grape growers, brewery workers, who keep a more or less constant level of blood alcohol throughout the day which allows them to carry out their job but has negative long term effects on health); *type* ε: binge drinker (see above).

According to Jellinek (1960), four phases in the development of alcohol addiction can be distinguished:

1. *The pre-alcoholic phase*: The alcohol consumer experiences the subjective positive effects and starts abusive use.
2. *Frequent thoughts about alcohol* (e.g., stocking up in advance), concealing actual volume of consumption, partial lack of memory following alcohol consumption.
3. *After about six months*, a lack of control becomes apparent. Although patients often want to drink less, attempts at abstinence fail. The physical addiction in the body causes them to solve morning withdrawal symptoms by consuming alcohol. Higher and higher doses are necessary to achieve the required effect; procuring alcohol and hiding the addiction become priority activities, whilst real tasks at hand are increasingly neglected. Social and professional decline begins at this stage if not before.
4. *In the chronic phase*, several-day spells of drunkenness and a reduction of alcohol tolerance due to organic damage to the central nervous system can be identified, which can lead to cerebral atrophy. Alcohol psychoses occasionally occur.

Other negative effects on the nervous system which affect non-addicts are: abnormal alcohol reaction, alcohol melancholy, pathological drunkenness, epilepsy; and amongst chronic consumers, polyneuropathy, Wernicke-Korsakoff syndrome, alcohol paranoia, alcoholic hallucination and *delirium tremens*. Physical consequences of chronic consumption are, for example, varicoses of the oesophagus veins due to a block in the venous blood flow in the cirrhotic liver and haemorrhage from these unnaturally extended veins (a common cause of death among alcoholic patients), reflux oesophagitis, chronic gastritis, duodenitis, ulcers, pancreatitis, fatty liver, liver cirrhosis, hypogonadism, alcohol-toxic (cardio-)myopathy, foetal alcoholism syndrome, and, caused by falls, brain atrophy and intracranial bleeding.

Two forms of addiction are distinguished, physical and psychological. Psychological addiction is characterised by an excessive longing for alcohol, whilst physical addiction is accompanied by withdrawal symptoms during abstinence from alcohol: shivering, sweating, nausea, vomiting, fear, depression, irritability, sleeping problems, epileptic attacks and *delirium tremens*, which was often lethal before psychopharmacological treatment became available.

Many, though not all, addiction mechanisms especially entail beta-endorphins, which is also true for alcohol addiction. Beta-endorphins are part of the reward system consisting of neuro-anatomical structures which are mainly localised in the limbic system. From an evolutionary biological perspective, endorphins probably originally played a role in channelling and optimising learning in the sense of classical conditioning, and later in phylogeny also affected operative learning functions (functional desire). Endorphins play an important role in social and sexual well-being. Synthetic opioids allow conditions which could not be achieved in the social reality.

Persons at higher risk for addiction have a reduced plasma beta-endorphin level and show greater increases in beta-endorphins following alcohol consumption than persons at lower risk (e.g., Blum *et al.* 1986; Seizinger *et al.* 1983), one could say that they compensate for the lack of psychological well-being while sober with alcohol intake, which is especially rewarding for this group. However, chronic alcohol consumption reduces, in the long run, endorphin levels even further when the person is sober. These lower beta-endorphin levels caused by chronic alcohol misuse probably increase the risk of a relapse after a period of abstinence, whilst the risk is also increased due to experiencing a stronger beta-endorphin release as a result of consumption. Besides stressful life events, these mechanisms are regarded as the underlying basis for developing an addiction. The effect of beta-endorphin rise following alcohol consumption can be pharmacologically suppressed using morphine antagonists. As clinical trials have shown, this can reduce the risk of an alcohol relapse (e.g., O'Malley *et al.* 1995; Volpicelli *et al.* 1995).

Other transmitters affecting the risk of a relapse also exist. They play an important role in treating depression, e.g., serotonin and noradrenalin. Psychiatric drugs which influence these systems can also have a positive affect on addictive behaviour. Yet there is still no sure cure for alcoholism today and high relapse rates are typical (Berman and Noble 1993) despite the efforts of specialists and self-help groups.

It has long been apparent that alcoholics are more common in certain families than others (Clifford *et al.* 1984; Cotton 1979; Kendler *et al.* 1992). Evidence of an inherited risk of addiction has been confirmed by studies on adopted children and twins. 30–40 per cent of those who have become addicted had one addicted parent (e.g., Hinterhuber 1982). Adopted children of addicted biological parents have a 2.5-fold higher risk of becoming addicted compared to adopted children whose biological parents were not addicted (Merikangas 1990).

Conclusion

From the time of its first production, beer has had good and bad effects on humans. In recent years the benefits of light to moderate consumption of alcohol have become obvious through various lines of research. Whereas it was first thought that the Mediterranean epidemiology with less cardiovascular diseases was due to the role of red wine, it has now become evident that alcohol as such is responsible for the reported beneficial effects. Beer contains many substances which can aid well-being and health. The caveat is, as Paracelsus said: the dose makes the poison.

Notes

1. RR means 'Relative Ratio'.
2. CI means 'Confidence Interval'.

References

Berman, S.M. and Noble, E.P. (1993) Childhood antecedents of substance misuse, *Current Opinion in Psychiatry*, 6:382–387.

Blum, K., Topel, H. (1986) Opioid peptides and alcoholism: genetic deficiency and chemical management, *Functional Neurology*, 1: 71–83.

Bode, C., Bode, J.C., Erhardt J.G., French, B.A. and French, S.W. (1998) Effect of the type of beverage and meat consumed by alcoholics with alcoholic liver disease, *Alcoholism, Clinical and Experimental Research*, 8: 1803–1805.

Borghi, L., Meschi, T., Schianchi, T., Briganti, A., Guerra, A., Allegri, F. and Novarini, A. (1999) Urine volume: stone risk factor and preventive measure, *Nephron*, 81 (Suppl 1): 31–37.

Brenner, H., Rothenbacher, D., Bode, G. and Adler, G. (1999) Inverse graded relation between alcohol consumption and active infection with Helicobacter pylori, *American Journal of Epidemiology*, 149(6): 571–576.

Cleophas, T.J. (1999) Wine, beer and spirits and the risk of myocardial infarction: a systematic review, *Biomedicine and Pharmacotherapy*, 53(9): 417–423.

Clifford, C.A., Hopper, J.L., Fulker, D.W. and Murray, R.M. (1984) A genetic and enviromental analysis of a twin family study of alcohol use, anxiety and depression, *Genetic Epidemiology*, 1: 63–79.

Cotton, N.S. (1979) The familial incidence of alcoholism: a review, *Journal of Studies on Alcohol*, 40: 89–116.

Criqui, M.H. and Ringel, B.L. (1994) Does diet or alcohol explain the French Paradox? *Lancet*, 344(8939–8940): 1719–1723.

Damerow, P. (1996) Food production and social status as documented in proto-cuneiform texts. In Wiessner, P. and Schiefenhövel, W. (eds) *Food and the Status Quest*, Berghahn, Oxford: 149–169.

Dixon-Shanies, D. and Shaikh, N. (1999) Growth inhibition of human breast cancer cells by herbs and phytoestrogens, *Oncology Reports*, 6(6): 1383–1387.

Dörfler, H.-P. and Roselt, G. (1990) *Heilpflanzen* (5th edition: original 1984), Urania Verlag, Leipzig.

Feldman, D., Stathis, P.A., Hirst, M.A., Stover, E.P. and Do, Y.S. (1984) Saccharomyces cerevisiae produces a yeast substance that exhibits estrogenic activity in mammalian systems, *Science*, 224(4653): 1109–1111.

Figueredo, E., Quirce, S., del Amo, A., Cuesta, J., Arrieta, I., Lahoz, C. and Sastr, J. (1999) Beer-induced anaphylaxis: identification of allergens, *Allergy*, 54(6): 630–634.

Gaziano, J.M., Hennekens, C.H., Godfried, S.L., Sesso, H.D., Glynn, R.J., Breslow, J.L. and Buring, J.E. (1999) Type of alcoholic beverage and risk of myocardial infarction, *American Journal of Cardiology*, 83(1): 52–57.

Gorinstein, S., Zemser, M., Berliner, M., Goldstein, R., Libman, I., Trakhtenberg, S. and Caspi, A. (1997) Moderate beer consumption and positive biochemical changes in patients with coronary atherosclerosis, *Journal of Internal Medicine*, 242(3): 219–224.

Groenbaek, M., Becker, U., Johansen, D., Tonnesen, H., Jensen, G. and Sorensen, T.I. (1998) Population based cohort study of the association between alcohol intake and cancer of the upper digestive tract, *British Medical Journal*, 317: 844–848.

Groenbaek, M., Deis, A., Sorensen, T.I., Becker, U., Borch-Johnsen, K., Mueller, C., Schnohr, P. and Jensen, G. (1994) Influence of sex, age, body mass index, and smoking on alcohol intake and mortality, *British Medical Journal*, 308: 302–306.

Groenbaek M., Mortensen, E.L., Mygind, K., Andersen, A.T., Becker, U., Gluud, C. and Sorensen, T.I. (1999) Beer, wine, spirits and subjective health, *Journal of Epidemiology and Community Health*, 53(11): 721-724.

Grossman, E.R. (1988) Beer, breast-feeding, and the wisdom of old wives, *Journal of the American Medical Association*, 259(7): 1016.

Henderson, M.C., Miranda, C.L., Stevens, J.F., Deinzer, M.L. and Buhler, D. (2000) In vitro inhibition of human P450 enzymes by prenylated flavonoids from hops, *Humulus lupulus*, *Xenobiotica*, 30(3): 235–251.

Hinterhuber, H. (1982): *Epidemiologie psychiatrischer Erkrankungen*, Enke, Stuttgart.

Hirvonen, T., Pietinen, P., Virtanen, M., Albanes, D. and Virtamo, J. (1999) Nutrient intake and use of beverages and the risk of kidney stones among male smokers, *American Journal of Edpidemiology*, 150(2): 187–194.

Hoffmeister, H., Schelp, F.P., Mensink, G.B., Dietz, E. and Boehning, D. (1999) The relationship between alcohol consumption, health indicators and mortality in the German population, *International Journal of Epidemiology*, 28(6): 1066–1072.

Janssens, J.P., Shapira, N., Debeuf, P., Michiels, L., Putman, R., Bruckers, L., Renard, D. and Molenberghs, G. (1999) Effects of soft drink and table beer consumption on insulin response in normal teenagers and carbohydrate drink in youngsters, *European Journal of Cancer Prevention*, 8(4): 289–295.

Jellinek, E.M. (1960) *The Disease Concept of Alcoholism*, Hill House Press, New Brunswick.

Jepson, R.G. Fowkes, F.G., Donnan, P.T. and Housley, E. (1995) Alcohol intake as a risk factor for peripheral arterial disease in the general population in the Edinburgh Artery Study, *European Journal of Epidemiology*, 11(1): 9–14.

Kauhanen, J., Kaplan, G.A., Goldberg, D.E., Salonen, R. and Salonen, J.T. (1999) Pattern of alcohol drinking and progression of atherosclerosis, *Arteriosclerosis, Thrombosis and Vascular Biology*, 19(12): 3001–3006.

Keil, U., Chambless, L.E., Doering, A., Filipiak, B. and Stieber, J. (1997) The relation of alcohol intake to coronary heart disease and all-cause mortality in a beer-drinking population, *Epidemilogy*, 8(2): 150–156.

Kendler, K.S., Heath, A.C., Neale, M.C., Kessler, R.C. and Eaves, L.J. (1992) A population based twin study on alcoholism in women, *Journal of the American Medical Association*, 268: 1877–1882.

Kerr, W.C., Fillmore, K.M. and Marvy, P. (2000) Beverage-specific alcohol consumption and cirrhosis mortality in a group of English-speaking beer-drinking countries, *Addiction*, 95(3): 339–346.

Klatsky, A.L. (1998) Alcohol and cardiovascular diseases: a historical overview, *Novartis Foundation Symposium*, 216: 2–12.

Kolata, G. (1984) Steroid hormone systems found in yeast, *Science*, 225(4665): 913–914.

Koppes, L.L., Twisk, J.W., Snel, J., Van Mechelen, W. and Kemper, H.C. (2000) Blood cholesterol levels of 32-year-old alcohol consumers are better than of nonconsumers, *Pharmacology, Biochemistry and Behavior*, 66(1): 163–167.

Kraepelin, E. (1899) Neuere Untersuchungen über die psychischen Wirkungen des Alkohols, *Münchener Medizinische Wochenschrift*, 46: 1365–1369.

Kraepelin, E. (1923) Neuere Arbeiten über die Beeinflussung des Seelenlebens durch Alkohol, *Internationale Zeitschrift für Alkoholismus*, 31: 266–284.

Marmot, M.G., Rose, G., Shipley, M.J. and Thomas, B.J. (1981) Alcohol and mortality: a U-shaped curve, *Lancet*, 8220(Pt 1): 580–583.

Meise, U. (ed.) (1993) *Alkohol, die Sucht Nr. 1*, Verlag Inegrative Psychiatrie, Innsbruck.

Merikangas, K.R. (1990). The genetic epidemiology of alcoholism, *Psychological Medicine*, 20: 11–22.

Milligan, S.R., Kalita, J.C., Pocock, V., Van De Kauter, V., Stevens, J.F., Deinzer, M.L., Rong, H. and De Keukeleire, D. (2000) The endocrine activities of 8-prenylnaringenin and related hop (*Humulus lupulus L.*) flavonoids, *Journal of Clinical Endocrinology and Metabolism*, 85(12): 4912–4915.

Niebergall-Roth, E., Harder, H. and Singer, M.V. (1998) A review: acute and chronic effects of ethanol and alcoholic beverages on the pancreatic exocrine secretion in vivo and in vitro, *Alcoholism: Clinical and Experimental Research*, 22(7): 1570–1583.

O'Malley, S.S., Croop, R.S., Wroblewski, J.M., Labriola, D.F. and Volpicelli J.R. (1995) Naltrexone in the Treatment of Alcohol Dependence, *Psychiatric Annals*, 25: 681–688.

Ottenjann, H. (1999) Trink-Tips fuer Harnstein-Patienten. Apfelschorle statt Bier (Drinking tips for patients with urinary calculi. Apple cider instead of beer), *MMW Fortschritte der Medizin*,141(37): 4–6.

Prescott, E., Groenbaek, M., Becker, U. and Sorensen, T.I. (1999) Alcohol intake and the risk of lung cancer: influence of type of alcoholic beverage, *American Journal of Epidemiology*, 149(5): 463–470.

Reinhardt, L. (1911) *Kulturgeschichte der Nutzpflanzen*, vol. 1–2, E. Reinhardt, München.

Renaud, S. and de Lorgeril, M., (1992) Wine, alcohol, platelets, and the French paradox for coronary heart disease, *Lancet*, 339(8808): 1523–1526.

Rimm, E.B, Giovannucci, E.L., Willett, W.C., Colditz, G.A., Ascherio, A., Rosner, B. and Stampfer, M.J. (1991) Prospective study of alcohol consumption and risk of coronary disease in men, *Lancet*, 338(8765): 464–468.

Schott, H. (2001) Das Alkoholproblem in der Medizingeschichte, *Deutsches Ärzteblatt*, 98: 1958–1962.

Schuurman, A.G., Goldbohm, R.A. and van den Brandt, P.A (1999) A prospective cohort study on consumption of alcoholic beverages in relation to prostate cancer incidence (The Netherlands), *Cancer Causes and Control*, 10(6): 597–605.

Seizinger, B.R., Boverman, K. and Maysinger, D. (1983) Differential effects of acute and chronic ethanol treatment on particular opioid peptide systems in discrete regions of rat brain and pituitary, *Pharmacology Biochemistry and Behavior*, 18(Suppl.1): 361–369.

Simons, L.A., McCallum, J., Friedlander, Y., Ortiz, M. and Simons, J. (2000) Moderate alcohol intake is associated with survival in the elderly: the Dubbo Study, *Medical Journal of Australia*, 173(3): 121–124.

Stevens, J.F., Taylor, A.W., Clawson, J.E. and Deinzer, M.L. (1999) Fate of xanthohumol and related prenylflavonoids from hops to beer, *Journal of Agricultural and Food Chemistry*, 47(6): 2421–2428.

Tekel, J., De Keukeleire, D., Rong, H., Daeseleire, E. and Van Peteghem, C. (1999) Determination of the hop-derived phytoestrogen, 8-prenylnaringenin, in beer by gas chromatography/mass spectrometry, *Journal of Agricultural and Food Chemistry*, 47(12): 5059–5063.

Teyssen, S., Gonzalez-Calero, G., Schimiczek, M. and Singer, M.V. (1999) Maleic acid and succinic acid in fermented alcoholic beverages are the stimulants of gastric acid secretion, *Journal of Clinical Investigation*, 103(5): 707–713.

van der Gaag, M.S., van Tol, A., Scheek, L.M., James, R.W., Urgert, R., Schaafsma, G. and Hendriks, H.F. (1999) Daily moderate alcohol consumption increases serum paraoxonase activity: a diet-controlled, randomised intervention study in middle-aged men, *Atherosclerosis*, 147(2): 405–410.

Volpicelli, J.R., Watson, N.T., King, A.C., Sherman, C.E. and O'Brien C.P. (1995) Effect of naltrexone on alcohol "high" in alcoholics, *American Journal Psychiatry*, 152(4): 613–615.

Wannamethee, S.G. and Shaper, A.G. (1999) Type of alcoholic drink and risk of major coronary heart disease events and all-cause mortality, *American Journal of Public Health*, 89(5): 685–690.

Woodson, K., Albanes, D., Tangrea, J.A., Rautalahti, M., Virtamo, J. and Taylor, P.R (1999) Association between alcohol and lung cancer in the alpha-tocopherol, beta-carotene cancer prevention study in Finland, *Cancer Causes and Control*, 10(3): 219–226.

Zernig, G., Saria, A., Kurz, M. and O'Malley, S.S. (eds) (2000) *Handbook of Alcoholism*, CrC Press LLC, Boca Raton, FL.

Zhang, Y., Kreger, B.E., Dorgan, J.F., Splansky, G.L., Cupples, L.A. and Ellison, R.C. (1999) Alcohol consumption and risk of breast cancer: the Framingham Study revisited, *American Journal of Epidemiology*, 14 (2): 93–101.

CHAPTER 3
BEER: HOW IT'S MADE – THE BASICS OF BREWING

Keith Thomas

Introduction

An advertising campaign promoted by the UK Brewers' Association in the mid 1930s contained the challenging title 'Beer is Best'. Intended to revive the poor sales at the time, it was an early statement of the long-held belief in the value of beer. Today that belief is being rigorously tested, not least in the light of ethanol's pathological effects, but also to accord credit where beer's nutritional content may provide unseen benefits. Moreover, beer is more than a flavoured solution of ethanol but an ingredient of culture contributing positively in many cases but negatively in others.

The Brewers' Association's claim that beer is best does have major historical support, not least in providing potable fluid intake when water supplies were commonly contaminated with cholera, typhoid and a choice of other diseases. In the UK in the 1700s and 1800s this was particularly true, at least until tea became an abstentionist alternative. Other countries have used beer or equivalent fermentations to similar effect. The level of alcohol in beer (3–10 per cent by volume) made it preferable for fluid replenishment compared to stronger drinks. Although this application of beer has been superseded by hygienic water supplies, factory-prepared bottled beverages and good social hygiene, beer has retained its popularity. It is also increasingly studied as a valuable dietary ingredient (Bamforth and Gambill 2007) and modified to increase its specific features (Jeney-Nagymate *et al.*. 2007; Muller *et al.*. 2007).

However, what afforded beer its protective ability against disease and why might it have any functional qualities beyond mere fluid? What specifically is beer – particularly compared to other beverages – and how exactly is it made? A consideration of these questions is the purpose of this summary view of the brewing process.

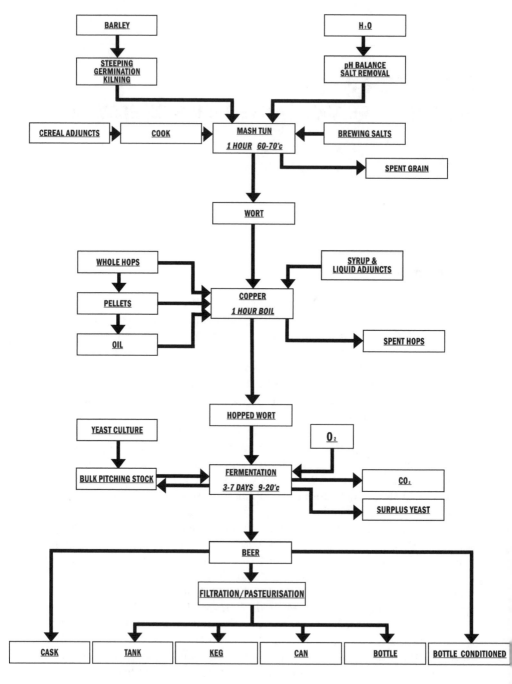

Figure 3.1   The Brewing Process from Barley to Bottle
(copyright Keith Thomas)

Definition

A good definition of beer is that imposed by the Institute of Brewing and Distilling on its examination candidates: '*A drink produced by the fermentation of sugars derived from malted barley flavoured with hops*'. The important part of this definition is the identification of two stages in the production – the extraction of sugars from malt and the fermentation of these sugars (Figure 3.1). Numerous fermented beverages are produced by simply fermenting a sugar extract – usually from fruits – to produce wines or ciders. Crude and sophisticated versions of these are possible according to whether the extract is pasteurised or not, further flavoured or fortified. Beer differs from these by using grains as a raw material. Grains contain sugar but unlike fruit have it in the form of the complex unfermentable starch polysaccharide rather than the simple mono- and di-saccharides most abundant in fruit. A preliminary process in brewing is the digesting of this starch to simpler sugars before fermentation is possible.

These grains are the seeds of a range of crops but particularly cereal species, most commonly barley, wheat, oats and rye. They are associated with temperate climates compared to the many fruits which are more abundant in warmer climates. They are also relatively dry and hard and contain their starch in well protected locations surrounded by impermeable cell walls and seed husks. This sugar is intended to provide energy for the future embryo to grow, not to attract animals to eat and distribute the internal seeds as in fruit.

At this point it is worth distinguishing between brewing and baking since the origins of both are interlinked and probably developed together in antiquity (Bamforth 2007; Hornsey 2003). Bread also uses cereal grains but does not require their starch to be digested to fermentable sugars. Bread also involves a fermentable step but only briefly uses the low levels of residual, or added, fermentable sugars to elevate the dough before baking. Carbon dioxide, the second major product of fermentation, is the active agent of baking, not ethanol. Starch remains in the dough and is made more digestible by the baking process so making bread a high energy food. In early antiquity bread may have been moistened and allowed to ferment further to produce a beer-like beverage (Samuel 1996; Hornsey 2003).

Malting and Mashing

For beer the starch in cereal grains must be more extensively digested. This occurs in two stages – malting and mashing. Malting initiates germination of the grains and activates the natural hydrolytic enzymes present to the point at which sufficient are present to digest the starch. Mashing uses these enzymes to digest the starch to produce a liquid extract, wort, which contains the resulting sugars as well as other digestion products – amino acids, polyphenols, minerals and vitamins also released from the cereal grains. It is this range of materials which partly accounts for beer's high nutritional status.

The types of cereals used in brewing should be noted. Today barley is the dominant cereal but wheat, rye and oats are all possible as they can be malted to obtain enzymes. Other grains, such as maize, rice and sorghum, cannot be malted, and although usable as sources of fermentable sugars, can only be added as adjuncts alongside barley malt or with endogenous enzymes to digest their starch. In antiquity, wheat was often a major cereal for brewing, but crop breeding developed barley in preference because of its higher enzyme synthesis and larger husk which is valuable as a filter to clarify the wort after mashing. Wheat is still a contributor to the grist in some beers, particularly continental wheat beers where it contributes specific flavours as well as giving strong head retention due to its higher protein levels (Delvaux *et al.* 2001). A further consequence of this is a greater haziness in the final beer.

Barley breeding has taken a contrary path in striving for low protein varieties with less than 1.5 per cent nitrogen. This provides for easier clarification in processing but does limit the areas for cultivation and requires careful growth management. Recent developments to produce barleys with low anthrocyanogen levels to reduce astringent mouth-feel have been promoted (McCaig *et al.* 2006) and the potential of genetically modified varieties is awaiting customer acceptance.

Malting

The standard malting process first soaks or 'steeps' grains for 24–36 hours with regular changes of water and forced aeration. Barley grains take up water to 44 per cent hydration and produce gibberellic acid which stimulates the synthesis of hydrolytic enzymes from the scutellum and aleurone layer surrounding the starchy endosperm. The maltsters target at this point is not to digest the starch but the endosperm cell walls and the protein matrix surrounding the starch grains. Amylase enzymes are also produced but remain largely unused until the later mashing stage.

At the correct stage the germinating malt is dried for storage and distribution to breweries. Drying is both critical and varied in order to produce malts of particular specifications. A careful sequence of airflow, temperatures and humidity is needed to preserve enzyme activity in pale malt. Temperatures above 100°C inactivate most amylase enzymes and so prevent later starch digestion. However, they do create additional flavours by caramelisation and by maillard reactions to produce the coloured malts required for dark beers (Gruber 2001). It is also believed that such malts may have functional benefits and may protect beer against the effects of oxidation (Coghe *et al.* 2003).

Today malting is conducted by specialist companies, often separate from breweries, but in the past malting and brewing were typically linked along with retail premises to create a full vertical integration. Today breweries purchase malt to specification and blend enzymatically active pale malt with coloured malts and cereal adjuncts into a grist for a specific beer. This grist is crushed before mashing and mixed with brewing liquor (water) to a target of between 4:1 and 2.5:1 liquor to grist reflecting a medium to thin porridge consistency.

Brewing liquor is a somewhat transparent but essential component of beer. Correct proportions are necessary to achieve target levels of alcohol, and its mineral components strongly affect the efficiency of production and contribute directly and indirectly to flavour. The pH and salt levels are strictly controlled and contaminants such as nitrate and pesticide levels regulated. In many cases complete removal of components is achieved by reverse osmosis and ion exchange methods. Subsequent addition of salts achieves a consistency which allows marketing to claim that an international brand is identical across the world. In turn it allows brands to be franchised for local production rather than shipping tanker volumes from the country of origin.

Traditional brewing before 1850 had little concept of water chemistry but had evolved beer characters according to the salt content of local supplies. Major distinctions related to the alkalinity due to bicarbonate salts and the sulphate:chloride balance. Along with calcium ions, alkalinity affects the pH of the mash so influencing enzyme activity. Sulphate and chloride impact directly on flavour with sulphate enhancing hop bitterness and chloride giving a smoother palate. Locations with particularly favourable water salt composition were able to produce specific and distinctive styles of beer, for example, bitter ales from Burton-upon-Trent with high sulphates and stouts from Dublin with high carbonates. Lager beers are generally lightly flavoured and developed in continental locations such as Bavaria, the Czech Republic and Slovakia, with generally low salt levels.

Mashing

Brewing liquor and grist are mixed in or on entry to a mashing vessel, generally large and shallow with robust construction and insulated against heat loss. Mashing temperature is critical to successful brewing. A relatively high initial 'strike' temperature is used to swell or gelatinise the starch grains and open them up to dissolution and digestion. Mashing temperature is important. Amylase enzymes are optimally active between 60 and 70°C and this is the typical temperature range of many systems. The exact temperature chosen, however, is complicated by the presence of two amylases, α and β, with different optima. α amylase, with an optimum between 65 and 70°C, digests starch chains internally, producing a range of sugars – glucose, maltose, maltotriose and larger dextrins. β amylase has a lower temperature optimum between 60 and 65°C and is denatured rapidly at higher temperatures. However, it digests maltose from the ends of starch chains and contributes greatly to the level of fermentable sugars and thus to the alcohol level produced.

Dextrins produced by α amylase action contribute instead to the body and thickness of the final beer. Choice of mash temperature thus influences beer character and may be matched for style – thin tasting pale ales and lagers, thick stouts and old ales. Mash temperature may be further managed according to malt quality where poorly modified grains require a temperature-programmed mash. This sequentially activates β glucanases to complete cell wall digestion at 35–40°C, proteases to complete protein digestion at 45–50°C and finally 65–70°C to conduct starch digestion. Today internal heating systems provide for such heating but continental brewing developed a modification termed decoction whereby an amount of mash is removed, boiled and returned to the mash to instigate each step increase. Less commonly practised today, some breweries retain decoction mashing for other perceived benefits including flavour and beer character.

Other modifications of mashing are required if cereal adjuncts are used. As these often have gelatinisation temperatures above 65°C they must be heated separately to swell the starch before adding to the mash. This is done in a separate cereal cooker and the extract blended to allow barley enzymes to conduct digestion. The use of cereal adjuncts is not a recent practice. Observations on brewing residues from ancient Egypt show mixtures of malted and unmalted grains (Samuel 1996). Mashing is typically conducted for one hour but in Victorian times and before it may have taken up to five hours or even overnight. It is unsure if this reflects poor quality malt requiring longer time to digest or a desire to maximise extraction of sugars and alcohol production. Traditional practices also included conducting one mash to produce two or more beers – a process termed 'party gyling' – a gyle being a single batch of beer. For this the initial run off would have higher sugar levels than later run offs and would have been used to produce a higher strength premium ale. Later run offs would be more dilute and used to produce cheaper table beer.

Extracting wort from the mash tun is a major difficulty in brewing. Ideally a clear run off is preferable as residual starch grains and coagulated protein cause hazes, flavour defects and staling. Today fine mesh screens and perforated plates provide a base for malt husks to conduct a fine separation or use mash filters in the case of bulk systems using finely ground grain (Andrews 2004; Braekeleirs et al. 2007). In early brewing, clarity was less critical and alternative filtration systems may have used juniper branches. In even cruder cases no separation is conducted and the mash is fermented semi-solid and drunk through straws as in indigenous African Bantu beer.

Typical processing of the completed mash includes washing or 'sparging' the digested grain residues with fresh liquor to remove residual wort and maximise sugar extraction. Initial runnings from the mash tun have high sugar levels of around 20 per cent. These are diluted by the sparge and a final collected wort of 12 per cent or 1050 original gravity is obtained and will produce a beer of 5 per cent alcohol by volume.

Boiling

This wort is collected in a boiling vessel, often termed a '*copper*' or '*kettle*'. Boiling achieves a number of aims, specifically sterilization, enzyme inactivation, flavour stabilization and physical stabilization. The first of these is a major reason for beer's safety advantages compared to unboiled water in past years. It may not, however, have been conducted in very early years resulting in beers very different from those we know today, most probably with a strong malt character, and possibly flavoured by herbs or honey. In the absence of boiling, such beers may well have retained enzyme activity and shown progressive changes as dextrins, proteins and other polymers were digested. This would mirror other short-term fermentation products such as are found in the Far East. Increasing alcohol levels would also be evident as the beer matures. Even with boiling, early beers before the use of hops in the fourteenth century would have had a variety of herbs added and current speculation on the choice of these has some relevance to the potential of beer's nutritional and possibly functional benefits.

Contemporary boiling is particularly focused on developing and stabilizing flavour and on minimising potential haze formation in the final beer. The major and distinctive flavour of modern beers is the bitterness produced from α acids or humulones in hops (Peacock 1998). α acids themselves have limited bitterness but become very bitter when isomerised to iso α acids, a reaction catalysed by heat. Boiling performs this conversion although, because the wort has a pH of around 5.3, it is typically no more than 35 per cent complete when using whole hops.

Developments over the past fifty years have produced a range of hop products with greater efficiencies of conversion including pellets of powdered hops and oils of fully isomerised humulones. A particularly specific hop product is tetra hop extract, stabilized against photodegradation. Beer produced by standard hops and packaged in clear glass bottles will show the results of photodegradation by the unmistakable aroma of 3-methyl-2-butene-1-thiol, the warning smell also produced by skunk anal glands. Tetra hop is another technical development allowing the marketing department to extend the presentation and image of beer.

Although dominant in contemporary beer flavour, hops have a controversial history. Initially appearing as a flavouring in continental beers in the fourteenth century, hops not only provided distinct flavour features, but also produced longer shelf life due to the strong antibacterial properties of iso α acids. All beers will inhibit microbial growth due to their low ph (3.9–4.2) and high alcohol levels, but beer is still susceptible to the growth of specialised microbes, particularly acetic and lactic acid bacteria. High acidity and off flavours make unhopped beer unstable and the near universal use of hops in boiling today has clear justification.

Hop plants themselves are tended by a highly specialised industry tending a 5-metre-tall perennial climbing plant which only grows in specific latitudes. The hop flower contains the active materials in its lupulin glands at the base of the flower bracts and is sensitive to deterioration by environmental stress and infestation by viruses, fungi and aphid diseases. In addition, to prevent deterioration, hop cones must be dried on the day of harvest. Different varieties have been developed over time and may be associated with specific beer styles for example the classic UK *Goldings* and *Fuggles* varieties with pale ales, and *Hallertau* and *Saaz* with continental lagers. More recent interest has focused on increasing α acid levels to enhance yield, on enhancing levels of aromatic oils, and on breeding dwarf hops which are easier to grow and harvest.

Hop oil is the second contribution of the hop plant to beer character. Over 300 specific compounds are involved (Moir 1994) and may be grouped into hydrocarbons, oxidised derivatives and sulphur compounds. The release of these during boiling depends on the volatility of the compound and the final beer flavour can be manipulated by choice of hop variety, dosing levels and time of addition. Skills in hop management are one element of successful brewing and the variety of hop features, including annual variations, explain why beer can be such a varied beverage.

Simple evaporation contributes to this variation by removing not only the hop volatiles but also other flavours carried over from mashing. Di-methyl sulphide is a major feature here and differs greatly between ale and lager, as malts are higher in lager and provide a distinctive cabbage, sweetcorn flavour.

Boiling's final contribution to brewing is to clarify the wort through precipitation of proteins and polyphenols. High levels of these in the final beer will cause hazes and their precipitation in boiling and in conditioning is carefully managed. To achieve a sound precipitation a vigorous boil is necessary. Hydrophobic proteins will selectively gather on the surface of water vapour bubbles and coagulate. The more bubbles present in the boil the greater and more rapid the coagulation. Active systems of pressurised boiling, and more recently thin film vapour evaporation (Bonacchelli *et al.* 2006), have both increased boiling efficiency and reduced time.

After boiling, rapid cooling is essential to avoid both contamination by microorganisms and oxidation of reactive compounds, particularly aldehydes and lipids. Open cooling in shallow trays was common for centuries and doubtless provided some of the above features as typical characteristics. Since the 1890s a variety of heat exchangers and refrigeration systems have achieved cooling within hours allowing rapid yeast pitching to follow boiling.

Fermentation

Fermentation is the second major reaction of brewing. It is a fundamental metabolic process common to many microorganisms as well as yeast. Ethanol and carbon dioxide are common products but in many bacteria lactic and acetic acids result. Yeasts are indigenous in the environment particularly on fruit and would have had no difficulty growing in the worts of antiquity.

Subsequent brewers realised that yeast was essential for fermentation despite having no concept of its cellular characteristics. In fact bitter arguments between early microbiologists and biochemists were only resolved by the elegant experiments of Louis Pasteur in the 1850s. By 1900 yeast was not only recognised as the agent of alcohol production but selected into specialised strains. For many years particular breweries were distinguished by the specific strains they used – often jealously protected, but in other cases shared cooperatively, with neighbours. The close attention of microbiology and molecular biology in recent years has provided a wealth of information on yeast genetics and physiology and provided an extensive base for the management of fermentation (Güldener *et al*. 2005; Nakao *et al*. 2009).

In traditional ale brewing yeast is pitched into freshly cooled wort at a concentration of ten million cells per ml. Rapid growth over the following 48 hours can raise this count fivefold producing surplus yeast for future fermentations. Observation of such fermentations illustrates a major feature of yeast physiology – flocculation – the ability of yeast to aggregate and form flocs which either rise to form a head in ale yeasts or sediment in lager yeasts. This distinction affords the classification of ales as top fermenting beers and lagers as bottom fermenting.

Although flocculation is not so clear-cut for every yeast strain as top fermenting, some yeasts may sediment; genetic analysis has shown clear differences between ale and lager yeasts. These differences appear to arise from early evolution whereby lager strains developed from a hybridisation of *Saccharomyces byanus* and *Saccharomyces cerevisiae* (Nakao *et al*. 2009). Ale strains are much more heterogenous in their genetics but in general terms produce less sulphite and ferment at higher temperatures of 16–25°C compared to lager yeasts at 9–13°C (Crumplen *et al*. 1993).

These differences are reflected in the many different fermentation systems evident in different breweries and different regions. Standard open vessels may conduct adequate fermentation, but convoluted systems to separate yeast for reuse led to the complexities of the Burton Union system and the Yorkshire Square. In many breweries today, tall conical fermenters are used because of their more rapid fermentation, ease of management and smaller floor area.

During growth, yeast ferments sugars to ethanol and carbon dioxide to obtain cellular energy. Although fermentation is inefficient in producing energy, the production of ethanol is believed to confer a selective advantage on yeast under natural conditions, where the antimicrobial action of ethanol inhibits competition from other microbes (see also chapter 1).

Ethanol and carbon dioxide are not the only products of fermentation. A range of other flavours is produced and these provide distinction amongst yeast strains. Higher alcohols, esters, aldehydes, ketones and sulphur compounds, particularly hydrogen sulphide and dimethyl sulphide (DMS), are most notable and vary with yeast strain. Contemporary beers are particularly prescribed for their levels of two important metabolites, DMS and diacetyl, with flavours of sweetcorn and butterscotch respectively. DMS can be produced by yeast or other microorganisms but most in beer arises from malt, as described earlier.

Diacetyl levels rise during fermentation as a consequence of amino acid metabolism and easily exceed the flavour threshold of 0.2 mg per litre. Post-fermentation assimilation of diacetyl by yeast allows for its reduction during maturation, as occurs naturally during prolonged storage of traditional lagers (Bamforth and Kanauchi 2004). More recently the use of immobilized enzymes achieves the same in shorter time, particularly with continuous fermentation systems (Yamauchi *et al.* 1994).

Maturation

Maturation can be regarded as a continuation of fermentation but generally relates to changes after ethanol production is complete. By this stage fermentable sugars will have been utilized but unfermentable dextrins remain providing a high specific gravity of 1012 for a 5 per cent beer. In comparison, wines and ciders lacking dextrins complete fermentation at a specific gravity of 990, and a much thinner mouth-feel. Maturation events also include a variety of flavour changes such as a reduction of green-apple-flavour, acetyl-dehyde, and an increase in fruit-flavoured esters as alcohols react with acids. An increase in carbon dioxide concentration may occur if the beer is held under pressure. Alternatively CO_2 or a CO_2 nitrogen mixture may be introduced to a target specification later at packaging.

A particularly important target of maturation is clarification by settlement of yeast, but also of further precipitation of proteins and polyphenols. Gravity will achieve this, but slowly. Accelerated settlement may be conducted using fining agents including isinglass proteins from fish swim bladders, alginates from seaweed, polyvinyl pyrolodine and silicates. All of these are relatively recent applications and it is likely that historic beers were hazy and, arguably, more nutritious than today's. Once again the traditional brewing process has been altered to provide for marketing demands.

Packaging

Packaging after maturation is another major area of marketing concern where package types – casks, keg, bottle or can – have common and individual challenges to preserve beer quality. There are important demands for visual appeal in designing bottle and can shape, colour and texture. In general, a common concern is to keep matured beer as free from oxygen as possible, with typical targets of less than 0.2 mg per litre. Higher levels are likely to cause oxidation resulting in stale flavours (Kaneda *et al.* 1999) and protein – polyphenol precipitation (Bamforth 1999) and so reduce shelf life. Pipework, storage vessels and filling systems are carefully designed to achieve this aim.

While standard processing results in direct packaging of a beer into containers, much bulk production involves fermentation at high gravity and dilution with sterile water before packaging. Naturally this water must be de-aerated and sterilized before use, but the overall process has economic advantages in reducing fluid volumes in processing.

In most cases beer is filtered and/or pasteurised to provide a sterile product with long shelf life of up to 18 months. Filtration involves a variety of media including fibre sheets but also mineral powders while pasteurisation requires high energy input. Both treatments may adversely affect beer character – filtration reducing foam by removing proteins and pasteurising accelerating oxidation. Foam is a major visual attraction of beer and has complex origins in materials and processing (Evans and Sheehan 2002).

There is a clear distinction in the packaging between draught beers packaged into casks and kegs, or even tanks, and small pack beer in bottles and cans. This generally reflects retail sales in bars and the take-home trade respectively, although bottle sales in some bars can be considerable.

Shelf life of draught beer is shorter than that of small pack beer due to the opportunities for interference and contamination during dispense (Walker *et al.* 2007). Initiatives to minimise biofilm in dispensing systems have been made but achieving high quality beer across a bar also requires skills in cellar management and hygiene. Traditional cask ale is particularly sensitive as air is introduced to the cask during dispense thus limiting shelf life to a few days. Filtered and artificially carbonated beer, either in keg or small pack are more consistent over time, but are significantly removed in character from traditional beer. They are, however, the vast majority of sales and have become the dominant character of beer around the world. Where once beer was ordered as specific styles or brands it is now often just 'beer'. Producers of traditional styles have a challenge to prove that their Beer is indeed Best.

References

Andrews, J. (2004) A review of progress in mash separation technology, *Technical Quarterly of the Master Brewers of the Americas*, 41: 41–49.

Bamforth, C.W. (1999) Beer haze, *Journal of the American Society of Brewing Chemists*, 57: 81–90.

Bamforth, C.W. (2007) Beer as liquid bread, *Technical Quarterly of the Master Brewers of the Americas*, 44: 15–18.

Bamforth, C.W. and Gambill, S.C. (2007) Fiber and putative prebiotics in beer, *Journal of the American Society of Brewing Chemists*, 65: 70–76.

Bamforth, C.W. and Kanauchi, M. (2004) Enzymology of vicinyl diketone reduction in brewers' yeast, *Journal of the Institute of Brewing*, 110: 83–93.

Bonacchelli, B., Tigel, R., Harmegnies, F. and Formesyn, B. (2006) Wort stripping technology to save entery – targets and new industrial results, *Technical Quarterly of the Master Brewers of the Americas*, 46: 288–292.

Braekeleirs, R., Vandenbussche, J. and Harmegnies, F. (2007) Practical experiences with mash filtration on thin-bed filters from brews made with several kinds of raw materials, *Technical Quarterly of the Master Brewers of the Americas*, 44: 121–126.

Coghe, S., Vanderhaegen, B., Pelgrims, B., Basteyns, A.V. and Delvaux, F.R. (2003) Characterisation of dark speciality malts: new insights in colour evaluation and pro- and antioxidative activity, *Journal of the American Society of Brewing Chemists*, 61: 125–132.

Crumplen, R., D'Amore, T., Slaughter, C. and Stewart, G.G. (1993) Novel differences between ale and lager brewing yeasts, *Proceedings of the Congress of European Brewing Convention*, 24: 267–274.

Delvaux, F., Gys, W., Michiels, J., Delvaux, F.R. and Delcour, J.A. (2001) Contribution of wheat and wheat protein fractions to the colloidal haze of wheat beers, *Journal of the American Society of Brewing Chemists*, 59: 135–140.

Evans D.E. and Sheehan, M.C. (2002) Don't be fobbed off: the substance of beer foam, *Journal of the American Society of Brewing Chemists*, 60: 47–57.

Gruber, M.A. (2001) The flavour contribution of kilned and roasted products to beer styles, *Technical Quarterly of the Master Brewers of the Americas*, 38: 227–233.

Güldener, U., Münsterkötter, M., Kastenmüller, G., Strack, N., Helden, J. van, Lemer, C., Richelles, J., Wodak, S.J., García-Martínez, J., Pérez-Ortín, J.E., Michael, H., Kaps, A., Talla, E., Dujon, B., André, B., Souciet, J.L., Montigny, J. de, Bon, E., Gaillardin, C. and Mewes, H.W. (2005) CYGD: The comprehensive yeast genome database, *Nucleic Acid Research*, 33: 364–368.

Hornsey, I. (2003). *A History of Beer and Brewing*, Royal Society of Chemistry, Cambridge.

Jeney-Nagymate, E. and Fodor, P. (2007) Analytical properties of vitamin-entriched beer, *Technical Quarterly of the Master Brewers of the Americas*, 44: 179–182.

Kaneda, H., Kobayashi, N., Takashio, I., Tamaki, I. and Shinotsuka, K. (1999), Beer staling mechanism, *Technical Quarterly of the Master Brewers of the Americas*, 36: 41–47.

McCaig, R., Sawatzky, K., Egi, A. and Li, Y. (2006) Brewing with Canadian hulless barley varieties, CDC Freedom, CDC McGwire, and CDC Gainer, *Journal of the American Society of Brewing Chemists*, 64: 118–123.

Moir, M. (1994) Hop aromatic compounds. In *European Brewery Convention Monograph XXII – EBC-Symposium on Hops, Zoeterwoude, The Netherlands, May/ June 1994*, Verlag Hans Carl, Nuremberg, Germany: 165–180.

Muller, R., Walker, S., Brauer, J. and Junquera, M. (2007) Does beer contain compounds that might interfere with cholesterol metabolism?, *Journal of the Institute of Brewing*, 113: 102–109.

Nakao, Y., Kanamori, T., Itoh, T., Kodama, Y., Raineri, S., Nakamura, N., Shimonaga, T., Hattori, M. and Ashikari, T. (2009) Genome sequence of the lager brewing yeast, an interspecies hybrid, *DNA Research*, 16: 115–129.

Peacock, V. (1998) Fundamentals of hop chemistry, *Technical Quarterly of the Master Brewers of the Americas*, 35: 4–8.

Samuel, D. (1996) Investigation of Ancient Egyptian baking and brewing methods by correlative microscopy, *Science*, 273: 488–490.

Walker, S.L., Fourgialakis, M., Cerezo, B. and Livens, S. (2007) Removal of microbial biofilms from dispense equipment: the effect of enzymatic pre-digestion and detergent treatment, *Journal of the Institute of Brewing*, 113: 61–66.

Yamauchi, Y., Kashihara, T., Murayama, H., Nagara, A., Okamoto, T. and Mawatari, M. (1994) Scaleup of immobilized yeast reactor for continuous fermentation of beer, *Technical Quarterly of the Master Brewers of the Americas*, 31: 30–34.

CHAPTER 4
INTERDISCIPLINARY INVESTIGATIONS INTO THE BREWING TECHNOLOGY OF THE ANCIENT NEAR EAST AND THE POTENTIAL OF THE COLD MASHING PROCESS

Martin Zarnkow, Adelheid Otto and *Berthold Einwag*

The ancient Near East was the homeland of beer brewing. Numerous written documents from the third millennium BC onwards inform us about the fundamental role of beer for daily alimentation and social events (Milano 1994). Considering the amount of consumed beer, brewing must have taken place on a large scale. However, no clear archaeological evidence for brewing has so far been found in a private or an official building at a Mesopotamian site.

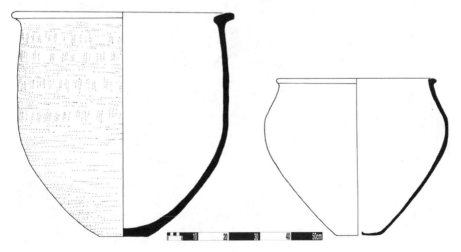

Figure 4.1 Large 'beer vat' (approximately 200 litre volume) and a vessel with a hole in the bottom (90–110 litre volume).

New Hints for Ancient Brewing at the North Mesopotamian Site of Tall Bazi

Excavations at Tall Bazi in Northern Syria have led to new insights into malt and beer making in ancient times (Zarnkow, Spieleder *et al.* 2006). At Tall Bazi, located in the Euphrates valley, fifty houses of the Late Bronze Age settlement (fourteenth to thirteenth century BC) served for residential purposes and for production of objects of all kinds. Unknown circumstances led to the sudden destruction of the city and the conservation of many objects of the daily life within these houses. The very similar organisation of the houses and their contents allowed detailed insights into the daily activities of the inhabitants (Einwag and Otto 2002).

One of the most remarkable features was the repeated combination of three ceramic vessels at a certain location in the houses: A large vat with a volume of up to 200 litres with a wide opening and a thickened rim was found in nearly every house (Figure 4.1). This largest vessel of the ceramic inventory was always set into the ground and immobile (Figure 4.2). Often associated was a slightly smaller vessel (ca. 90–110 litres) with a hole in the bottom (Figure 4.1). Large storage jars, which served for storing solid food and often still contained carbonised barley, completed the set. The question was; which liquid the vat and the large vessel may have contained? Drinking water can be excluded,

Figure 4.2 A large beer vat and a grinding installation in two neighbouring rooms of house 17 at Tall Bazi.

because the vat could not be cleaned thoroughly, and the microbial growth in water must have been considerable in the warm climate. Other liquids which were consumed at that time such as oil, wine or honey are unlikely, because storage jars have in general narrow openings for easy closing. The position of the large vat near the entrance and under the staircase showed that good ventilation was sought. These considerations in combination with our knowledge about the high amount of beer consumption in the ancient Near East made beer a good candidate for these vessels.

This state of the question made scientific residue analysis necessary. In order to identify the liquid, sherds of the above-mentioned pots and of other vessels which presumably might have been connected with beer and wine were subjected to spot tests (Feigl 1960). In some instances, residues of tartrate were found, which indicates that they contained wine. Several of the above-mentioned vats and vessels with a hole in the bottom were found to contain residues of oxalate. Oxalate crystals are formed when grain is mixed with an excess of water. After a 24-hour steep of 200g of barley in 0.5 l of water, 7.6 mg/l of oxalate was formed (Zarnkow, Spieleder *et al.* 2006). As oxalate can arise from other plants, for example rhubarb (290–640 mg of oxalic acid/l: Souci, Fachmann *et al.* 2000), an oxalate find does not necessarily provide evidence for beer. However, the probability is high. As no tartrate was found in these vessels, wine or grape juice can be eliminated as a starting medium for fermentation (yeast cells on the surface of the grapes). Some yeast cells were also found in isolated cases. Yeasts are, however, ubiquitous in the vicinity and thus only an indication for fermentation though not a compelling proof. A further indication is provided by sporadic starch grains found on the fragments. Important utensils such as stirring spoons or reed mats as working tools were not found because they were made of organic materials which are seldom preserved in archaeological sites. These utensils can, however, be assumed to have been used by the inhabitants of Tall Bazi.

The first conclusion that can be drawn is that the large vessels possibly had a role in the brewing process. This is indicated by the fact that the beer vessel is fixed in the floor. This presupposes that what it contained was not hygienically vulnerable because the vessel could not be completely cleaned. On the other hand, contact with the floor ensured that there was a cooling effect, something that must have been of particular interest in summer. As the vessel was only half sunk into the earth and the remainder was exposed to the influence of the ambient temperature, a temperature difference arose during fermentation (only 2.7 per cent of the total energy is chemically bound in the anaerobic phase, the remainder is heat energy (Narziss 2005), leading to a circulation within the vessel.

However, in order to achieve a greater degree of certitude about the possibility of ancient brewing at Tall Bazi, it was necessary to brew a 'Bazi beer' on location and with equipment similar to the ancient one, taking into account the conditions of the antiquity.

The Climatic and Botanic Situation

Tall Bazi lies at the edge of the rain-farming zone. It can be assumed that the climate in the Late Bronze Age was similar to that of the present day (Wirth 1971). The Euphrates region was then covered with sparse alluvial forest, and the few trees were used more in construction than as firewood. Twigs and animal dung were used in the latter case. A palaeobotanic analysis of grain showed up mainly multi-rowed barley, and rarely naked wheat and emmer. Some barley grains showed clear signs of germination.

The Technological Situation

It has to be assumed that the male and female beer brewers of Tall Bazi had a more than adequate technological range of experience. These people were very well trained in handicrafts and were in a position to make a product in a reproducible manner which was seen to be valuable enough to find mention in numerous written documents (Röllig 1970). There are other aspects associated with beer production that will be dealt with below. One asset is that it is possible to have a drinkable beverage in storage and keep it suitable for drinking as a result of the low pH value, because the occurrence of pathogenic germs is prevented (Back 1994). Furthermore, beer is a nutritious beverage with many physiological benefits. As the cuneiform texts do not inform us which grain was used in which state for malt and beer making, it has to be made clear right from the beginning that, from a technological standpoint, malt was and is a fixed feature of beer preparation. Otherwise, the nutritive and alcoholic yield is much too low because the required amylolytic enzymes that are capable of converting native cereal starch to a sugar which can be fermented by yeast are not present. Extensive preliminary trials showed that high alcohol yield is possible only with malt. Most fermentations based on unmalted grain had no appreciable alcohol yields. Boiled, therefore gelatinisised, unmalted barley grist was the only one having a small yield, comparable to half the alcoholic content when using malt grist (Zarnkow, Spieleder et al. 2006). Consequently, amylolytic enzymes are present in sufficient measure only when the grain has germinated and thus malted. Another important aspect is the adequate presence of amino acids in the malt wort for supporting yeast growth, allowing multiple yeast cycles without any problem. Repitching use of yeast is the most conceivably sensible variant. It is hard to imagine that a male or female beer brewer would not have recognised the benefit of a 'live' fermenting foam cover of a top-fermenting fermentation. This in no way indicates that only malt was used. It was certainly also the case that unmalted starch sources were used (Jennings, Antrobus et al. 2005). Forms of pre-gelatinised starch such as bulgur (boiled, unmilled grains) or bread are conceivable.

Brewing Experiments According to the Technology of Antiquity

On the basis of the archaeological, climatic and botanical conditions described, brewing tests were directed towards producing a drinkable beer without artificial heat input. This very unusual technology has to be regarded as a basic technology of the Bazi brewers of 3,200 years ago. This basic technology can be extended in every direction (heating, flavouring, etc.). Cold mashing involves having an enzyme potential present and that the starch has to go through pre-gelatinisation. Malt can provide both of these conditions to a sufficient extent. Malt bread cannot be considered as pre-gelatinised starch due to the site conditions (no baking moulds) and the extremely liquid dough that arose in the tests.

Malting

We found that the hole-bottomed vessels were extremely suitable as steeping and germination vessels. Germination could be carried out, on the one hand, in vessels and, on the other hand on mats (we used mats). The local rooms, built from sun-dried mud bricks in the same way as the ancient rooms millennia

Figure 4.3   Spreading out green malt on the roof for kilning.

earlier, assured a constant pile temperature of about 24°C during germination. The green malt was turned over twice a day by us, and germination was completed after four days. Kilning took place on the flat roof of the houses, consisting of mud (Figure 4.3). Here, an important factor emerged. 60°C was reached in the summer months without any problem whereas only 45°C was measured in April (but in both cases water contents of the malted barley were under 14%, therefore storage conditions were reached). This could be an indication of seasonal malting, supported by the fact that the barley varieties still used today require a long dormancy (germination power 09/2004: 50 per cent and 04/2005: 82 per cent; both from the 04/2004 crop). After approximately one year dormancy, it was possible to malt the barley into better malt.

Milling the Malt

The dry malt was milled on a saddle quern with a grinding stone (Figure 4.4), both consisting of basalt or coarse-grained limestone. Mortars were also found in Bazi but we preferred the saddle mill in a practical comparison of both milling systems. In some instances the milling installation was carefully set on a floor plastered with sherds (Figure 4.2); more frequently, however, milling took place at a better ventilated area, namely on the roof of the house.

Figure 4.4 Grinding the Bazi malt on a saddle quern.

Mashing, Wort Preparation and the Fermentation Process

Mashing-in was carried out at 34°C, with vigorous stirring for 15 min, using a grist/water mixing ratio of 1:8.3. A mixture of *Saccaromyces* and *Schizo-saccharomyces* yeasts as well as *Lactobacillus* species were added to the mash subsequently, and the mix was allowed to rest for 36 hours at about 24°C. A mixture of alcoholic and lactic acid fermentation is the most conceivable probability, as shown by pre-tests. With a view to a low alcoholic content, the resulting beers were mashed in very dilute form because the ancient beers must have been drunk by all sections of the population including children (Stol 1994). The obtained experimental beers had the anticipated low alcoholic content (1.6 vol per cent). They were highly fermented (final attenuation 87.0 per cent), standard in terms of saccharification (0.118 in the photometric iodine sample) and, with a pH of 3.90, provided a certain degree of safety against microbial contamination. The beers were stable for over two months under modern storage conditions (6°C). The much diversified taster panel assembled on location certified the beers as having a pleasant lively character with enjoyable consumption potential.

Summary

Based on a multiplicity of archaeological and palaeobotanical circumstantial evidence, we succeeded in discovering a conceivable process for ancient oriental malt and beer production for the period around the fourteenth/thirteenth century BC, using experimental test series on location. This is a cold mashing process in large beer vessels with malt or malt surrogates which had been previously steeped and germinated in base-tapped vessels. Germination could also be continued and completed on a mat. The mashing process was followed by a heterogeneous fermentation which most probably resulted from intentional propagation. Many questions are still open in relation to Bronze Age malt and beer production. With this interdisciplinary approach (archaeology, brewing technology), a new effort is made to investigate the many remaining questions about ancient beer brewing.

References

Back, W. (1994) *Farbatlas und Handbuch der Getränkebiologie, Teil 1. Kultivierung/ Methoden, Brauerei, Winzerei*, Fachverlag Hans Carl, Nürnberg.

Einwag, B. and Otto, A. (2002) Tall Bazi 1998 und 1999 – Die letzten Untersuchungen in der Weststadt, *Damaszener Mitteilungen*, 13: 65–68.

Feigl, F. (1960) *Tüpfelanalyse, Band II, Organischer Teil*, Frankfurt a. Main.

Jennings, J., Antrobus, K. L., Atencio, S. J., Glavich, E., Johnson, R. Loffler, G. and Luu, C. (2005) Drinking beer in a blissful mood. Alcohol production, operational chains, and feasting in the ancient world. *Current Anthropology* 46(2): 275–303.

Milano, L. (1994) *Drinking in Ancient Societies, History of the Ancient Near East/Studies 6*, Padova.

Narziss, L. (2005) *Abriss der Bierbrauerei*, Wiley-VCH, Weinheim.

Röllig, W. (1970) *Das Bier im Alten Mesopotamien*, Gesellschaft für die Geschichte des Brauwesens e.V., Berlin.

Souci, S.W., Fachmann, W. and Kraut, H. (2000) *Die Zusammensetzung der Lebensmittel Nährwert-Tabellen*, CRC Press, Boca Raton.

Stol, M. (1994) Beer in neo-Babylonian times. In Milano, L. (ed.) *Drinking in Ancient Societies, History of the Ancient Near East Studies 6*, Padova: 155–183.

Wirth, E. (1971) *Länderkunde Syrien*, Wissenschaftliche Buchgesellschaft, Darmstadt.

Zarnkow, M., Spieleder, E., Back, W., Sacher, B., Otto, A. and Einwag, B. (2006). Interdisziplinäre Untersuchungen zum altorientalischen Bierbrauen in der Siedlung von Tall Bazi/Nordsyrien vor rund 3200 Jahren. *Technikgeschichte* 73(1): 3–25.

CHAPTER 5
BEER IN PREHISTORIC EUROPE

Hans-Peter Stika

Introduction

In contrast to wine, which is made from sugars derived from fruit, beer production is based on starch. Cereals were, and still are, used in brewing. Other starch sources (manioc, yam, sweet potato, quinoa, etc.) may be used. Yeast is also necessary for fermentation. This fungus turns sugar into alcohol but cannot work on starch which is the main component of cereals. Therefore, it is necessary during the brewing process to convert the starch into sugar. This is normally done by germinating the grain which induces the production of the enzyme to split the starch into maltose. After drying, the malt can be ground, dissolved in warm water to convert most of the starch into sugar, and, finally fermented by yeast into raw beer. Additionally, it has to be purified and ripened until it reaches the preferred quality of beer. In modern beers hops are always added not only to improve the taste but also for better quality and durability (Stika 1998; see also chapters 3 and 4).

Other traditional methods for facilitating fermentation are

- chewing the millet (traditional African *sorghum* and *pennisetum* beers or old type Asian millet beers),
- thermal treatment by cooking or baking (ancient Egyptian and Mesopotamian beer bread partly made of malted cereals), and
- the application of mold fungus on rice (Far Eastern rice beers).

After this short introduction to the biological basics of brewing I shall consider historical and prehistorical information about beer.

In ancient Greek and Roman sources, beer is mentioned with regard to several tribes (including Celts and Germans) and described as their main drink (various authors, in particular Tacitus, cited in Lenz 1859). In ancient Greece and Rome, beer was known but wine was the preferred drink if it was available. The Mesopotamian and Egyptian beer production and its importance is depicted in reliefs, paintings and inscriptions from as early as Neolithic times. In these regions light beer was used as 'daily bread' as well as payment for work, offerings, grave goods and medicine. As little is known from written and iconographic sources for European prehistoric times, one has to search for indications of beer production and consumption unearthed at excavations.

Indications of Beer in Archaeological Excavation

What kinds of indications, apart from those from iconographic sources, can be gleaned from archaeological excavations for prehistorical periods? There are the remains of the malt, the residues of wort and liquid, the tools and vessels used for brewing, the features where the brewing activities took place, the flavouring additives, the transportation and storage vessels, or special drinking sets. But how indicative of prehistoric beer in Europe are these different finds?

Finds of Malt

Van Zeist (1991) listed some charred finds of germinating cereal grains from Roman times onwards. From Bronze Age sites in Spain, there are records of germinated grain, which may have been due to brewing activities (Hopf 1991). Coarsely ground malt from Celtiberic Numantia in central Spain was found in hand-driven rotation mill-stones, which is indicative of the first steps of a brewing process (Juan-Tresserras 1995). Furthermore, a large amount of lightly germinated barley grain was found in charred preserves unearthed in the early Celtic settlement of Hochdorf in south-western Germany. It is believed that these grains could be residues derived from an accident from burnt-down malting activities (Stika 1996). However, aside from the germinated grains, there must be certain special circumstances and some other indications in order to interpret the finds as brewing activities.

   It is possible that the grain could have germinated because of wet conditions in the fields before harvest or due to storage in a damp environment. To stop germination and to make it suitable for consumption, it may have been dried. It is also possible that an intentional malting could have occured to produce sweetened grain so that it could be consumed either directly or for ritual purposes, for example as funeral gifts (e.g., Roman Augst in Switzerland cf. Jacomet 1986).

Residues of the Wort and the Liquid

The first archaeochemical evidence for beer was found in an Upper Egyptian site called Hierakonpolis dating to 3500–3400 cal BC (Maksoud *et al.* 1994).

Using different chemical and physical methods of studying residues from a vat, a total of twenty-five compounds were identified which are components of fermentation processes. Desiccated organic residues on the surface of pottery vessels from the New Kingdom in Upper and Middle Egypt were studied under scanning electron microscopy (Samuel 1996a, 1996b). Organic crusts were derived from Deir el-Medina close to Luxor (dating to 1550–1307 BC) and from Amarna close to Valleys of the Kings and Queens (dating to 1350 BC). The microstructure shows starch granules which were pitted, channelled, and hollowed by enzymatic attack as well as desiccated yeast cells in the process of budding, indicating active growth at the time of desiccation. Based on these results and contrary to the traditional views about ancient Egyptian brewing, malted grain was found to be part of the brewing process.

The kinds of desiccated residues found in the deserts of Egypt have not been found in Europe. However, what have been found are dried-out brewing residues. This liquid forms a crust, for example on ceramic sherds, and this is known as 'beer-stone'. After micro-sieving these beer-stones, the following components can be found using microscopy: phytoliths of cereal epidermis cells, starch granules with signs of enzymatic attack, yeast cells, and oxalate crystals. These components can be indications of beer residues, but proof lies in the chemical analyses. There are some finds from Spain dated from the late Bronze Age, early Iron Age and Iberic Iron Age, which provide evidence of being residues of beer (Juan-Tresserras 1995).

Tools and Vessels Used for Brewing

In prehistoric times we would expect tools and vessels made of timberwork to have been used as well as huge ceramic pots. As is the case with most excavation in Europe, organic tools and vessels are rarely preserved. Differentiation between storage pots and fermenting pots is impossible if there are no residues of beer-stone found on their surfaces.

Features Where the Brewing Activities Took Place

It is difficult to find structures in the soil which are diagnostic of brewing activities. However, in Roman Grossprüfing, close to Regensburg in Bavaria (dated at 200 AD), features were found which may indicate a brewery (Rötzer 1993). A well, a basin for watering the grain to start germination, a place for malting, and a drying-kiln for producing roasted malt were excavated. But a Roman brewery is only one possible interpretation of these features. Going further back into European prehistory, it is even more difficult to find evidence for 'breweries' because stone and mortar were not, or were only rarely, used before the Roman period. The case of early Celtic Hochdorf will be explained in detail later in this chapter.

Flavouring Additives

In Europe, additives for flavouring beer, in particular sweet gale (*Myrica gale*) and hops (*Humulus lupulus*), started in the early Middle Ages and these are documented as being used on a larger scale in high and late mediaeval times (Behre 1999). Around the time of the birth of Christ, gale may have been used locally in the northern Netherlands for brewing but there are no indications for its use earlier. A lot of other herbs have, at one time or another, been used as beer additives (listed by Behre 1998), but there is no prehistoric evidence of this in a brewing context.

Transportation and Storage Vessels and Drinking Sets

Some years ago, a mug and several Roman ceramic vessels (type *dolium*) from the early Celtic period were excavated in southern Germany which were interpreted by archaeologists as typical containers for beer and brewing activities. But a critical examination by natural scientists could not prove this archaeological interpretation (Hopf 1963, 1976).

As shown above indications for beer and brewing are scarce for European prehistory.

Traces of an Early Celtic Brewery in Eberdingen-Hochdorf, Kreis Ludwigsburg, South-West Germany

The excavations of an early La Tène settlement (fifth century BC) north west of Stuttgart unearthed, among other structures, ditches (Stika 1996). These ditches were carefully constructed, long and straight (5–6 m long, 0.6 m wide and up to 1.1 m deep) with a U-shaped profile (Figure 5.1). As no traces of erosion were observed, it appears that wooden boards supported the walls in ancient times. At the bottom of the trenches, a layer of charred cereal grains was found. The cereals were almost free of contamination of chaff and weeds and consisted of barley grains which showed evidence of germination (Figure 5.2). The layer of weakly, but evenly, germinated, pure hulled barley grains must be the result of intentional production of malt on a greater scale. In the upper part of the grain layer, pieces of charcoal were mixed in and on top of that charred layer. Dried and partly burned mud bricks were also found.

Germination and charring experiments on recent barley grains (Figure 5.3) obtained results close to the archaeological finds of Hochdorf. The malt from the Celtic settlement at Hochdorf might have been an excellent starting point for a high quality beer if it had not been destroyed by accident. But without the fire no charred grain and no residues of the Celtic beer would have been found by later archaeologists.

Figure 5.1 Ditch with charred grain at the bottom, early Celtic Hochdorf.

Figure 5.2 Barley grains which show evidence of germination, early Celtic Hochdorf (the scale is 0.5 mm long).

Figure 5.3 Modern germinated grains of hulled barley.

An attempted reconstruction of these finds could be as follows: The ditch may have been used for germinating the grains after watering. For even germination and the production of high quality malt, moist hulled barley should be exposed under low temperatures to humid, but ventilated air in the dark. These conditions would have existed in that ditch if it were covered. After several days of germination with the occasional turning of the grains, keeping them moist, they would have reached a stage where enough enzyme was produced to mobilize the starch but not too much energy to cause germs to develop. To stop the germination, the green malt has to be dried. Again the ditch might have been used: this time as a drying-kiln. On the top of the ditch it seems that a structure of dried mud bricks was attached carrying a wooden frame with a cover made of woven reed, willow or textile. The grains were deposited on this structure and were heated at a low temperature in order to dry them. Accidentally, it would seem, a fire began and the construction, especially the organic cover, started to burn. The cover carrying the grains broke lengthwise, the malt fell into the ditch, and the burning structure fell in after it. The grains became charred and could not be used for brewing. The whole structure was filled first with the remaining mud brick and then with thrown-in loose clay, which preserved it.

The function and use of this ditch cannot be deduced with complete certainty. However, what further traces of a Celtic brewery could be found today, when no stone constructions were used and all wooden material would have completely decayed? Several questions are left open concerning beer production in Hochdorf, but the finds are widely accepted to be residues of a Celtic brewery.

At Hochdorf there is archaeological evidence of another alcoholic drink used by the Celts, namely mead. From the late Hallstatt princely burial mound of Hochdorf, mead production is documented. It seems to have been used as grave goods (Körber-Grohne 1985). A crust in a huge bronze vessel was palynologically and chemically analysed to be residues of mead production. In some early celtic excavations in south-west Germany, imported wine aphorae were found, which give indications for a third alcoholic drink enjoyed by the upper class Celts: namely, wine.

The Reconstructed Taste of Celtic Beer

There is no detailed information on the brewing technique of the Celts. But looking at the results of the excavation and with the help of theoretical aspects we can come close to working out what this beer of antiquity was like. The way of drying the green malt may have affected the taste of the beer. The open fire would have caused a smoky taste and the uneven heat may have led to malt which was partly dark. The amount of lactic acid bacteria probably was comparatively high because of the slow drying conditions. The malt then was coarsely ground and mashed. The heating of the wort was done using hot stones out of fires. The malty liquid may have caramelised at the surface of the hot stones which would give it a special flavour. No hops appear to have been added. The fermentation started spontaneously which could easily have happened by using yeast-contaminated brewing equipment or through spores of yeast carried in the air and infecting the brew by chance. This yeast must have been a type of pale beer (*Weissbier*) yeast, an old type which works at higher temperatures and rises to the top of the fermenting liquid. The other northern type of yeast needs ice cooling during fermentation and was introduced to southern Germany on a large scale after the ice-machine was invented in the nineteenth century. The lactic acid bacteria caused a low pH-level which would have helped to preserve the brew and give it a slightly sour taste. The Celtic beer may have had a totally different taste compared to our modern beers.

References

Behre, K.-E. (1998) Zur Geschichte des Bieres und der Bierwürzen in Mitteleuropa. In Both, F. (ed.) *Gerstensaft und Hirsebier, 5000 Jahre Biergenuß*, Isensee, Oldenburg: 49–88.

Behre, K.-E. (1999) The history of beer additives in Europe – a review, *Vegetation History and Archaeobotany*, 8: 35–48.

Hopf, M. (1963) Untersuchungen am Inhalt des römischen Doliums aus Alzey, *Jahrbuch des Römisch-Germanischen Zentralmuseums Mainz*, 10: 68–75.

Hopf, M. (1976) Bier. In Hoops, J. (ed.) *Reallexikon der Germanischen Altertumskunde*, Walter de Gruyter, Berlin/New York: 530–533.

Hopf, M. (1991) South and Southwest Europe. In van Zeist, W., Wasylikowa, K. and Behre, K.-E. (eds) *Progress in Old World Palaeoethnobotany, A retrospective view on the occasion of 20 years of International Work Group for Palaeoethnobotany*, Brookfield, Rotterdam: 241–298.

Jacomet, St. (1986) Verkohlte Pflanzenreste aus einem römischen Grabmonument beim Augster Osttor (1966), *Jahresberichte aus Augst und Kaiseraugst*, 6: 7–53.

Juan-Tresserras, J. (1997): *Procesado y preparación de alimentos vegetales para consumo humano. Aportaciones del estudio de fitolitos, almidones y lípidos en yacimientos arqueológicos prehistóricos y protohistóricos*, Ph.D. Thesis at the Department of Prehistory, Ancient History and Archaeology, University of Barcelona.

Körber-Grohne, U. (1985) Die biologischen Reste aus dem hallstattzeitlichen Fürstengrab von Hochdorf, Gemeinde Eberdingen (Kreis Ludwigsburg). In Küster, H. and Körber-Grohne, U., *Hochdorf I*, Forschungen und Berichte zur Vor- und Frühgeschichte in Baden-Württemberg 19, Theiss, Stuttgart: 85–265.

Lenz, H.O. (1859) *Botanik der alten Griechen und Römer*, reprint 1966, Wiesbaden.

Maksoud, S.A., El Hadidi, M.N. and Amer, W.M. (1994) Beer from the early dynasties (3500–3400 cal BC) of Upper Egypt, detected by archaeochemical methods, *Vegetation History and Archaeobotany*, 3: 219–224.

Rötzer, S. (1993) *Museen in Regensburg*, Lankes & Spaan, Regensburg.

Samuel, D. (1996a) Archaeology of ancient Egyptian beer, *Journal of American Society of Brewing Chemists*, 54: 3–12.

Samuel, D. (1996b) Investigation of ancient Egyptian baking and brewing methods by correlative microscopy, *Science*, 273: 488–490.

Stika, H-P. (1996) Traces of a possible Celtic brewery in Eberdingen-Hochdorf, Kreis Ludwigsburg, southwest Germany, *Vegetation History and Archaeobotany*, 5: 81–88.

Stika, H-P. (1998) Zu den biologischen Grundlagen des Brauen und der Kultivierungsgeschichte der Getreide. In Both, F. (ed) *Gerstensaft und Hirsebier, 5000 Jahre Biergenuß*, (Isensee), Oldenburg: 11–38.

van Zeist, W. (1991) Economic aspects. In van Zeist, W., Wasylikowa, K. and Behre, K.-E. (eds) *Progress in Old World Palaeoethnobotany: A retrospective view on the occasion of 20 years of International Work Group for Palaeoethnobotany*, Brookfield, Rotterdam: 109–130.

CHAPTER 6
BEER AND BEER CULTURE IN GERMANY

Franz Meussdoerffer

The German Question

The subject of beer culture in Germany embraces two variables: beer in respect of its impact on culture on the one hand, and on Germany on the other. Beer and beer brewing have been part of cultural activities from its recorded advent about 4,000 BC in Mesopotamia (Nelson 2005). Much more difficult to identify for the purpose of discussion is the question of Germany. Germany has, except for very short periods of her history, never been a united, centrally governed country. For most of the time states diverse in population density, dialect, economy, and culture formed a more or less close alliance. In particular, the great natural divide, formed by the mountain ranges of the Erzgebirge, the Franken- and Thueringer Wald and the Harz; and the rivers, Weser and Elbe, has roughly marked out the political and cultural borders over long periods in history. The extent of Roman influence in antiquity, the relationship with the Carolingian empire and the Federal Republic of Germany until 1989 were also relevant. This divide until the twentieth century also roughly marked out the boundaries of Roman Catholic south-west and protestant north-east. Most importantly, this divide separated, at least until the eighteenth century, two culinary cultures, as climatic conditions and consequently agricultural prerequisites differed. The northern cuisine descended from Germanic alimentation, characterised by the absence of bread and an ample consumption of meat and beer, augmented, from the seventeenth century on, by potatoes. In contrast, the southern cuisine evolved from the Roman Mediterranean tradition based on wheat, bread (later noodles) and wine (Montanari 1993). Not surprisingly, drinking habits corresponded to associated cultural preferences (Engs 1995). Only when grape cultivation in the north tapered off, due to climatic changes and wars from the fourteenth century onwards, and when the idea of a German nation was shaped in the sixteenth century, did beer become the preferred drink of the indigenous Germans, and at the same time an integral part of nutrition in most German-speaking lands. However, distinct northern and southern beer cultures can be differentiated. Moreover, due to local peculiarities there are as many different brewing traditions as there are cities. Thus, German beer culture is characterised by its amazing variety.

Beer and Nationhood

Cornelius Tacitus never travelled to Germany. All he encountered were the German slaves readily available in the Roman and Gallic markets and the abundant rumours spread by soldiers and merchants. Thus, when he wrote his famous tract on *Germania, de origine et situ Germanorum liber* in 98 BC, his description, as he himself admitted, was not very accurate and more of a moral teaching on Roman decadence. Contrasting Roman artificial luxury with the natural innocence of the barbarians, he also commented on food. In chapter 23 of his book he reports that the Germans brewed beer and consumed it in huge quantities. When the Germans in the Renaissance learned to read Latin, they eagerly promoted the tale of their noble, beer drinking ancestors. The famous cartographer and humanist, Abraham Ortelius, (1527–1598) edited a refined version of the Tacitus book under the title of: '*Aurei saeculi imago sive Germanorum veterum vita, mores, ritus et religio…*' (Image of the golden age or life, customs, culture and religion of the ancient Germans…) (Ortelius 1596). At a time when German humanists set out to define the German character, they felt inferior to the more learned and civilised Italians and French. Ortelius reminded his contemporaries that frugality and honesty were the true German values (Dann 1996). And that they drank beer. Accordingly, Germans began to fancy themselves as great beer drinkers.

To be sure, beer had ever been an integral part of the diet of farmers and artisans in the German-speaking countries. In the north, where grape cultivation proved to be rather unproductive, even the nobles and clergymen resorted to beer as their daily drink and duties on brewing contributed to the sovereign's revenue (Bartscherer 1967). Furthermore, brewing became rooted in the commercial activities of the cities, the vast majority of which had only been founded after 1,000 AD and enjoyed far reaching liberties. Heirs to the Viking trade routes and trading centres, the Hansa, a powerful association of cities dominating the trade between the Baltic sea and the Atlantic ocean, became the nucleus of the northern German brewing tradition. Their access to the rich grain supplies of the fertile lands in the East provided them with the essentials for brewing: grain, hops, and malt. After average temperatures began to decline noticeably in the fourteenth century, beer – hopped beer – became a commodity in the cities on the shores of the North and Baltic Seas. Hopped beer had been brewed before in the eighth century (Nelson 2005), when average temperatures had been equally low (Moberg *et al.* 2005). However, the necessity to sustain sailors and soldiers aboard their ships with large quantities of a wholesome and stable drink as well as the prospect of selling this beer with good profit along the sea coasts, allowed members of the 'German Hansa' to develop a remarkable brewing capacity (Blanckenburg 2001). This large scale production of hopped 'export' beers of course required special production methods. Oats, the traditional mediaeval brewing cereal, were replaced during the fourteenth and fifteenth centuries by barley and wheat (Blanckenburg 2001; Unger 2001). As the ratio of relative prices of beer to wine changed from 1:4 to 1:12 over the sixteenth and seventeenth centuries (Huntemann 1970), beer production spread in the cities of central and north-ern Europe. As widely varying local factors like the availability of grains and beer additives, water quality and fermentation facilities determined the respec-tive beer quality, an astonishing diversity of beer styles emerged. As a result, northern beers were of excellent quality and could sell at premium prices all over Germany, Scandinavia and the Netherlands. At approximately the same period the mediaeval universalism was finally replaced in Europe by new governmental structures based on territories and new perceptions of social distinctiveness and confraternity (Knape 2000). The Protestant reformation with its German Bible and German sermon contributed much to the percep-tion of a distinct German culture. The centre of German Protestantism was in the northern states; its adversaries prevailed in the south. At a more popular level, Catholics had their wine and Protestants their beer (Nelson 2004). While these different drinking habits played no particular role in the ensuing confes-sional polemic (Holt 2006), drinking, particularly beer drinking, was to become an attribute of the very German character in the perception of the neighbour-ing nations. The English, French and Mediterranean travel reports of the sixteenth and seventeenth century abound in amusing tales of the simple-minded, beer-addicted Germans (Austin 1985; Room 1988; Tlusty 1994).

The Emergence of a German Beer Culture in the Nineteenth Century

During the seventeenth and eighteenth centuries the flourishing beer culture in northern and middle Germany decayed. The once excellent and celebrated beers of Hamburg, Wismar, Einbeck, Braunschweig, Hannover, Danzig, Torgau, Freiberg or Breslau depreciated to diluted, sour and – due to the frequent addition of inorganic or organic dopes – unwholesome brews. The reasons for this development were manifold. The thirty years war had destroyed infrastructure and capital. A grossly disproportional taxation and inflexible, outdated regulation of beer production and trade squashed innovation and development. Most of all, nutritional habits changed. The traditional northern diet based on beer, porridge and soup gave way to food based on bread and potatoes. Concomitantly the growing availability of spices, sugar, coffee and tea changed preferences dramatically. By 1800 AD beer had lost its top position among beverages to coffee, tea and chocolate. Most noteworthy, hard liquor replaced beer as the favourite alcoholic drink of peasants and artisans.

While the approximately three hundred autonomous territories comprising the Holy Empire of German Nations tried to maintain their cumbersome equilibrium, the revolution across the Rhine River created a vigorous French nation, based on the principles of civic liberties. After the Napoleonic wars the remaining forty-one German sovereign states formed a loose association as the German Confederacy. As a thoughtful observer, Madame de Staël, noted, Germany lacked any established and well-proven political institutions, a prerequisite for the existence of a nation (Staël 1813). Therefore, Germans had to shape their concept of a nation once more by drawing on a carefully modelled glorious past and their alleged distinctiveness from their neighbours (James 1991). In this context they remembered Tacitus and the beer guzzling Germans. In particular, students assumed a leading role in the efforts to create a united German state. Freed temporarily from civil necessities by the war, they fashioned a simple life far from responsibilities, bureaucracies and intellectual sophistication. Drinking beer and smoking long pipes ranked high among their activities. Allegedly, Johann Wolfgang v. Goethe rhymed:

Bestaubt sind unsre Bücher;
der Bierkrug macht uns klüger.
Das Bier schafft uns Genuß,
Die Bücher nur Verdruß
(From Spengler 2007: 241)[1]

While dust collects on our books,
The beer mug makes us wiser.
While beer makes joyful looks,
Books cause frowns like a miser.[2]

The students developed specific drinking rituals for their conventions and set trends for mugs and glasses. As the students made their way into civic life, the student customs moved with them. Weekly meetings at regular tables (*Stammtisch*) and personalised beer mugs became a tradition among middle-class men in Germany. Two other popular movements rooted in the post-Napoleonic period further contributed to the particular (male) sociability, characteristic of the German beer culture: the gymnastic clubs and the men's choral societies (Klenke 1998).

The strong movement towards a united German state among the middle classes initiated first the economic unification within the Zollverein (customs union) in 1834 and later the political unification under Prussian domination (1871). As a result, urbanisation and industrialisation progressed rapidly. These developments precipitated a new thriving industry in beer brewing. The basis for the resurgence of beer was a brewing technique devised in the South, in Bavaria. A popular English dictionary observed in 1844: 'The Germans from time immemorial have been habitually beer-drinkers, and have exercised much of their technical and scientific skill in the production of beer of many different kinds, some of which are little known to our nation, while one at least, called Bavarian, possesses excellent qualities, entitling it to the attention of all brewers and consumers of this beverage' (Ure 1844).

In the south, knowledge of the ancient brewing technology had survived in the cellars of numerous monasteries. Even the Roman designations *celia* and *cervisia* were further used for different types of beer. The falling average temperatures in the fourteenth and fifteenth century initiated the production of hopped beer not only in the Hansa cities in the north, but also in the Franconian and Thuringian regions bordering Bavaria to its north. However, unlike the Hanseatic brewers, the brewers in Franconia applied a different fermentation process taking advantage of their cellars deep in caves in the sandstone rocks of their region. Their wort fermentation proceeded at lower temperatures and was consequently slower. A maturation phase had to follow the fermentation, thus extending the time required for a brew. Moreover, another yeast type, which at the end of the fermentation process settled at the bottom of the vat, had to be used for this 'bottom' fermentation. As low temperatures were absolutely prerequisite for this type of brewing, beer production was restricted to the time between September/October and March/April. In spite of all this complexity, the resulting beers were much superior with respect to stability and palatability. Bottom fermentation consecutively spread from Franconia into Bavaria proper at the beginning of the fifteenth century (Hackel-Stehr 1987).

Around 1500 AD grape cultivation in Bavaria abated quickly and wine was supplanted by beer as the dominating popular beverage. Nothing exemplifies this change better than the famous Bavarian purity law of 23 April 1516. For the first time a state, not just a city, took the lead in forming the drinking habits of its subjects and in regulating brewing in detail. As the bottom-fermentation technique was improved over the seventeenth and eighteenth centuries, beer became an indispensable part of Bavarian life. While spirits were popular in the north, their consumption in the southern rural areas producing wine (Hörmann 1912) or beer (Zimmermann 1832) was almost negligible. Thus, in the years 1840–1842, in Bavaria, only 3 litres of spirits were consumed per capita per year, but 123 litres of beer and 11 litres of wine. In contrast, in Prussia the consumption of spirits was 7.9 litres per capita per year while beer and wine consumption remained at 24 litres and 2 litres per capita per year respectively. It is noteworthy, that the overall alcohol consumption in Prussia and Bavaria was comparable at 8.8 and 8.4 litres pure ethanol per capita and year respectively (Tappe 2004). It is interesting that the famous brewing institute at Weihenstephan in Bavaria should bud off a school for agriculture in 1865, while the equally renowned brewing institute in Berlin was founded in 1874 as a research station for the spirit-producing industry.

After the liberalisation of business regulations in the wake of the Napoleonic wars, numerous breweries opened in Bavaria. The enterprising spirits of distinguished brewers, the inventions of skilled engineers and the pioneering theories of excellent academics propelled brewing to the top of a rapidly expanding scientific and economic movement, with its base rooted on the stolid popularity of the product, beer. Soon the superior qualities of the Bavarian beers were recognised in other parts of Germany and new breweries using the Bavarian brewing process arose all over the German confederacy. A revolution in brewing technology, microbiology and preservation techniques accompanied this development. The rise of beer consumption was propelled by the rapid urbanisation and industrialisation in the years between 1865 and 1900. Beer consumption spread even in wine-producing areas as a result of tourism and the ensuing urbanisation (Haid 2003). While wine retained its status of an upper-class beverage (Teuteberg and Wiegelmann 1986), the working class emerged as major beer consumers, even if only after better working conditions and adequate remuneration had been achieved (Seidel 1997). The significance of beer in the nutrition of the working classes is best illustrated by the 'beer riots' which sometimes followed rises in some beer prices (Carpenter 1998). At the end of the nineteenth century beer had become the most popular beverage in Germany, while huge quantities were exported all over the world. No wonder that beer was perceived then as part of Germany's cultural identity by its citizens and by foreigners alike. The eminent French biologist Louis Pasteur, embittered by the injury of his only son and the damage to his beloved institute in the course of the Franco–German war of 1870, aimed at this special cultural and economic relevance of beer for Germany, when he set out to create a superior French 'beer of revenge' (Baxter 2001).

At about the same time, the preferences of the consumers changed. The beer glass increasingly replaced the pottered mug and in parallel the slightly turbid, sweet, dark beers gave way to the strongly hopped light beers. The latter originated in the Bohemian city of Pilsen, where the Bavarian brewer Joseph Groll had created this type of beer in 1842. Bottled beer and beer halls contributed further to the image of beer as an everyday beverage. However, beer production started to exceed demand from 1900 on and the creation of brands and advertisement became increasingly a necessity. The advertisements in turn reinforced the perception of beer as the time-honoured regional drink. Due to the Bavarian origin of modern German beers, ostensible Bavarian accessories were incorporated into the advertisements and shaped the perception of German beer culture during the twentieth century.

Today beer consumption is receding. The prohibitionist attitude of most societies, climate change and the tendency of globalisation to fix the price ratio of beer to wine again at approximately 1:4 might have contributed to this development. However, even today Germany is perceived by its citizens as well as by foreigners as a beer-drinking country par excellence. This might be true, considering the number of breweries, the per capita consumption, the variety of brands and beer types. A great German beer culture and tradition still exist, which reflect the diversity of modern Germany.

Notes

1. This poem is credited to Goethe, but the lines are most likely anonymous, albeit often quoted, taken here from Spengler in his attempt to summarize some of his ideas on beer and beer drinking.
2. Translation by Wulf Schiefenhövel.

References

Austin, G.A. (1985) *Alcohol in Western Society from Antiquity to 1800: A chronological history*, ABC-Clio Information Services, Santa Barbara, California.

Bartscherer, A. (1967) Vom Magdeburger Bärm-Amt und dem Kampf um dessen Ende, *Gesellschaft für die Geschichte und Bibliographie des Brauwesens, Jahrbuch 1967*, Institut für Gärungsgewerbe, Berlin: 67–79.

Baxter, A.G. (2001) Louis Pasteur's beer of revenge, *Nature Reviews Immunology*, 1: 229–232.

Blanckenburg, C. von (2001) *Die Hanse und ihr Bier*, Böhlau Verlag, Köln/Weimar/Wien.

Carpenter, K.N. (1998) *'Sechs Kreuzer sind genug für ein Bier!'. The Munich beer riot of 1844: social protest and public disorder in mid-19th century Bavaria*, Ph.D. thesis, Georgetown University.

Dann, O. (1996) *Nation und Nationalismus in Deutschland 1790–1990*, C.H. Beck Verlagsbuchhandlung, München.

Engs, R.C. (1995). Do traditional Western European drinking practices have origins in antiquity? *Addiction Research and Theory*, 2: 227–239.

Haid, O. (2003) Early tourism and public drinking. In Jacobs, M. and Scholliers, P. (eds) *Eating out in Europe*, Berg, Oxford: 105–124.

Hackel-Stehr, K. (1987) *Das Brauwesen in Bayern vom 14. bis 16. Jahrhundert*, Gesellschaft für Öffentlichkeitsarbeit der Deutschen Brauwirtschaft e.V., Bonn/Bad Godesberg.

Holt, M.P. (2006). Europe divided: wine, beer and the Reformation in sixteen's century Europe. In Holt, M.P. (ed.) *Alcohol, A Social and Cultural History*, Berg Publishers, Oxford: 25–40.

Hörmann, L. von (1912) Genuss- und Reizmittel in den Ostalpen, *Zeitschrift des Deutschen und Österreichischen Alpenvereins*, 43: 78–100.

Huntemann, H. (1970) *Bierproduktion und Bierverbrauch in Deutschland vom 15. bis zum Beginn des 19. Jahrhunderts*, Dissertation der Wirtschafts- und Sozialwissenschaftlichen Fakultät der Georg-August-Universität zu Göttingen.

James, H. (1991) Germans and their nation, *German History*, 9: 136–152.

Klenke, D. (1998) *Der singende deutsche Mann*, Waxmann, Münster.

Knape, O. (2000) Humanismus, Reformation, deutsche Sprache und Nation. In Gardt, A. (ed.) *Nation und Sprache*, Walter de Gruyter, Berlin: 103–138.

Moberg, A., Sonechkin, D., Holmgren, K., Datsenko, N., Karlen. W. and Lauritzen, S. (2005). Highly variable Northern Hemisphere temperatures reconstructed from low- and high-resolution proxy data, *Nature*, 433: 613–617.

Montanari, M. (1993) *Der Hunger und der Überfluss: Kulturgeschichte der Ernährung in Europa*, C.H. Beck Verlagsbuchhandlung, München.

Nelson, B.F. (2004) The reluctant Europeans: protestantism, nationalism and European integration. Conference paper at the annual meeting of the American Political Science Association, Chicago, Illinois, 2–5 September 2004.

Nelson, M. (2005) *The Barbarian's Beverage*, Routledge, Taylor & Francis, London/ New York.

Ortelius, A. (ed.) (1596) *Aurei saeculi imago sive Germanorum veterum vita, mores, ritus et religio, iconibus delineati et commentariis ex utrumque linguae auctoribus descriptae*, Philip Galle, Antwerp.

Room, R. (1988) Cross-cultural research in alcohol studies: research traditions and analytical issues. In Towle, L. and Harford, T. (eds) *Cultural Influences and Drinking Patterns: A focus on Hispanic and Japanese populations*, NIAAA Research Monograph 19, Publication No. (ADM) 88–1563, USGPO, Washington: 9–40.

Seidel, C. (1997) Arbeiterbewegung und Bierkultur, *Jahrbuch der Gesellschaft für Geschichte und Bibliographie des Brauwesens e.V*, Berlin: 171–187.

Spengler, J. (2007) Wer von Bier spricht, muss von Geschichte reden, *Jahrbuch der Gesellschaft für Geschichte des Brauwesens (GGB)*, Berlin: 221–248.

Staël, A.L.G. de (1813) *De l' Allemagne*, Nicolle, Paris.

Tappe, H. (2004) Alkoholkonsum in Deutschland im 19. und 20. Jahrhundert. In Teuteberg, H.J. (ed.) *Die Revolution am Esstisch*, Steiner Verlag, Stuttgart: 282–294.

Tlusty, B.A. (1994) Defining drunk in early modern Germany, *Contemporary Drug Problems*, 21: 427–451.

Teuteberg, H.J. and Wiegelmann, G. (1986) *Der Wandel der Nahrungsgewohnheiten unter dem Einfluß der Industrialisierung*, Vandenhoeck & Ruprecht, Göttingen.

Unger, R.W. (2001) *A History of Brewing in Holland*, 900–1900, Brill, Leiden.

Ure, A. (1844) *Recent Improvements in Arts, Manufactures and Mines, Being a Supplement to his Dictionary*, Longman Brown Green and Longmans, London.

Zimmermann, A.F. (1852) *Ausführliches Lehrbuch der Bier-Brauerei: Vollständige theoretisch-praktische Anleitung zum rationellen Betriebe des Bier-Brauerei-Gewerbes*, 2nd edition, E.H. Schroeder, Berlin.

CHAPTER 7
EUROPE NORTH AND SOUTH, BEER AND WINE: SOME REFLECTIONS ABOUT BEER AND MEDITERRANEAN FOOD[1]

F. Xavier Medina

Introduction

The aim of this chapter is to offer a brief reflection on how beer, as an ancient drink in the Mediterranean area, has been traditionally excluded from the 'Mediterranean diet' model. As Montanari (1996) said, two 'classic models' exist in Europe: the 'Northern model' (pork and beer) versus the 'Southern model' (bread and wine). However, we cannot forget that beer had an important role in Egypt (in the eastern Mediterranean basin) and that the most ancient vestiges of beer in Western Europe were found in the Mediterranean area. If the 'Mediterranean diet' is a social construction, then why is beer not actually part of it?

There is no doubt that beer is now one of the most popular drinks around the world. The success of beer, in its various types, strengths, tastes, etc., goes beyond all frontiers and is increasing on the five continents. However, at the level of a conceptual classification, and leaving aside actual figures, beer continues, at least in Europe, to belong to a diet which is associated with the North and, especially with Anglo-Saxon, German and Scandinavian societies. This is attested to by the brewing varieties, labelling, packaging and marketing strategies.

On the other hand, we find the concept of the southern, 'Mediterranean', pattern is one in which the wine-based civilisation contrasts with that which is based on beer. This creates in the European imagination two models that are clearly constructed into an opposition which, in most cases, is much less real than is generally assumed.

Beer, as a Mediterranean food

Surely, wine is the staple drink within the Mediterranean food model. As Torres (1996) points out, for grape growing it is worth distinguishing between the countries of the Mediterranean basin and those of central Europe, where viticulture differs due to climatic factors. In the Mediterranean, grapes reach full ripeness and when harvesting comes, they have all the natural elements necessary for the production of good wine. Central European countries, as well as the centre and north of France, have to resort to *chaptalisation* (the artificial addition of sugar to must) in order to obtain an adequate balance of musts. Within the duality of wine versus beer, beer is the one which is the logical one to be produced and consumed in northern countries which lie above the climatic borders of wine, where, as Braudel (1994: 21) argues, evidence of Charlemagne's vast empire is omnipresent in the places where brewers made good beer.

Yet the same author points out that beer was known in ancient times, in Babylon and in pre-dynastic ancient Egypt. As Luján (1996) similarly observes, the national and original drink was beer, although wine was also present (see also Torrent 1998: 256). The oldest remains of beer have been found in Upper Egypt and date from 7,000 BC. However, this drink is found not only in the eastern Mediterranean, but also further west. In Europe, the most ancient remains of beer found so far (wheat, malt, starch and yeast), date from around 5,000 BC at Can Sadurní (Begues, Barcelona) (*cf.* Edo, Blasco and Villalba 2004). The other two most ancient remains in Western Europe are also in Spain: The Ambrona Valley (Valle de Ambrona, Soria) dated around 2,100 BC (*cf.* Rojo and Velasco 2004) and Genó (Lleida) dated from 1,100–1,000 BC (*cf.* Juan-Tresserras 1998). These three finds have also clearly been made in the Mediterranean region. Thus, beer was not, even in ancient times, an alien ingredient to the Mediterranean food system. The construction of this kind of model, although relatively recent (during the latter half of the twentieth century), is based on historical interpretations and adaptations.

Towards a Creation of Food Models in Europe

From the Middle Ages onward, as Italian historiographer Massimo Montanari (1996) points out, a new definition of a European food model was invented from the confluence of Roman and Germanic cultures. These were initially different and even contrasting: field versus forest; cereal, vine, and olive agriculture versus hunting and animal husbandry. The culture of bread, wine and olive oil against the culture of meat, beer and butter. On the one hand, the Roman world was ideologically organised around the economic and cultural values of agriculture, a society for which bread was the prime food value, the symbol of their civilisation. On the other hand, Montanari (1996) goes on to argue that in the German world the staple food, which was not a plant, but an animal, the pig,[2] was the core not only of economic and food practices, but also of a whole universe of myth, symbol and ritual. This argument provides an interesting contrast in concepts and symbolism, even if nutritionists would be uneasy in calling any meat a 'staple'.

According to Montanari, in the Middle Ages two food models were born: the 'Germanic' and the 'Mediterranean'. In spite of their clear differentiation in the collective imagination, they were in close and intensive contact. In these models, the primary value of meat (mainly pork) combined with the equally primary values of bread, wine and beer; olive oil combined and alternated with animal fats. The pig, food symbol of many northern European countries, also played an essential role in the Mediterranean European cultures; consider, for example, Spain and Italy and the 'ham culture', which began spreading in these countries in the Middle Ages (even before, in Roman Times, in specific areas, like Cerdanya, the Roman *Ceretania*, in North Catalonia on the Spanish–French border).

Pork has been excluded and eliminated from the various typologies of food 'diets', not only from the 'Mediterranean diet',[3] despite the importance of its consumption. Swine husbandry has had a prime role within the Mediterranean food system, in the countryside as well as in the city, in almost all the northern regions of the Mediterranean, since it ensures useful and inexhaustible supplies of salted products, stuffed sausages and fresh meat for the daily diet.

Although the consumption of pork products has been almost fundamental in the non-muslim Mediterranean, the same is not true of beer, despite its presence in this area from ancient times. As Braudel (1994: 22) observes, outside the domains of vine-growing, beer was abundant in the broad area of northern countries, from England to the Low Countries, Germany, Bohemia, Poland and Russia. In the Mediterranean area, wine prevailed, but the spread of beer towards the South was almost as fluid as that of wine towards the North. Braudel observes that in Paris, in the sixteenth century, beer was consumed, but regarded as a 'drink for the poor' (Braudel 1994: 23), and its consumption increased only during times of economic difficulties and was affected by wine prices. Also, beer consumption was not unknown in southern areas like Seville or Bordeaux.

Yet the model of consumption patterns was already fully established: beer was the 'Northern' drink, and southern countries still preferred wine. As Braudel points out, the passion for beer shown by Emperor Charles I of Spain and V of Germany attests to the fact that the monarch was Flemish. He did not renounce this drink even during his retirement in the monastery of Yuste (Extremadura, Spain).

Beer and Tradition

As centuries went by, the separation of these two models in the European collective imagination became a dynamic image. Putting aside the cider-producing regions such as those in the north of Spain, west of France and west of

England, two areas may be roughly identified: the *wine countries* and the *beer countries*. This does not mean that in areas where beer production was predominant, wine was not produced or consumed (e.g., Germany or northern France) or vice versa (e.g., Spain, Italy or Greece). Despite high levels of beer consumption in typically Mediterranean countries like Spain[4] or Italy, and despite the existence of long established breweries in certain areas, the images which are offered and reproduced in relation to such drinks are geographically typified. Good wines are assumed to be produced in Spain, France and Italy, while good beers are thought to come from central or northern Europe (Alsace, Belgium, Holland, Bavaria, Hungary, Denmark, etc.).

In southern European countries, despite their own considerable and popular beer production (for beer consumption in Spain mainly hinges on local brands), the drink is sold through the evocation of a 'Northern' imagery. This association is exemplified by the characteristics summarised below:

- Kind of beer: Pilsner, Lager, Bock, etc., all of which come from northern European regions.
- Direct or indirect mention of the place of origin (if imported) or by evocation: Alsace, Denmark, Holland, etc.
- Typefaces resembling those of the North: such as the traditional German Gothic ones.
- Logos and slogans evoking northern regions or directly written in Saxon or Germanic languages.
- Written advertisements and commercials which portray images, symbols, and characters which are recognisably north European.

Although both beer consumption and brewing have a strong tradition in southern Europe, all the above characteristics and more point to an imagery which clearly refers to the regions in northern Europe. The production and consumption of this popular drink in the south of Europe appears to be, by this perspective, clearly underrated.

As one example among many others, one of the several beer encyclopaedia (Verhoef 2001b)[5] published in Spain in the last few years, devotes individual sections to the beers of most northern European countries,[6] whereas Mediterranean Europe in its entirety gets one chapter of only four pages. This briefly summarises production and consumption in Spain, Israel, Italy, Malta, Portugal, and Turkey. For Spain only one brand is mentioned, which, popular as it is, is not the most important one. This *Encyclopaedia of Beer* is not the definitive work on this subject, as there are many others of similar characteristics. However, the information in it provides a good example of what has been presented in this chapter. Additionally, it is all the more enticing to scrutinise, as it has been translated and published in Italy and Spain (Verhoef 2001a),[7] two Mediterranean countries of which it presumedly provides information.

Some data throw light on the points made in this article. A few observations can be made based on the encyclopedia's entry on Spain: The author asserts that yearly beer consumption in Spain amounts to more than 65 litres per person,[8] which is much more than in Greece, Italy or France (Verhoef 2001b: 256). This looks strange, when one considers that in the case of Spain, only one brand is mentioned, whereas France is represented by no fewer than 39 brands! Even for Mediterranean Italy, where, according to the author, beer consumption is lower than in Spain and is overall the lowest in Europe and the world, three different kinds of beer are named.

Another interesting aspect about the kind of image held of Mediterranean beer consumption is disclosed by Verhoef's commentary. The high temperatures of the Iberian Peninsula, he argues, encourage consumption of drinks which quench the thirst of the 'hordes of tourists' who visit the Spanish coasts every year. As holiday-makers mainly come from beer-drinking countries like Holland and Germany, beer is the most popular drink. As a consequence, says Verhoef (2001b), yearly beer consumption in Spain is more than 65 litres per person, far more than in Greece, Italy, or France.

Certainly, Verhoef's assertion is risky, if not mistaken. To assert that beer consumption is by the 'hordes of tourists' who spend their summer holidays in Spain betrays a poor knowledge of facts. After all, Greece, Italy and France are all countries which receive a large amount of northern visitors every year. His commentary is nevertheless significant, as it concerns the image of beer that Verhoef has devised and transmitted. Beer is mainly drunk by citizens of northern and central Europe, such as Holland and Germany, and, according to this author, Mediterranean people do not consume it. This assertion is, to say the least, puzzling.

Beer Consumption in Major Countries in 2004, compiled by the Japanese Kirin Breweries (Kirin Research Institute 2005) places Spain as the ninth world beer consumer, only after China, USA, Germany, Brazil, Russia, Japan, UK and Mexico. So, according to this source, in 2004 it was the fourth highest consumer in Europe in millions of litres, lower only than Germany, Russia and UK, and of course higher than other 'classic' 'Northern' countries like Hungary, Czech Republic or Holland.

As for production, Verhoef's (2001b: 256) claim that the total production of beer in Spain is higher than that of, for example, the Czech Republic, Holland, or Belgium, countries which are big beer consumers per capita, comes as a surprise to the reader. In these three cases, the author lists, respectively 48, 112 and 140 brands of beer, which stand out if compared to the single Spanish option. Yet, without even carrying out an exhaustive search one can recall over twenty Spanish beer brands at least.

Verhoef is right when he asserts that Spanish producers are influenced by northern and central European styles and that much of Spanish beer production consists of lagers of the Pilsner type. Once again the image and the practice of what a good beer must be is linked to the stereotypes from north and central Europe.

Another recent and useful example of this bias is the American webpage: 'How much does beer consumption vary by country?',[9] in which only four European countries are mentioned, the Czech Republic, Ireland, Germany and the UK.

Beer Production, Tradition and 'Northern' Models: A Catalan Example

As has been argued so far, the (shared) imagery of beer production and consumption is mainly a 'Northern' one. 'Good beer' is, generally speaking, what is produced in northern and central Europe and so brewers tend to reproduce these models in the making of beer, in the design of bottles, in the visual, printed and broadcast advertising and in the presentation and promotion of their products.

This does not imply that there is no beer tradition in southern European countries, as some of the most important Spanish and Italian brands date from the nineteenth century. Such tradition exists,[10] and, despite its reference to the Northern/Germanic model, it is another element relevant to commercial exploitation and market promotion.

One of the most important beer brands[11] in Spain comes from Catalonia and it has recently celebrated its 130th anniversary. In order to commemorate the 125th anniversary, in 2001, the company launched a new kind of beer, named after the founder of the brand: an Alsatian who emigrated to Barcelona and set up his beer business in 1876. Over the years, the products of this company became one of the most important traditions in this part of Spain.

That the company advertised itself as a 'traditional beer' brewery is significant: one of the advertisements refers to '1876 Barcelona', a city that had gone through industrial, economic and urban expansion. This gave the brand-founder the opportunity to make what he knew best, that is, traditional Alsatian beer, which was then practically unknown in the Mediterranean.

According to the company's 'traditional' promotion, the new beer created on the occasion of the anniversary is also a traditional product (with the name of the founder as a heading and the legend '1876 original method' as a subtitle). It is a beer of the lager type, has a mild taste, and, as the advertising stresses, is 'produced from natural products'.[12] The label reads: 'This beer has been brewed with malts and hops selected according to the *traditional Alsatian recipe* brought to Barcelona by (founder's name), founder of (company name) in 1876'.

As regards the way the brand and the product itself are presented, several main points can be stressed: first, there are the above-mentioned references to Northern/Germanic imagery, and, more specifically, the reference to the Alsatian origin of the founder and the brewing tradition of the company, as well as to the Alsatian 'original recipe'. Furthermore, the advertisement mentions explicitly that the beer has been produced 'with hops from the German region of Hallertau, properly ripened'. Finally, the legend, the bottle and label design graphics also refer to an easily identifiable Northern/Germanic image.

There is a clear and specific reference to 'tradition': What is emphasised about this product is the company's 125-year experience of the making of beer of the 'original' type, that is, the old-fashioned one. Furthermore, this beer is targeted at those who have 'always trusted our experience'.

To sum up, this product is promoted commercially as 'traditional', so its quality is made to sound like it is associated with experiences acquired through the years; and with its *naturalness*, that is, the use in its production of natural, healthy ingredients (without any explicit mention of the industrial process) and with its 'slow ripening in cellars'. In other words, beer is presented as a product which is produced carefully and without haste.

The above-mentioned aspects show an imported tradition, imported because, obviously, the origin, the recipe, and the brewing skills are from Alsace. The brand's tradition has, however, a 'Spanish' history: the company has been brewing beer in Spain for almost one and a half centuries and it is to such a background that the advertisement refers. What is ultimately being sold to consumers is 'Spanish' traditional knowledge. This means that the north-European imagery coexists with an identifiable Spanish beer tradition and this can be used as the vehicle for commercialisation.

Conclusions

In the Mediterranean area, beer is still considered to be part of a 'Northern European' food pattern, despite its wide and increasing consumption and the fact that it is one of the most popularly consumed drinks in Mediterranean countries such as Italy and Spain. For this reason it has been excluded from the Mediterranean food model and from the promotions linked to the so-called 'Mediterranean diet'. This is in contrast to wine, a drink which is (carefully and under control) recommended for a healthy heart inside the framework of the Mediterranean diet, and in spite of its ancient relationship to medical advice. Even if in this respect beer can be also a healthy drink; one can cite Boëns' (1878) essay, '*La bière au point médical, hygienique et social*' (Beer from a medical, hygienic and social perspective), presented at the Academie Royale de Médecine de Belgique (Royal Academy of Medicine of Belgium) or various articles published in the 1930s on hygienic, physiological, nutritional and food aspects of beer (Torrent 1998: 261–263). And more recently, other different medical studies on this subject.[13]

We move among socially constructed models that serve specific interests, which do not always seek to reach a global, holistic vision of the facts that they intend to analyse. We should remember that neither food systems nor food models are unchangeable, despite the fact that they feed on specific mythologies which seem to be culturally necessary. Rather, they are dynamic and may be transformed over time. In this sense, the presence of beer in the Mediterranean is not new or insignificant. Yet, at the level of the imagery beer still belongs, and presumably will continue to do so, to a Northern European food model.

Notes

1. Translated by Monica Stacconi.
2. The pig was very much appreciated in the Roman world and later until now in non-muslim Mediterranean Europe (Fàbrega 1996).
3. This topic has been dealt with more extensively by Medina (2005).
4. E.g., a few years ago, a press article was headlined: '44% of Spanish young people aged 15 to 25 drink twenty glasses of beer weekly' (*Barcelona y m@s*, 23 May 2001, p. 8).
5. *The Complete Encyclopedia of Beer. An Expert and Comprehensive Directory of the Beers of the World.* Lisse, Rebo Productions, 1998. We have used the Spanish edition of this work (Verhoef 2001b).
6. Namely, Denmark, Finland, Sweden, England, Ireland, Scotland, Germany, Holland, Belgium, France, Czech Republic, Austria, and Switzerland.
7. *Enciclopedia della birra*, Vercelli, White Star, 2001, with late reprints.
8. The author does not mention the year of such data. They do not correspond to the figures concerning beer consumption per person in Spain in 1999. That year consumption averaged 54.9 litres per person per year (see *La alimentación en España 1999*, 2000: 391). It is possible that the data used by Verhoef are a year before 1994, when beer consumption in Spain was more than to 64 litres per person. From then until 1999, consumption has declined despite some recovery more recently (2000: 395). The national association *Cerveceros de España (Brewers from Spain)* mentions that the consumption per person in Spain was 78 litres in 2003.
9. http://snippets.com/how-much-does-beer-consumption-vary-by-country.htm (accessed 1 September 2009).
10. On the role played by tradition in relation to food see Medina 1998.
11. The company's name is not mentioned here, in order to avoid advertising it.
12. The relationship between 'tradition' and 'naturalness' has often been highlighted elsewhere (see Medina 1998; Seppilli 1992).
13. As different contemporary examples, see: Brewers Association of Canada: http://www.brewers.ca/default_e.asp?id=9; The Brewers of Europe. The Benefits of a Moderate Beer consumption: http://www.brewersofeurope.org/docs/publications/pdf-Mei04.pdf; Fundación Cerveza y Salud (Beer & Health Foundation): http://www.cervezaysalud.com/html/body_quienes_somos.htm (accessed January 2009, July 2009 and May 2005, respectively).

References

Boëns, M. (1878) *La biere au point de vue médical, hygienique et social*, Société Royale Belge de Médicine, Brussels (cited in Torrent 1998).

Braudel, F. (1994) *Bebidas y excitantes*, Alianza Editorial, Madrid.

Edo, M., Blasco, A. and Villalba, P. (2004) Las cervezas prehistóricas. Estudio de caso: Can Sadurní (Begues, Barcelona). Paper presented at the 20th meeting of the International Commission on the Anthropology of Food, *Beer in Prehistory and Antiquity,* University of Barcelona, Barcelona, 3–5 October 2004.

Fàbrega, J. (1996) La cultura del cerdo en el Mediterráneo: entre el rechazo y la aceptación. In Medina, F.X. (ed.) *La alimentación mediterránea. Historia, cultura, nutrición*, Icaria, Barcelona: 217–238.

Juan-Tresseras, J. (1998) La cerveza prehistórica: investigaciones arqueobotánicas y experimentales. In Maya, J.L., Cuesta, F. and López Cachero, J. (eds) *Genó: un poblado del Bronce final en el Bajo Segre*, Publicacions de la Universitat de Barcelona, Barcelona: 239–252.

Kirin Research Institute of Drinking and Lifestyle (2005) *Beer Consumption in Major Countries in 2004*, Report vol. 29, 15 December 2005. [Online] Available at: http://www.kirinholdings.co.jp/english/ir/news_release051215_1.html. (accessed 8 August 2009).

Lujàn, N. (1996) Nacimiento y evolución de la cocina mediterránea. In Medina, F.X. (ed.) *La alimentación mediterránea. Historia, cultura, nutrición*, Icaria, Barcelona: 47–56.

Medina, F.X. (1998) Mediterranean food: the return of tradition, *Rivista di antropologia*, 76 (suppl.): 343–51.

Medina, F.X. (2005) Cows, pigs and... witches! On meat, Mediterranean diet and food in the Mediterranean area. In Hubert, A. and Avila, R. (eds) *Man and Meat*, University of Guadalajara (México), Guadalajara: 155–164.

Ministerio de Agricultura, Pesca y Alimentación (2000) *La alimentación en España 1999*, Ministerio de Agricultura, Pesca y Alimentación, Madrid.

Ministerio de Agricultura, Pesca y Alimentación (2004) *La alimentación en España 2003*, Ministerio de Agricultura, Pesca y Alimentación, Madrid.

Montanari, M. (1996) El papel del Mediterráneo en la definición de los modelos alimentarios en la Edad Media: ¿espacio cultural o mar de frontera? In Medina, F.X. (ed.) *La alimentación mediterránea. Historia, cultura, nutrición*, Icaria, Barcelona: 73–80.

Rojo, M. and Velasco, A. (2004) *La cerveza más antigua de Europa* (film), Servicio de medios audiovisuales de la Universidad de Valladolid, Valladolid.

Seppilli, T. (1992) Consumo di pane nella società dei consumi. In Papa, C. (ed.) *Antropología e storia dell'alimentazione. Il pane*, Electa Editori Umbri, Perugia: 201–205.

Torrent, J. (1998) La cerveza en la historia. In Maya, J.L., Cuesta, F. and López Cachero, J. (eds) *Genó: un poblado del Bronce final en el Bajo Segre*, Publicacions de la Universitat de Barcelona, Barcelona: 253–263.

Torres, M.A. (1996) Producción y comercialización del vino en el Mediterráneo. In Medina, F.X. (ed.) *La alimentación mediterránea. Historia, cultura, nutrición*, Icaria, Barcelona: 197–206.

Verhoef, B. (2001a) *Enciclopedia della birra*, White Star, Vercelli.

Verhoef, B. (2001b) *La Enciclopedia de la cerveza*, Libsa, Madrid.

CHAPTER 8
LIVING IN THE STREETS: BEER ACCEPTANCE IN ANDALUSIA DURING THE TWENTIETH CENTURY[1]

Isabel González Turmo

Introduction

The title of this chapter is not accidental. Drinks usually facilitate social relationships and these, where the climate permits, mainly take place outside the home. Of all drinks, beer is perhaps the one which is most frequently consumed 'in the street', that is to say, in pubs[2].

People's taste for draught beer and the need for mechanisms and quantities which allow drawing it properly make the existence of pubs an essential condition for the consumption of certain kinds of beer. However, it so happens that each place and each region constructs its own taste values and its own ways of drinking beer. This is what I will endeavour to explain in relation to Andalusia and the city of Seville.

First, I will briefly expose the current data and habits relative to beer consumption. Secondly, I will go through the history of such consumption in the last 150 years, placing particular emphasis on the changes recorded in recent years (González Turmo 1996). Lastly, I will try to explain how changes in the smell, taste and colour of beer are perceived by consumers; which new blends have been added; which timetables, places and manners can be observed in relation to its consumption; in what kinds of drinking establishments beer is served; and to what kind of customers it is served. In order to make the reader familiar with this topic I will provide some preliminary data on Andalusia and Seville.

Andalusia is located at the farthest southern edge of Spain as well as of Europe. Its territory stretches over 87,267 km^2 and is crossed by the river Guadalquivir, whose basin occupies almost 70 per cent of the region, from the north-east to the south-west. This region is very warm. Spring and autumn are mild and short. Summer is very long and hot with temperatures reaching or exceeding 40 degrees centigrade. Cities with an extended and densely populated historic central area are numerous in this region and Seville, among them, is the one that has the biggest historic area in Europe.

These characteristics may help explain why people are so keen on spending so much of their life in the streets. Andalusians do not entertain in their homes. Travellers have been complaining for centuries about the scarce hospitality of Andalusian people and about their bad entertaining practices. Usual complaints have been that tables are not set properly, domestic cellars are poor, food is light and very simple.

As compensation, Andalusians, like many other Mediterranean people, are experts in street life (Garine 1996). Furthermore, the peculiar environmental and climatic conditions have triggered a taste for very cold, almost frozen beer, to the extent that empty glasses are stored in the freezer in order to keep the drink cool after serving. Besides, beer must be light, with an alcohol content that is not too high since, due to the heat and dehydration, people drink copiously. Andalusian beer and, above all, Cruzcampo beer, which is originally from Seville, is a lager of only 4.8 per cent alcohol by volume, about average for European beers.

It is now time to make a brief historical survey of how beer consumption has changed in the city of Seville. I will provide a summary of the results obtained from six years of research. About the middle of the nineteenth century there were in Seville 100,000 inhabitants and 446 taverns: one for every 225 people. Considering that women, children and clergy did not go to taverns, that figure is rather high (Romero de Solís 1989). Only wine was served. The tavern was mainly a place for poor people, workers and artisans who were, according to the contemporary census, 45 per cent of the urban population. Big landowners and the middle class each had their own places to frequent; so people from the different classes tended not to mix and they tended to go to different casinos, coffee shops, restaurants and hotels.

Beer started to be consumed from 1865 onwards, when the first brewery was opened in the city. It is likely that beer was home-brewed before this date, but there is no record of its production, distribution or consumption. The brewery inaugurated in 1865 was located right in the town centre; it included a bakery and was open to customers. It was owned by an English widow, called Mrs. Witman. Nine years later, in 1874, a second brewery, Dekinder and Unzalu, was opened. The warehouses for beer importation made their appearance in 1882. The first one was called *Deposito de Cerveza Inglesa y Alemana* (English and German Beer Warehouse) and it was owned by Williams Anderson & Son.

They were all foreign: German, English, Dutch, Italian, Norwegian and even Basque. It is evident that beer was neither a habitual business nor a common product of consumption for Andalusian people. The same is true of the expensive pubs where beer started to be consumed. Their owners were Swiss, Dutch and Italian. Establishments were not yet as specialised as they are now. In the same place one could sleep, eat, drink beer, have coffee and cakes, play cards or billiards. There were not many such places, just fourteen in all, which is very few when compared to the almost 500 taverns existing at the time.

These pubs were all located in the most expensive streets and were owned by only a few people, who usually ran more than one establishment. Furthermore, they were part of national or international chains of pubs. That is to say, they could also be found, with the same names and sometimes the same owners, in Madrid, Barcelona and other big Spanish cities, and probably in the rest of Europe as well.[3] These establishments had names like Café Universal, Europeo, Emperadores, etc.

Among them, the cafeterias were the first ones which started to be called *cervecerías* (beer houses). This happened in 1870, six years after the first brewery had been opened. They were immediately successful. Shortly afterwards, all of them started to be called *pubs* and they were modernised. It was a steady, though slow, development since customers were few, mainly landowners and members of the middle class. Yet, beer became fashionable within this small number of people. It was *chic* and trendy to drink beer with German sausages and cold meat. This practice lasted up to the 1940s, when isolation and the embargo imposed on Spain during Franco's regime put an end to European importation, including that of beer and sausages.

However, one limitation on beer acceptance on the part of Andalusians lay in the difficulties in serving it cold. In 1875 the first ice mill was opened in Seville. Two years later there were two. This does not mean that ice had never been consumed before this date in such a hot city. In fact, according to the records, for centuries the snow had been brought from the Serranía de la Ronda, 150 km away, by means of pack trains of mules (González Turmo 1993). However, having it in the city itself was, of course, a completely different matter from bringing it all the way from the mountains. Furthermore, it cannot be assumed that from that moment onwards beer would always be consumed cold since, after all, the various beers came from places as different as England, Holland and Norway, and they were therefore characterised by very diverse qualities and alcohol levels. Yet, it was from this date on that people had the opportunity to drink cold beer and the pubs, which could provide it, would ensure a successful business. At the beginning of the twentieth century, beer ceased to be the drink of only a few people. In those years a remarkable increase in the population of the city took place. Iron and steel production doubled; other industries and electricity production quintupled. The electricity supply reached all the streets and premises and, as a direct consequence, the leisure hours of the citizens increased. The city swarmed with labourers coming from the poor rural areas nearby and these new customers created new demands. Besides wine, they now drank lemonade and beer.

In 1905, the company Cruzcampo was inaugurated and it soon monopolised local production. Its success was immediate. Newly arrived immigrants crowded the cheaper establishments set up by this company, which soon multiplied. From 1902 on, such places thrived and increased at a constant pace and then at a faster rhythm until their number had multiplied by 27 in only 28 years.

Obviously, such a growth involved the development of various kinds of establishments. To start with, there were café-pubs, beer warehouses and foreign ale houses. Only landowners and members of the middle class could have access to all of these. New kinds of shops were also opened; little cellars where one could find not only wine, like in taverns, but also beer. Or kiosks, small wooden stalls from which passers-by could buy beer and other drinks. Here people started to drink beer while standing in the street, in the way that most Sevillians do now.

As for pubs, they were located either in the centre or in the outer suburbs of the city; some were rich, some poor. Together with the pubs a new fashion made its appearance, which was already triumphing in Madrid: the appetizer and, even more important, the *tapas*! Such little portions of food which now seem to be the very gastronomic essence of the city, were born at that time. For those customers who did not like taverns or could not afford to go to a restaurant, tapas represented the opportunity of eating something outside of the home.

However, it was not until 1922 that the first territorial expansion of pubs and their increase in number took place.[4] The word, *bar* appeared for the first time, and such is the name by which most drinking establishments are known nowadays. This name was incredibly successful. Ten years later, in 1932, all pubs were called *bars*. At the same time they spread around the poor areas of the city. The date is not an arbitrary one. It was the year following the declaration of the Second Spanish Republic. The labourers' movement was rather powerful at the time. Sevillian labourers already had the right to gather in groups and they opened their own bars.

In little more than half a century Seville, a place where beer had hardly ever been consumed became the city with what Cruzcampo claimed to be a world famous bar. This bar was called Baturone, and was no more than a wooden stand. It no longer exists.

The Cruzcampo Brewing Company ultimately became an institution in Seville and in almost all Andalusia. Nobody drank any other beer in Seville. Part of the salary earned in the brewery was paid in kind: a can of beer which workers received at lunch time. The founding families were the owners of the brewery throughout most of the twentieth century. Later, in 1995, they sold out to Guinness and in the year 2000 the company was bought by Heineken, the leading European beer company, which also took over the Spanish beer, El Aguila.

The concentration of property in the hands of multinational brewing conglomerates is at present a clear tendency. Currently, Heineken has improved its Sevillian factory, which has become the head office. The company's aim is to increase the exportation of its Sevillian brand to the rest of Europe and restaurants in the USA.

This process of concentration has also implied a tremendous rise in production. According to MERCASA (2008) Spain is the third producer in Europe, after Germany and the UK. However, when it comes to consuming, Spain only occupies the thirteenth position, a very low one if one considers that part of such consumption rests on tourism.

The control exerted over the Cruzcampo company by multinational enterprises has entailed some serious changes of various kinds. In the first place, economic: many jobs have been lost (Delgado 1998: 75) and the traditional bond with national barley producers has been altered. In fact, one of the first measures of the new owners has been the elimination of the technical production department which supervised the quality control of raw materials. The purchase from Spanish farmers has been discontinued and globalisation has altered the origin and quality of the ingredients.

This has caused a change in flavour which is very easily detected by beer lovers. Yet most consumers still stick to the brand name regardless of the altered taste. In fact, the meaning attached to the brand, the identification process it implies for the consumer, neutralises any change in taste, which must have been noticeable. Taste is not the only important factor which has been transformed. Multinational enterprises are modifying consumers' habits. Next to Cruzcampo kegs, Heineken now places some of its other brands. The demand for Cruzcampo is still unrivalled, but other brands are also taking hold. Beer is also mixed with other drinks, and alcohol-free beer has now become very popular in Spain.

The need to preserve the symbolic bond with the brand name has been perfectly planned by the multinational company. On the one hand, it has given more impetus to the spreading of its iconography. It has created a school of hotel management and franchises of both the Irish pubs in Seville and bars in general. The first Gambrinus pub, named after the character representing Cruzcampo, was opened in the Basque Country in 1997. That same year another three were inaugurated in Spain, 24 in 1998, 40 in 1999 and 191 more in 2009. The speed of increase was a vertiginous one.

Cruzcampo's iconography in these pubs was exploited to the extreme extent when they were turned into small museums. The idea which the company was trying to sell was that nothing had changed. The pivotal element is, without doubt, Gambrinus, the character which has always appeared printed on Cruzcampo beer labels. He is a legendary figure of obscure origin. One of the legends says that he received the recipe for brewing beer from the Egyptian goddess, Isis. Many beer houses in Germany and in other European countries, e.g., Romania, carry his name, as does a beer brand in the Czech Republic. His image was brought to Spain from Bavaria at the beginning of the twentieth century, when the factory was looking for German technicians who might reproduce the characteristics of German beers in Seville. In the long run this Gambrinus has become a very important Sevillian. He represents a happy, friendly man whose pot belly is the emblem of satisfaction.

Yet that beer belly, of which he has been proudly boasting for more than ninety years, is getting alarmingly slimmer. Gambrinus probably went on his first diet when Guinness bought the brand. His second loss of weight took place after Heineken took over. He is no longer a fat man. Consumers not only have to forget the taste change; they also have to believe that beer is not fattening. Curiously enough, when I started writing this text, I asked the company to give me information on sales, exports, etc., and to provide me with two images of Gambrinus, before and after his weight loss. The data I received were not periodic and rather simple. I had to keep phoning various departments for one and a half months. Only when I said I would make the company's secrecy public, did I obtain half a dozen examples of data. Gambrinus's image was never given to me. They explained that the company did not recognise that Gambrinus had got slimmer. Certainly, it must be a miracle. Be that as it may, Heineken has achieved 37.5 per cent of the Spanish beer market (MERCASA 2008).

This phenomenon has nothing to do with the transnationalisation which existed in Sevillian breweries and pubs in the second half of the nineteenth century. At that time too they belonged to European chains. But the Swiss, Italian or German businessmen who ran the establishments settled in Seville, used local services and industries and even transformed their surnames in order to make them sound more Spanish. The great-grandchildren of such entrepreneurs still live in Andalusia.

The current situation is rather different: Heineken and other multinational beer companies try to gain control of brands which are already very well established in both regional and national markets. Together with the brand, they also buy distribution networks, which allow them to introduce their other beers and brands, modifying, as mentioned above, the consumer's taste. In order to broaden market niches, new bottles and cans have been introduced and subsequent advertising campaigns have targeted young people, since the future of this sector rests heavily on its ability to increase sales among these new consumers (Delgado 1998: 75-8).

Nowadays, Cruzcampo is sold, more than ever, as a Sevillian beer – but it is no longer Sevillian. One of their breweries is in the city of Seville, but the property, raw materials, formulas and design are all alien. Likewise, a model of a typical *bar* is being exported, which includes Sevillian *tapas*, a bright and noisy atmosphere and the smell of frying food, but Andalusian people do not profit from it.

Modifications in Beer Consumption

In Spain, the National Anti-Drugs Campaign has now identified the national average age at which people start drinking as 16.8 (Ministerio de Sanidad y Política social 2008). However, teenage consumption is the most significant. They hardly ever drink at home, but they do it in the streets at night and they literally take over some areas of the city. They not only drink in bars, but also in the street itself, by their motorcycles and cars. These young people consume beer together in huge groups, which we call *botellones*. Although only people over eighteen can legally buy beer, younger people may have the drink brought to them by somebody else or obtain it through enterprises which specialise in this kind of supply, the so-called *tele-botellón*. With a simple telephone call, the purchasers may have the drinks delivered to their car in a few minutes.

Sometimes the movement of young people to find areas of entertainment goes beyond the limits of their city. Every weekend they seek fun in nearby villages and towns.

Their favourite drinks have a high alcoholic content and they also like cocktails and various combination drinks (Ministerio de Medio Ambiente y Medio Rural y Marino 2008). Their attitude towards drinking differs from that of older generations, but not really because they are driven by a greater compulsive behaviour. For a few hours young people seek within their group of friends the ambiguity provoked by an alteration of the daily routine. Lights, rhythm, alcohol and life at a fast pace now flourish in the image that young people want to have of themselves and believe exists. Yet sometimes the result is stupor, or ethylic coma, mainly caused by the mixture of alcohol and pills.

This situation causes alarm among parents, health authorities and public institutions. As a consequence, on 18th April 2001 the Andalusian Parliament unanimously approved a broadening of the Anti-Drugs Law, in order to prosecute uncontrolled sales of alcohol at filling stations and unauthorised establishments. Selling alcohol in the street and during the night is now forbidden, and *tele* shops have also been prohibited. On the other hand, the authorities insist on the observance of the Law of 2003 which prohibited the sale and consumption of alcoholic drinks with an alcoholic content exceeding 20° (LEY 12/2003) in high schools and universities, health centres, public administrations, sports facilities and service areas. These measures are likely to coincide with the effort made by multinational companies in order to increase beer sales among young consumers. In any case, it is clear that both the brewing sector and the consumers' practices have undergone important transformations which are worth considering and studying.

In conclusion, the popularisation of beer-drinking in Andalusia is relatively recent, in comparison with other regions in Europe. Its Andalusian adaptation has changed the characteristics of the general environment and the social habits of the population. In fact, it is all part of the tendency for globalisation of this industry, which affects everything from the production and distribution to the drinking habits and the need to regulate these.

Acknowledgement

This study was carried out within the research group, Territorio, Cultura y Desarollo, PAI, Junta de Andalucía (TECUDE. PAI. SEJ-418).

Notes

1. Translated by Monica Stacconi.
2. Use of the word 'pub' here is because it is the word that is used for some beer houses in Seville.

3. Their surnames were Swiss, Italian, Basque and Catalan; e.g., Dosch, Pulini, Garrastazu, Fallola, Lebrún. Frapoli, Olgiati, Franconi and Lhardy.
4. The breweries were at first forty-two, after two years fifty-three and they would go on growing like this: in 1924 there were eighty-two; in 1926 hundred and three; in 1930, hundred and eight; and in 1932 hundred and thirty-eight.

References

Delgado, C. (1998) *El nuevo libro del vino*, Alianza Editorial, Madrid.
Garine, I. de (1996) Alimentation Méditerranéenne et realité. In González Turmo, I. y Romero de Solís, P. (eds) *Antropología de la Alimentación: nuevos ensayos sobre la dieta mediterránea*, Universidad de Sevilla y Fundación Machado, Sevilla.
González Turmo, I. (1993) Introducción y anotaciones sobre aspectos alimenticios al documento "Bosque de Doña Ana. A la presencia de Felipo Quarto, Católico, Pio, Felice, August, Año 1624", *El Folk-lore andaluz, No.9*. Seville.
González Turmo, I. (1996) *Banquetes, tapas, cartas y menús. Sevilla, 1863–1996*, Servicio de Publicaciones del Ayuntamiento de Sevilla, Seville.
LEY 12/2003, de 24 de noviembre, para la reforma de la Ley 4/1997, de 9 de julio, de Prevención y Asistencia en materia de Drogas, modificada por la Ley 1/2001, de 3 de mayo.
MERCASA (2008) Alimentación en España 2008. Available at: http://www.mercasa.es/nueva/alimentacion_08/index.php.
Ministerio de Sanidad y Política social (2008) Observatorio español sobre drogas. Available at: http://www.pnsd.msc.es.
Ministerio de Medio Ambiente y Medio Rural y Marino (2008) *Informe Socioeconómico del Sector de la Cerveza en España, 2007*, Madrid.
Romero de Solís, P. (1989) 'La *Taberna* en España y Amérique'. In Renaudin, Y. (ed.) Boire, a monograph supplement of *Terrain*, Paris: 63–71.

CHAPTER 9
THE THIRST FOR TRADITION: BEER PRODUCTION AND CONSUMPTION IN THE UNITED KINGDOM

Paul Collinson and *Helen Macbeth*

Introduction

This chapter represents an attempt to draw together various themes related to the changing nature and context of drinking habits in the United Kingdom (UK) during recent decades, with a specific focus on the brewing and consumption of beer. We begin by presenting an overview of the main developments within the brewing industry in the UK since the late 1970s, noting in particular the trend towards consolidation of production and the concomitant decline of regional and local breweries. These observations are related to changing patterns in the way beer is now produced and marketed in the UK. The second section of the paper concentrates on the place where, traditionally, most beer in Britain was consumed – the public house or 'pub'. The chapter goes on to demonstrate that changing patterns of consumption and production of beer have influenced and are influenced by the way in which the traditional functions of the pub have evolved over recent years. The final section of the paper draws these themes together by arguing that these developments should be understood in the light of wider sociocultural forces related to the responses to modernity and the rise of the 'post-modern society'.

Types of British Beer

In discussing the nature of the brewing industry in the UK, it is necessary first to distinguish between the different terms associated with beer, since the terminology differs from that used in other countries. The two major categories of beer, among the drinking public, are dark beer (or ale) and 'lager', which is a paler and more gaseous drink. There are many different types of drink which fall under the general heading of 'ale', including 'bitter', 'mild', 'porter' and 'stout' (of which Guinness is the most famous example). Within the category ale a further distinction is between 'cask' beers, often called 'real', 'draught' or 'hand-pulled' ales – i.e., beers which ferment in the usually wooden casks – and 'nitro keg' beers which arrive at the point of sale in sealed, usually metal, kegs. The latter types of beers are pasteurised and filtered before leaving the brewery gate, and are therefore far more stable and 'reliable' and so more profitable than 'real ales', which require careful conditioning in the cellar of the pub. There is a further difference in the way these beers are delivered to the glass: real ales are usually delivered by hand-pump, whereas keg beers, because they contain far less natural gas, have to be infused with a mixture of carbon dioxide and nitrogen and are often transferred from cellar to bar via electric pumps. Real ales are unique to the British Isles.

There have been some notable shifts in consumer habits over recent decades. Although beer remains the UK's most popular alcoholic drink, there has been an overall decline in the amount of beer drunk relative to other beverages (Figure 9.1). As of July 2008, beer sales were at their lowest level since the 1930s (British Beer and Pub Association 2008). The type of beer drunk has also changed markedly, with a general increase in the popularity of lager since 1970, and a corresponding decline in the sales of ale. Meanwhile, there has been a strong growth in sales of 'packaged', as opposed to 'draught' or 'tap' beers during recent years. This has been accompanied by a resurgence of bottled ale consumption, fuelled partly by a rise in its availability cheaply in supermarkets. These trends will be revisited below.

The UK Brewing Industry

In Britain, the brewing industry was one of the few traditional manufacturing industries to survive the recessions of the 1970s and 1980s comparatively unscathed. In 2000, the industry employed over 830,000 people, with over £15 billion being spent on beer and lager by the public. However, the past decade has seen a general decline in the industry, something which has been compounded by the global economic downturn during 2008 and 2009. The brewing industry has lost over 200,000 jobs in the past nine years, and, in parallel with consumer tastes, has undergone some fundamental changes in recent years.

The most significant trend relates to the general rationalisation of much of the industry and the concentration of most of the production in the hands of a small number of conglomerates. The four main producers are all foreign-owned: the Dutch company Heineken, Belgian-based Anheuser-Busche InBev (the world's largest brewing company, which owns two former British brewing rivals, Bass and Whitbread), Coors of the USA and Denmark-based Carlsberg. These four together now account for 80 per cent of the total beer brewed in the UK, their dominance fuelled by an aggressive expansionist regime since

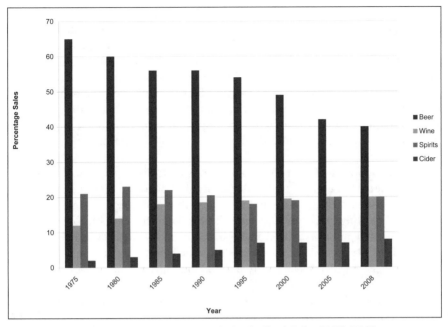

Figure 9.1 Sales of different types of alcoholic drinks 1975–2008
(Source of data: British Beer and Pubs Association 2008: 30).

the early 1980s. This in turn has led to the disappearance of many local and regional breweries (Protz 2001: 6). Although this trend has been partly offset by a growth of microbreweries (very small breweries supplying a handful of outlets) in recent years – which means that the number of breweries in the UK (711) is now the highest as at any time since 1945 (CAMRA 2009) – there were 37 major brewery closures in the UK between 1997 and 2008 (British Beer and Pub Association 2008).

The exponential success of the principal breweries in recent years in expanding their market share has been underpinned by a distinctive marketing approach. The strategy of these large companies has been focused on exploiting the pre-existing high level of brand loyalty to the smaller breweries among the beer-drinking population. The companies have achieved this by diversifying the range of brands they produce, keeping the former names of the small breweries they absorb, while gaining economies of scale by concentrating production in a decreasing number of manufacturing centres. Indeed, the principal aim of companies in buying up regional breweries seems to be the control of the brand name and the market tied to it, rather than the beer production itself (see also chapter 8).

This 'brand is all' approach is reflected in the marketing of beer in the UK. In their publicity, many brands seek to emphasise 'tradition' and 'continuity' in both the ways the product is made and the context in which it is consumed.

Brand loyalty among the beer-drinking public is particularly related to geography; until recent decades, beer-drinking was dominated by regional breweries which controlled their own geographical market, maintaining their position by also controlling the pubs selling their beer through the 'tied house' system.[1] The Oxford brewery, Morrells, for example, closed in 1998 and all its production was transferred to a contract brewing plant in Dorset. However, the company still owns a large number of pubs in and around the Oxford area, and in a promotional brochure published in 2001, the importance of geographic loyalty to a particular brand is thrown into sharp relief. The Morrells brochure states that:

> [T]here is more to Oxford than its famous dreaming spires, noble lawns and ancient, honey-coloured colleges. Real Oxford life blends a rich cultural heritage with the here and now ... with eights week rowing in May, languid punting on the meandering Cherwell and the clamour of a varsity march, and a pint or two of Morrells in celebration. Morrells has been part of Oxford life since 1782, so there's not much they don't know about the city ... classic Morrells beers are an essential part of real Oxford life.

Nowhere does the brochure mention that the beer is no longer brewed in Oxford, but in an anonymous brewery over sixty miles away (cited in CAMRA 2001: 565).

The UK Pub Industry

The number of pubs in the UK has fallen dramatically in recent years. The rate of decline is also accelerating: between 2000 and 2005, pub closures were running at a rate of two per week; this had risen to 54 per week by July 2009 (British Beer and Pub Association 2009). Of the 68,000 pubs in the UK in 2000, only 57,500 remain.

The consolidation in the industry has also been reflected in a shift in the way pubs are run in the UK, with a general decline in the number of 'free houses', which are those pubs not tied to a particular brewery. However, this trend has not been the result of the greater dominance of the breweries: in 2008, only 16 per cent of UK pubs were owned by breweries, compared to 30 per cent in 2000 and over 50 per cent in 1985 (Brewers and Licensed Retailers Association 2001; British Beer and Pub Association 2009). The situation has been complicated by the rise in importance of the 'pub chains' over the past decade, most of which are exclusively retailing operations and have no interest in the production of beer. The result of this is that, whilst many of the larger breweries no longer control pubs themselves, there has been a consolidation in the control of pubs, with a handful of pub-chain companies now running a substantial proportion of Britain's pubs (Table 9.1).

Table 9. 1   Major pub chains in the UK in 2008

Pub Chain	Approximate Number of Pubs
Punch Taverns	8,384
Enterprise Inns	7,783
Admiral Taverns	2,700
Greene King	2,400
Mitchell & Butlers	1,892
County Estate Management	950
Wellington Pub Company	855
JD Weatherspoon PLC	690
Trust Inns	602

(Sources: British Beer and Pub Association 2008: 103–105; *Guardian* newspaper 9 Sept 2009: 29).

The rise of the pub chain has led to a far greater level of homogeneity among UK pubs, particularly within urban areas of the country. Almost all towns and certainly all cities now contain a number of pubs belonging to the major chains. Each pub within such a chain is fitted to a largely identical standard and serves the same types of beers no matter where in the country they are located. These chains are often based on a particular marketing concept or theme, representing a further way of establishing brand loyalty among pub consumers.

One of the most interesting examples of this phenomenon is the Irish theme pub, of which there are at least four national chains in Britain. Mitchell and Butler's O'Neill's chain, for example, is designed to mimic the 'authentic Irish pub experience'. Adorned with images of Ireland (including Celtic symbols, street signs, standing stones, fiddles and, of course, pints of Guinness), O'Neill's website promises a 'guarantee of a warm welcome' and 'great *craic*', where one can 'unwind' in a 'laid-back but friendly setting'. All these pubs serve a range of stouts and 'Irish food'; signs and menus are written in Gaelic script and interiors are furnished using genuine or replica items from real Irish pubs in Ireland. The plaster on the walls is deliberately cracked and roughened, and is painted with a pale yellow ochre wash to indicate nicotine staining. Together with the faded black and white photographs, antique agricultural implements, bottle-glass windows and the 'spit and sawdust' floors, the overall effect is one which seeks to emphasise age and tradition. Yet the first O'Neill's pub only opened in 1992. It is notable that O'Neill's is just one of twenty-two pub brands owned by Mitchell and Butlers, each of which is targeted at a distinct consumer market.

The growth of the pub chains means that pubs in Britain are now far more than mere drinking establishments and the diversification of services offered by pubs during the past two decades is a major factor which separates them from their counterparts in continental Europe. It is now unusual for pubs not to offer a full range of meals and many now double up as restaurants. Pubs may also have accommodation, and, particularly in rural areas, play areas for children; this emphasises the fact that they are acceptable places for families. Families may now go for a 'day out' not to the beach or the countryside, but to the pub. Usually this is the only way these pubs are able to survive.

Preserving our Heritage: The Campaign for Real Ale

During the past two decades, there has been a reaction among consumers against these trends, led predominantly by a pressure group called the Campaign for Real Ale (CAMRA). Established in 1971 originally as the Campaign for the Revitalisation of Ale, it is one of the largest consumer organisations in Europe, with over 100,000 members. CAMRA has been partly responsible for ensuring that cask ale, which was in danger of dying out during the 1970s, remains available in most pubs in the UK. It has also campaigned against the monopolisation of the brewing and pub industries by large conglomerates. Although the championing of cask ale represents the organisation's raison d'être, the essential focus of its campaigns is on preserving tradition, be this in the way beer is brewed, in maintaining a diversity of different brands, in campaigning against the decline of 'free houses' or in halting the closure of pubs. The organisation also seeks to retain the regional character of British beer, and, with varying success, has called for all companies to state clearly on pumps where their brands are brewed.

CAMRA has been campaigning against the closure of rural pubs for a number of years. The organisation's annual publication, *The Good Beer Guide*, set out the purposes of the campaign in 2001:

> [The campaign] would, we planned, draw attention to some of Britain's best loved and most historically important buildings where traditionalism still rules, native and stranger are united, and the ghastliness of the theme pubs and slick city wine bars are left far behind. Pubs where one can draw up a chair to the blazing log-filled inglenook or sit in the open air and revel in the beauty of Britain's glorious landscapes. Sepia pictures on the walls are likely to be genuine, and the subsidence that caused the sloping floor probably took place in the 18th Century ... For locals the pub is the hub of village life, a place to meet and chew the cud. It continues traditional games – shove-halfpenny, skittles and dominoes – which have, for the most part, died out elsewhere. For visitors, with a more romantic viewpoint, the country pub is as much an intrinsic element of the British countryside as safely grazing sheep and sky larks ascending.
>
> (Smith 2001: 7–8).

In a similar vein, CAMRA's website states:

> The role of the rural British pub as a cohesive centre of its community has never been more important than it is today, and yet a record number have

ceased to trade in recent years ... Beyond the chatter and laughter of the rural bar room crowd on a busy Sunday lunchtime, there are also the quiet times mid-week in February when no one bar the publican and his dog venture past the front door. In previous centuries, these were the times when the local agricultural workers or skilled craftsmen would have popped in to warm themselves, exchange a little gossip and indulge in a pie and a pint. But times change; the agricultural workforce has dwindled as mechanisation has taken root, and many of the traditional village-based craftsmen have long ceased their particular trades. Even the beer is now largely delivered in metal casks, and coopers are a rare breed. In short, there are times when all is too peaceful, when tranquility can transcend viability.

(CAMRA 2009: 4–5)

In the quotations above, there is a sub-text which seems to hark back to some long forgotten 'golden age', an age in which the production and consumption of beer was motivated not by market forces but by the landlord's love of the beer he sold and the 'responsibilities' he felt towards the local community he served. For this mythical figure, making a profit was clearly a secondary consideration, if it was a consideration at all. This sub-text can also be discerned in the description of the images associated with the rural pub, images which are probably shared by a large majority of CAMRA's membership.

Despite CAMRA's partial successes, it remains the case that much of the younger drinking population (by far the most important market for the breweries and pub owners) prefers to drink lager, particularly of the bottled variety, and the 'foaming pint' of ale is no longer as fashionable as it once was. Lager dominates the British beer market, and accounted for 58 per cent of all bottled or canned beer sold in 2008, compared to a figure of just 26 per cent for ale. 'Ghastly theme pubs' (Smith 2001: 7) are also extremely popular, and so, profitable!

Nevertheless, the appeal to tradition is an important commodity in the brewing industry, and it is clear that CAMRA and the brewing companies are locked in competition over the rights to Britain's beer heritage and authenticity, with both sides seeking to convince the public that each has a moral stake within it. One might ask why over 100,000 people in Britain appear to be concerned about 'preserving their heritage' in this way? To answer this question, it is necessary to change tack somewhat, and to focus on 'the pub' as a concept, on the role it plays, or (in the case of many areas of the country) used to play, in British social and cultural life, and on the image presented today, for example, by the tourist industry.

The Pub as a Concept

It is probably true to say that the pub represents – or is perceived of as representing – a central component in Britain's national identity. Indeed, in a European context, the British pub may be considered virtually unique, since, with the exception of Ireland, there is no other country in which the pub or its equivalent has attained comparable status as a national cultural symbol. Despite increased competition from other leisure activities in the post-modern, consumer-driven and service-led society, pubs remain extremely popular and they undoubtedly retain an important social role. It is worth noting that the word itself is an abbreviation of 'public house', a highly revealing term. Moreover, the images engendered by the quotations above are very definite: pubs are viewed as inherently egalitarian establishments, representing centres of community life; they are also meeting places; they are often a focus for entertainment, for bonhomie and laughter, and above all, they are places for buying and drinking beer. Like cask ale, they also signify continuity and tradition, bulwarks of stability against the uncertainties created by a rapidly changing world.

Pubs also represent something mildly dangerous. Just as the alcohol that they serve produces an altered psychological state, few other social contexts offer the same possibilities for manipulation of the normal social order or for alteration of defined social roles pertaining in the world outside. They are places where people are able to talk to strangers, for example, without being regarded as somehow unusual, or as mentally unbalanced. This is particularly true of large cities, where the population has become conditioned into assuming that someone who approaches a stranger and engages them in conversation outside the confines of a pub is potentially dangerous, whose motivation may be robbery, or worse.

However, as we have mentioned, the traditional functions of the pub are being challenged at the present time. Not only have large breweries been partly responsible for changing the nature of beer consumption in the UK, through their aggressive marketing of more profitable lager and nitro-keg beers, but also beer drinking has been affected by the rise in popularity of wine, particularly red wine, in recent years. This is something which, in this volume, provides an interesting comparison to the increasing consumption of beer in the traditionally wine-drinking countries (see other chapters in this volume, especially chapter 7). Furthermore, more people buy beer and wine in supermarkets, which they drink at home. This seems to be due both to their cheap availability in supermarkets and to changes in patterns of home life, with both partners working, with television and the internet significant pastimes and with child care by both parents.

The impact of these developments has been disproportionately felt in rural areas of the country. Only one-third of all rural parishes in the UK have a pub today, compared to well over half only two decades ago. Furthermore, the role of rural pubs has altered to the extent that they can no longer be considered as the centres of community life. In short, the images expressed above may now be more imaginary than real. Where that image of the rural pub as a tranquil, pastoral idyll is maintained, it is probably deliberately maintained to attract outsiders.

The above observations were borne out by the results of a small-scale survey of the beer-drinking habits of residents of a village in north Oxfordshire in

2001 (Macbeth, Collinson and Collingwood-Bakeo 2002). This survey found that most people in the village did not drink beer at all in the week surveyed or drank it only infrequently. Few people drank regularly in pubs, while some went to clubs and many purchased beer in supermarkets to be drunk at home. It is very likely that these trends have deepened since that survey was conducted, in line with national trends. Thus, while the traditional image of the country pub is an important marketing tool, that image of its role in the rural community may no longer be reflected in reality. Survival of pubs now owes as much or more to the patronage of visitors, be they nearby urban dwellers or tourists, than to their traditional local market, and that patronage is encouraged by the image of tradition, as well as by the restaurants, play areas, etc. mentioned above.

The Thirst for Tradition

In this chapter, we have sketched out some of the main developments in the brewing and pub industries in the UK, and noted the way the marketing of beer often seeks to appeal to 'continuity' and 'tradition' as a way of retaining brand loyalty among its consumers. We have also highlighted reactions against recent trends, which have usually been couched as a call to 'tradition' in the production and consumption of beer. Later in the chapter, we presented evidence which suggests that the images often associated with the rural pub no longer reflect reality.

In conclusion, one can suggest that our observations might be explained with reference to an influential paradigm in the social sciences at the present time, namely post-modernist theory. According to this thesis, the service-led economies of the Western and developed world may be characterised as 'post-modern', a term which seeks to describe a fundamental alteration in social relations and personal and group identities. In the post-modern society, there is a process of commodification of virtually any phenomena, and a change in forms of social organisation based on productive relations to ones that are, in Baudrillard's words, based on 'consumption and seduction' (quoted in Kneafsey 1994: 107). This type of society is characterised by the fragmentation of familial and social relationships and a concomitant dislocation of traditional networks of interaction. A number of authors have argued that this has given rise to a need for people to search out specific experiences and contexts which provide a sense of 'continuity' and 'tradition' otherwise lacking from their everyday social worlds (see, for example, Harvey 1990; Featherstone 1990; Waugh 1992). Often these are to be found in rural areas, which are perceived as having a more 'authentic' identity and as being imbued with a more developed 'community spirit' in comparison to the fast-paced, often alienating urban environment (Kneafsey 1994).

We have mentioned that the concept of the pub may be considered to be one that is inherently related to those images associated with the small, local community. Wherever pubs may be located, they are, first and foremost, gathering places, associated with community life. People in the atomised environment of a large city often crave a sense of community, such as that perceived to be found in rural areas, and pubs often meet that demand. The trends occurring within the industry noted earlier, particularly in relation to the rise of pub chains and theme pubs, may be viewed as exploiting such a need. In many countries now, Irish theme pubs, for example, are specifically tailored towards a marketing concept which emphasises 'tradition', through the deliberate creation of an antiquated environment within each pub. They may also be seen as an example of the way culture itself has become a commodity, with an inherent economic value which may be marketed, bought and sold in the same way as any other, more tangible, asset. In the same vein, the value which the large breweries clearly place upon controlling regional brands of beer and their brand names further exemplifies the importance to the industry of maintaining (or inventing) tradition, as well as representing a commodification of regional cultures and identities. These trends towards imitation – in beer production as well as in the rise of the pub chains – are consistent with the essential characteristics of the post-modern society, in which authenticity itself becomes a highly-prized and contested asset, and therefore an increasingly diffuse and ultimately meaningless phenomenon.

Viewed from this perspective, then, organisations such as CAMRA and the campaign to save rural pubs may be considered to be examples of a general reaction against trends within wider society, exemplifying the need to search out more grounded, 'authentic' and ultimately more 'real' social experiences. This, fundamentally, is perhaps a reason for the continued importance of the pub in the social and cultural life of the country. For it is clear that, for many people in the UK at least, the pub retains an extremely significant role, one of the last bastions of *Gemeinschaft* in an increasingly *Gesellschaft*-oriented world. However, in the context of the current recession and competition from supermarkets, many pubs, particularly those in rural areas, no longer remain economically viable. It remains to be seen how the clear contradictions between the social functions of the pub and the commercial priorities of the industry are resolved in the future; from the evidence presented here, it seems that, for the moment at least, it is the latter which have the upper hand.

Notes

1. This system allowed breweries to ensure that only their own beer was sold in the pubs they owned, collectively referred to as the breweries' 'estate'. Following an investigation by the Monopolies and Mergers Commission in the late 1980s, regulations were altered to allow tenants to sell beer from other breweries as well as the one to which they were tied, and a number of the larger breweries were forced to sell off some of their estates.

References

Breweries and Licensed Retailers Association (2001) Beer and pub facts. Available at http://www.beerandpub.com/.

British Beer and Pub Association (2006) *British Beer and Pub Association's Statistical Handbook 2006*, British Beer and Pub Association, London.

British Beer and Pub Association(2008) *Statistical Handbook. A Compilation of Drinks Industry Statistics*, Brewing Publications Ltd., London.

British Beer and Pub Association (2009) *Statistical Handbook. A Compilation of Drinks Industry Statistics*, Brewing Publications Ltd., London.

CAMRA (2001) *Good Beer Guide 2002*, CAMRA, St. Albans.

CAMRA (2009) *Good Beer Guide 2010*, CAMRA, St. Albans.

CAMRA (2009) *Saving your Local Pub: A guide for local communities*, CAMRA, St. Albans.

Countryside Agency (2001) *The Pub is the Hub*, (Report number CA 95), HMSO, London.

Featherstone, M. (1990) Global culture: an introduction, *Theory, Culture and Society*, 7: 1–14.

Harvey, D. (1990) *The Condition of Postmodernity*, Blackwell, London.

Kneafsey, M. (1994) The cultural tourist: patron saint of Ireland. In Kockel, U. (ed.) *Culture, Tourism and Development: The case of Ireland*, Liverpool University Press, Liverpool.

Macbeth, H., Collinson, P. and Collingwood-Bakeo, A. (2002) Changes in beer-drinking and pub-going habits in UK: indications from a small Oxfordshire study in 2001, *Alimenta Populorum*, 2(1): 11–21.

Protz, R. (2001) Save Britain's brewing heritage. In CAMRA *Good Beer Guide 2002*, CAMRA, St. Albans.

Smith, S. (2001) Thatched or despatched. In CAMRA *Good Beer Guide 2002*, CAMRA, St. Albans.

Stafford, N. (2001) Small fish to fry. In CAMRA. *Good Beer Guide 2002*, St Albans: CAMRA.

Waugh, P. (1992) *Practising Postmodernism/Reading Modernism*, Edward Arnold, London.

CHAPTER 10
BEER IN THE CZECH REPUBLIC

....

Jana Parízková and *Martina Vlkova*

There are several reasons to write about beer in the Czech countries, not only because of a long tradition and the great local popularity of this beverage, but also because of one statistic: the Czech Republic has the greatest consumption per capita and per year in the world (Food and Agriculture Organisation of the United Nations 2009). This is similar to neighbouring Bavaria, where local consumption of beverages generally differs little from that of the Czechs. The consumption of beer and of other alcoholic beverages has been stable over the last few decades, even when significant changes in the political, social and economic situation have occurred (Figure 10.1).

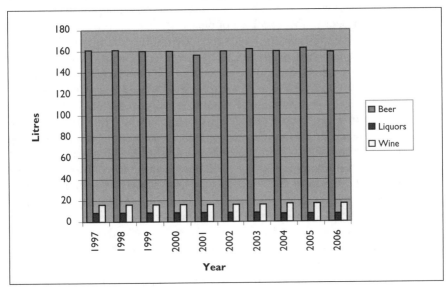

Figure 10.1   In the Czech Republic the ratios of beer, liquor and wine consumed per capita per year (1997–2006) changed little
(Source: Český statistický ú řad (Czech Statistical Office) 2007a)

Average general consumption of alcohol in Central and Eastern Europe is also high, with a relatively large proportion of unrecorded consumption estimated as ranging from one litre in the Czech Republic and Estonia to 10.5 litres in Ukraine; this varies with gender, being lower in women. Consumption levels of alcohol during recent periods in this part of Europe have been correlated positively with levels of detrimental health outcomes (Kubicka 2006; Popova *et al.* 2007). Effective and cost-effective programmes to improve this situation have been implemented in the Czech Republic. Increased drinking since the 'Velvet Revolution' in 1989 has caused concern: for example, in women in the capital, Prague, whose lifestyle has entailed an expansion of social contacts. This has been particularly true for those working in freelance jobs and/or involved in the newly emerging trend for self-employment (Kubicka *et al.* 1995).

Increased consumption of alcohol and especially of beer has also been considered as among the causes of an increased prevalence of overweight and obesity, but this has not been confirmed in some studies in the Czech population (Bobak *et al.* 2003). The level of consumption causing a risk to health in Czech men was found to be age-related, with the climax at 35 to 44 years of age and with linear decreases with educational level. No statistically significant relationship between unhealthy alcohol consumption and age or education level was found in women (Kubicka and Csémy 2004). However, moderate beer consumption may help to maintain, for example, homocysteine concentration levels in the normal range due to high folate content; this reduces the risk of cardiovascular diseases (see Kaiser *et al.*, this volume). As revealed in a study in the Czech population, folate from beer may thus contribute to the protective effect of alcohol consumption on cardiovascular disease in a population with generally low folate intake from other nutrients (Mayer *et al.* 2001). This positive effect could also contribute to the increased popularity and high consumption of beer in the Czech Republic.

Environmental conditions for beer production in the territory of the Czech Republic have long been favourable. The soil has a characteristic composition (e.g., iron content), which is good for the cultivation of hops (*Humulus lupulus* L.). According to the Český Svaz Pivovarů a Sladoven (Czech Beer and Malt Association) (2009), there is also a suitable quality of water, which has an important role in the successful production of beer. The high quality of the hops has always allowed Czechs to prepare beer with 10 grades[1], the less intoxicating of which can be consumed in greater quantities as a refreshing beverage.

The history of brewing is also long; the first historical record comes from the year 859. Czech hops had been cultivated and exported via the Elbe River to Hamburg for the famous hops market, *Forum Humuli*, since the year 1101. The first mention of brewing beer in Bohemia comes from the foundation charter of *Vyšehrad capitula* in Prague, issued by Vratislav II in the year 1088, which decreed that each priestly estate should supply one bucket of mead and one bucket of beer each harvest.

In the centuries that followed, there were more references to beer: Olomouc Bishop Bruno in the years 1258 and 1267 granted to twenty poor singers bread and beer every day for a whole year. Members of the Ostrov monastery and serfs in Úhonce in 1388 got for breakfast, bread, cheese and beer (Šimon 2009). The great expansion of beer drinking was followed by St. Vojtěch's (St. Ethelbert's) prohibition against drinking beer, under threat of exclusion from the church. Pope Innocence abolished this ban in the Czech countries, after the intercession of King Vaclav IV (Wenceslas IV).

The Golden Bulla of Karel IV (Charles IV) established that all citizens had the right to brew beer. A special brewing profession did not exist, as beer was produced in the home like other food and drink (Šimon 2009; Večerníček 2009). The foundation of the royal cities also gave rise to the issuing of various rights and privileges, including the licence to brew beer. This was badly received by the aristocracy, who defied this royal law and used their privileged status for the benefit of their own breweries. In 1517 King Ludvík Jagellonský gave permission for aristocrat breweries to be established in a concession called the 'St. Wenceslas reconciliation'. Since that time noble breweries have enjoyed great prosperity. By the middle of the sixteenth century, 1,000 breweries existed in Czech territory. Later the long-settled citizens in cities began to take possession of this law, monopolised it, and did not allow the more recently settled citizens to have the same rights. There was a 'mile law', which stated that beer could not be brewed, or malt produced, or beer sold in pubs opened less than one mile from a city (Cihlár 2003).

In rural areas the right of brewing by households passed to the proprietors of farms. Therefore, the aristocracy and knights claimed this right for their own use in order to produce malt and to brew beer. This law was confirmed by King Vladislav II Jagellonský in 1485. At the beginning, the aristocracy considered that brewing was not honourable enough for them, and passed on this right to their subjects or to the cities. Their objective was to attract settlers to the new cities, which was useful for increasing their wealth. At first, the cities denied the aristocracy the right to buy houses, and to trade and to open pubs. The reason was because the aristocracy produced the malt and brewed the beer, but did not allow city dwellers to sell beer in their territories. On the other hand, the aristocracy complained in 1484 that the cities not only had increased the prices of malt and beer, but also that the aristocracy could not do as they wished with their wealth. This movement was led by the powerful Vilém from Pernštejn, who got rich just from the production of beer. King Vladislav II Jagellonský wanted to support the cities, but after the aristocracy helped him during the war against Hungary, he did not permit any more construction of breweries and pubs in other territories. The cities defended themselves, but in 1517 they were forced to permit the nobility to brew beer in the cities at first for a period of only 6 years, in return for gaining certain other political privileges, which had not been secured until that time. This law later became permanent, by decree of Ferdinand II in 1627 (Večerníček 2009).

After 1517, a great change occurred in the brewing of beer. First, the number of breweries in the rural areas increased significantly, along with the pubs. Večerníček (2009) suggests that by the end of fifteenth century there existed villages with more than twenty pubs; and in cities and towns each eighth or ninth house was an ale house. According to Český Svaz Pivovarů a Sladoven (2009), in the sixteenth century there existed over 3,000 breweries. Beer was called 'liquid bread' and people drank it for breakfast, lunch and dinner (Šimon 2009). Later, the Thirty Years War brought great harm to Czech brewing, as it did in other European countries. Beer began to be brewed from ingredients of low quality (e.g., rootstock, stubble, turnips, etc.), and many well-established breweries were destroyed; their proprietors and workers were killed or had to escape, move elsewhere or emigrate.

In the seventeenth century, the preparation of beer was thought to be something mysterious, and instructions for its preparation were sold at great expense (Šimon 2009). Brewing was accompanied by the singing of appropriate songs, and there were various superstitions about how a successful brewing could be guaranteed by special conditions of wizardry. For example, it was believed that for beer to be successfully finished, a true virgin had to spin a thread, which was soaked in wax from an altar candle, and this thread had to be wound around the beer tap. Such a thread also could be laid under a barrel of beer to assure its quality. Or if the beer was spoiled, it was recommended that one take two handfuls of ground juniper plus some measure of pine bark and white flour, and dissolve this mixture with beer from all the barrels: only then would the beer start to ferment successfully (Česal and Herzinger 2002).

The Jesuit Jan Barner translated the book called *O moci piva* (The Power of Beer) by Kryštof Fischer (in 1706) and claimed that the Good God supplied beer to the countries where wine was scarce. He claimed that beer is a healthy drink, as it is prepared from barley or wheat, from which the strength of beer is derived rather than from the hops or the water. His other advice included that wine can harm circulation and other parts of the body, but beer, when drunk in moderation, does not harm the brain or kidneys; also that soup can be prepared from beer. Similarly, he suggested that when ginger and cinnamon are added to beer, stomach troubles, which originate from other foodstuffs or drink, can be relieved, and when cumin is added to beer, stomach pains disappear. When one is tired from a journey, a beer compress can relieve pain and tiredness in the feet. Toothache is relieved by tepid beer. Bakers can use yeasts from beer for bread fermentation. When breeding poultry, hens will become fatter after drinking beer. Much other advice was given on how to use beer for many purposes (Sládek 1995).

During all of these periods, beer was prepared manually in homes and in individual breweries. Therefore, each beer had its special character and differed individually. Brewing beer was mostly linked to a pub, where not only beer, but also food like pork, sausages and goose were served as well (Večerníček 2009). Only in the eighteenth century did a Czech brewer, F.O. Poupě, introduce some scientific principles and regulations in his book called *Die Kunst des Bierbrauens* (The art of beer brewing); for example, he wrote that the temperature during brewing should be monitored. He also founded a school and educated many brewers who continued the tradition of brewing beer in other countries (Šimon 2009). Some larger breweries were founded at that time, but some of them are even older, for example, Platan, Regent, Samson, etc. (Cihlář 2003).

In 1842, a large brewery was established in Plzeň (Pilsen) (see Table 10.1), where there were good conditions for brewing beer (water of the right composition, sandstone cellars for storing beer, etc.). The city significantly supported this enterprise, and the production of beer increased steadily (Šimon 2009). The processes for brewing were continually improved. Beer produced in this way was consumed not only in the Czech countries, but also was more and more often exported to other countries around Europe, and also later to the USA and Canada.

Table 10.1   Some trademarks of various breweries in the Czech Republic

Brewery	Trademark(s)
Plzeňský Prazdroj – Pilsner brewery	Pilsner Urquell, Gambrinus, Master, Klasik, Primus
Plzeňský Prazdroj – Radegast brewery	Radegast, Birell
Plzeňský Prazdroj – Velké Popovice brewery	Velkopopovický kozel
Budějovický Budvar	Budweiser Budvar, Carlsberg, Pardál, Bud Super Strong
Braník	Braník
Staropramen	Staropramen
Heineken Czech	Krušovice, Starobrno
Platan	Platan, Prácheňská perla
Bohemia Regent	Regent,
Budějovický měš'anský brewery	Samson
PMS Přerov – Přerov brewery	Zubr
PMS Přerov – Litovel brewery	Litovel
PMS Přerov – Hanušovice brewery	Holba

(Source: Český Svaz Pivovarů a Sladoven 2009).

Many other breweries have developed since then which continue the Czech tradition of beer production. These brand names are well known internationally, mainly Pilsner Urquell, Staropramen (Old Source), Budweiser Budvar, Radegast, Gambrinus and Velkopopovicky kozel (Buck from Great Popovice); all are highly esteemed (Table 10.1). There exist about seventy breweries of various trademarks, for light or dark beer, with special characteristics.

One well-known brand name, Budweiser Budvar, produced beer in the southern Bohemian city of České Budějovice, and later became a cause for legal action. This conflict primarily concerned the brand name: American producers started to produce this beer in St. Louis at the end of the nineteenth century and also used the name of Budweiser. This controversy continues today between Anheuser-Busch and the Czech producers of Budweiser Budvar. Because of this legal dispute, American producers of Budweiser do not export their beer to European countries such as France, Italy, the Czech Republic, Slovakia, etc., and Czech producers do not export beer with the trademark of Budwar to North America (Čuban 2000).

In Prague, there are many traditional breweries as well as new ones established later. One of the most famous is the beer restaurant *U Fleků*, which was founded in 1499. This large pub, with many halls, a garden restaurant and a cabaret, has its own well, and is a 'must-see' in Prague. They serve thirteen grades of dark beer with a very special taste; it is much stronger than is normally expected by most beer lovers. Other breweries, e.g., those of the New City of Prague, and the breweries of Smíchov, Bráník, and Holešovice are also much appreciated. All have their special characteristics. Smíchov specialises in producing a light beer at a lower cost, which is very popular. Another famous beer restaurant is *U Kalicha*, where many scenes of *Dobrý voják Švejk* (The Good Soldier Svejk) took place in the famous books of Jaroslav Hašek.

Under the socialist regime, it was the custom to have student work-brigades, which helped with the hops harvest, when mechanisation was less frequent than it is today. This work was accompanied by a number of festivities, including the bringing of a hops wreath to the statue of St Wenceslas in Wenceslas Square, in Prague, where so many important political demonstrations occurred later. A very popular musical film, with pleasant melodies, which still appears on TV and in cinemas today, was shot here.

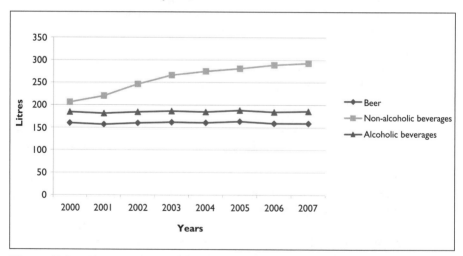

Figure 10.2   Changes in the consumption of alcoholic and non-alcoholic beverages and beer (in litres) per capita and per year in the Czech Republic over the period 1997–2006

(Český statistický ú řad 2007b).

Since pagan times, hops were thought to have a mischievous and lascivious character, which led to loss of chastity and virginity; similarly hops were an ancient symbol of fertility, and newlyweds were covered with hops as a promise for having many offspring. Still today, the hop is called 'Czech gold'.

Consumption of beer in the Czech Republic has remained stable even with the dramatic increase in non-alcoholic beverages over the last decade (Figure10.2). In fact, one comparison of beer consumption in 2003 (Figure 10.3) showed that in the Czech Republic it was the highest per capita in the world (Food and Agriculture Organisation of the United Nations (FAO) 2009). *Pivo*, the Czech synonym of beer, is an old Slavonic word and means the commonest and most widespread beverage. One explanation of the high consumption is that 'Let's have a beer' belongs to the most cordial of invitations among friends and colleagues, not only for drinking, but also in order to chat and discuss urgent political, professional, personal, and other problems. The pleasant ambiance resulting from beer drinking thus helps solve a number of problems, which would be more difficult without beer.

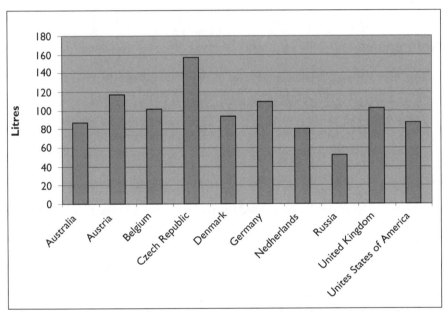

Figure 10.3   Comparison of beer consumption (in kg) per capita and per year in various countries in 2003

(Source: FAO 2009).

Most Czechs cannot enjoy the typical Czech dishes without having a beer with the meal. This is due also to the character of Czech meals which have traditionally been quite heavy : *Veprova pecene* (pork) or *Kachna se zelim a knedliky* (duck with dumplings and sauerkraut), *Hovezi svickova s knedliky* (beef sirloin with dumplings) or *Gulas s knedliky* (Goulash with dumplings) 'must' be served with a cold half litre of beer. Research by the Centrum pro výzkum veřejného mínění (Public Opinion Research Centre) (2008) shows that about 90 per cent. of men and 50 to 60 per cent of women drink beer and these statistics have been stable over the last few decades. The average amount of beer consumed varies from 7.9 to 9.5 half litres of beer per week per man and 1.9–2.4 per woman. The biggest consumers are men aged 45–59. On the other hand, because of the total prohibition of driving under the influence of alcohol, in the last few years non-alcoholic beer has become popular (Figure 10.2).

In summary, the tradition of beer drinking remains lively in the Czech Republic, having survived all political, social, economic and other changes, all of which bear witness to the essentially favourable character of beer.

Notes

1. See 'alcohol content' in Glossary.

References

Bobak, M., Skodova, Z. and Marmot, M. (2003) Beer and obesity: A cross-sectional study, *European Journal of Clinical Nutrition*, 57: 1250–1253.

Centrum pro výzkum veřejného mínění- Sociologický ústav AV ČR (2008) *Konzumace piva v České republice v roce 2008* (Beer consumption in the Czech Republic in year 2008), online. Available at: http://www.cvvm.cas.cz/upl/zpravy/100828s_OR81022a. pdf (accessed 5 September 2009).

Česal, A. and Herzinger, R. (2002) *Magická řemesla* (The magic trade), Rodiče, Praha.

Český statistický úřad (2007a) Spotřeba alkoholických nápojů a cigaret na 1 obyvatele. In Český statistický úřad, *Práce, sociální statistiky* (Work and Social Statistics: Consumption of alcoholic beverages and cigarettes per capita in the Czech Republic), Český statistický úřad, Praha.

Český statistický úřad (2007b) Spotřeba nejdůležitějších druhů potravin na 1 obyvatele. In Český statistický úřad, *Práce, sociální statistiky* (Work and Social Statistics: Consumption of most important foodstuff per capita in the Czech Republic), Český statistický úřad, Praha.

Český Svaz Pivovarů a Sladoven (2009) *Pivovarství a sladařství v českých zemích.* (Brewing and Malt in Czechia), online. Available at: http://www.cspas.cz/pivo.asp?lang=1 (accessed 4 September 2009).

Cihlář, T. (2003) *Pošumavské pivovary: Po stopách starých pivovarů a pivovárků západního Pošumaví aneb od Albrechtic až do Žichovic* (Breweries of the Bohemian forest: Old breweries in the western Bohemian forest, from Albrechtice to Žichovice), Nakladatelství Dr. Radovan Rebstöck, Sušice.

Čuban, J. (2000) *Americký Budweiser čechům nevoní* (The Czechs do not like the American Budweiser), online. Available at: http://ekonomika.idnes.cz/americky-budweiser-ceskym-pivarum-nevoni-fgt-/test.asp?c=2000M114T01D (accessed 5 September 2009).

Food and Agriculture Organisation of the United Nation (FAO) (2009) *FAOSTAT: Consumption: Crops Primary Equivalent*, online. Available at: http://faostat.fao.org/site/609/default.aspx#ancor (accessed 4 September 2009).

Kubicka, L. (2006) Alcohol use in the country with the world's highest per capita beer consumption – the Czech Republic, *Addiction*, 101: 1396–1398.

Kubicka L. and Csémy L. (2004) Analýza sociodemografického kontextu požívání alkoholických nápojů v dospělé populaci České republiky z hlediska zdravotního (An analysis of the sociodemographic context of alcohol use in the Czech adult population from the health perspective), *Časopis Lékařů Českých*, 143: 435–439.

Kubicka, L., Csémy, L. and Kozeny, J. (1995) Prague women's drinking before and after the 'Velvet revolution' of 1989: A longitudinal study, *Addiction*, 90: 1471–1478.

Mayer, O. Jr., Simon, J. and Rosolová, H. (2001) A population study of the influence of beer consumption on folate and homocysteine concentrations, *European Journal of Clinical Nutrition*, 55: 605–609.

Popova, S., Rehm, J., Patra, J. and Zatonski, W. (2007) Comparing alcohol consumption in central and eastern Europe to other European countries, *Alcohol Alcohol*, 42: 465–73.

Sládek, M. (ed.) (1995) *Malý svět jest člověk aneb výbor z České barokní prózy* (Human being is a small world: Selection of Czech baroque prose), H&H, Jinočany.

Šimon, P. (2009) *Dějiny pivovarnictví v Čechách* (History of brewing in Czech countries), online. Available at: http://www.pivety.com/DejinyCechy.htm (accessed 5 September 2009).

Večerníček, J.N. (2009) *Djiny piva: Od zrození po konec Středověku* (Beer history: from the neolithic to the 16th century), Computer Press, Brno.

CHAPTER 11
ALCOHOL CONSUMPTION AND BINGE DRINKING IN GERMAN AND AMERICAN FRATERNITIES: ANTHROPOLOGICAL AND SOCIAL PSYCHOLOGICAL ASPECTS

Gerhard Dammann

Introduction

Excessive beer-drinking is a characteristic aspect of college or university student life, especially when it is organised in fraternities.

In German-speaking countries (Germany, Austria and Switzerland) certain kinds of fraternities, the *Verbindung* (which literally means, bonding or union), have a long tradition. Most are restricted to male membership. Some have a nationalistic ideology, but most are politically neutral. Some are affiliated with a religious denomination (especially of the Catholic church), but many are secular. Members of *Studentenverbindungen* (the student fraternities) normally wear a ribbon and a cap in the colours of their fraternity to show their affiliation. Fraternities still have much influence in politics and business, as a consequence of younger members being supported by older members.

Some retain the ritual of the '*Mensur*' (literally, measure) that refers to fencing. Students use a straight-bladed sabre in duelling bouts. Duelling is illegal these days, but the *Mensur* persists, in a regulated form. Two members of different fraternities fence to prove themselves and the honour of their fraternities. Injuries occur but today these are never lethal due to protective clothing, although the '*Schmiss*' (a particular facial scar) is a proud badge of honour.[1]

Three different sources continue to influence the tradition and rituals of the German fraternities: those from the few universities whose foundations date back to the Middle Ages; those derived from the democratic movement of the early nineteenth century; and those resulting from secret societies in the Age of Enlightenment. Such fraternities in Europe were places where young men could prove themselves and show they were not afraid of pain, nor would they flinch if their honour should be tested.

The history and traditions of the North American fraternities and sororities are very different. Most of them are 'Greek letter fraternities' (most notable of which is Phi Beta Kappa, which is a purely scholastic society), but there are also fraternities without Greek letters, sometimes called secret societies, the most notorious of which is 'Skull and Bones', a secret society at Yale University. Most of the Greek letter fraternities and sororities have programmes of philanthropy carried out by their members, such as fundraising and charitable activities. Originating from literary societies in colleges and universities, North American fraternities and sororities promote scholarship, rhetoric and ethical conduct. Some were founded as early as the 1770s,[2] yet certain symbolic traditions are maintained. There are special handshakes, passwords, songs and rituals of initiation. Membership of both German and American fraternities is lifelong.

Drinking in American Fraternities

In the last ten years, a considerable amount of research has focussed on the use and abuse of alcohol among American college students (e.g., Wechsler *et al.* 1994). Most of the American studies on binge drinking are very critical of these activities; often emphasising the negative (and even sometimes fatal) effects and risk factors, they demand more preventative programmes. One such dangerous ritual is the '21-for-21'. For this, twenty-one glasses of beer must be drunk on one's twenty-first birthday. Another is binge drinking, which Reeves Sanday (1996) discusses in relation to the rape of female students. Wechsler *et al.* (1998) found an almost equal number of students who drink alcohol but do not binge drink as those who binge drink, being almost 40 per cent in each category. They also found that the frequency of those who abstained totally from alcohol was about equal to those who drank very often, totalling about 20 per cent. Not surprisingly this diversity of drinking habits is likely to have a bearing on how students respond to the alcohol policies of colleges. Wechsler *et al.* (1998: 66) write:

> Fraternities and sororities continue to be at the center of the campus alcohol culture. Despite highly publicized tragedies and continuing examinations of alcohol policies, 2 of 3 fraternity and sorority members are still binge drinkers. For those fraternity and sorority members who live in Greek houses, the statistics are even more extreme: 4 of 5 of these students are binge drinkers and half are frequent bingers.

If colleges and universities are to alleviate their alcohol problems, many authorities argue that they must drastically change this drinking culture. Although fraternity membership makes up only a small part of the national student population, it has a far greater influence. On many campuses the fraternities provide a centre for social activities; on some traditional campuses, the proportion of Greek letter fraternity students is high (Lee *et al.* 1998). It is interesting therefore to note that there is no published medical, public health-related or social psychological report in the scientific literature on the negative effects of binge drinking in *European* fraternities, nor on fraternity-related forms of rape.

For the USA, however, there is a wide literature. Turrisi *et al.* (2006) argue that excessive consumption of alcohol and its consequences create a serious problem for American universities. Each year in the USA, alcohol causes 'fatalities, assaults, serious injuries, and arrests in college students' (Turrisi *et al.*: 401). De Simone (2007) suggests that fraternity membership influences the likelihood of binge drinking, but individual factors also play an important part. In a study of members of male fraternities and of female sororities, Larimer *et al.* (2004) found that the perceptions of the students about their alcohol consumption significantly correlated with their pattern of drinking at the time, while their views on the acceptability of drinking gave a significant prediction of their drinking a year later, as well as of their symptoms of dependency and other consequences related to alcohol. Neighbors *et al.*'s (2007) study showed that powerful social norms are good indicators of alcohol consumption in this population and suggested that drinking to cope with adverse life situations predicts later problems with alcohol.

Cashin *et al.*'s (1998) results based on 25,411 students indicated that students in the fraternity system had more drinks per week, took part in heavy drinking sessions more frequently and, with a few exceptions, more often incurred negative consequences of drinking than did non-fraternity students. Leaders of such fraternities and sororities especially tended to consume large quantities of alcohol and experience negative consequences at levels as high as or higher than those of other American fraternity members. Generally members of such university fraternities and sororities expressed beliefs that alcohol promoted friendship, socialising and sexuality to a greater extent than did non-fraternity-students.

Several reviews have systematically examined the scientific literature on the effect of fraternity membership on alcohol-related beliefs and behaviours (e.g., Turrisi *et al.* 2006). Barry (2007) states: 'By charter, national Greek organizations (i.e. fraternities and sororities) place an emphasis on upholding personal integrity, academic scholarship, and development of campus leaders. Recent concerns, however, assert that the drinking behaviors of members of Greek organizations are antithetical to the mission of their universities.' The findings 'suggest that Greek members comprise a subgroup that consumes alcohol in greater quantities, underscores and misperceives the risks of alcohol abuse, and emulates a social environment and culture in which drinking alcohol is a key part of life' (Barry 2007: 307).

In a national sample of nearly 17,600 American students at 140 colleges and universities, Wechsler *et al.* (2002) found that 44 per cent had been involved in binge drinking during the two weeks just before the survey. In this study, binge drinking for men was defined as having five or more drinks in a row, or as having four or more drinks in a row for women. Drinking habits acquired in high school often continue in higher education. Those who had been binge drinkers in high school were found to be much more likely to carry on being binge drinkers as undergraduates. Being white, involved in sports or a member of a fraternity or sorority group also positively affected the likelihood for a student to be a binge drinker. Few of these students, even among the very frequent binge drinkers, considered that they had an alcohol problem, although some 3 per cent had sought professional help. However, compared with non-binge drinkers, more binge drinkers had had alcohol-related problems since the beginning of the academic year (Wechsler *et al.* 2002).

Wechsler *et al.* (2002) also found that frequent binge drinkers had suffered other serious problems. Examples include missing class, getting behind in studies, unplanned sex, often without contraceptive protection, trouble with campus police, injury, etc. (Presley *et al.* 1993; Ryan *et al.* 1994). In her book, *Fraternity Gang Rape*, Reeves Sanday (1990) described the discourse, rituals, sexual ideology, and practices that contribute to some American fraternity environments being rape-prone. Not surprisingly, the reaction of fraternity members to her book was mixed. Most reported that incidents of a 'pulling train' (gang rape) on campus were linked to fraternities (Reeves Sanday 1990: 19). Weitzman *et al.* (2003) characterised binge drinking as 'anomic', without rules, in a Durkheimian sense.

Drinking in German Fraternities

Beer drinking in German fraternities involves, besides cultural and amuse-ment aspects, elements of both initiation and mock duel. The tradition of student fraternities dates back to the Middle Ages. Itinerant scholars studying in Bologna or Paris organised themselves into groups by their country of origin and lived together in student hostels (*bursa*). First-year members ('foxes') of these groups, or fraternities, were often subjected to extreme initiation rites. Elements of initiation persisted in the sometimes excessive drinking rituals. Such elements included introduction to secrets, taboos, promotion to full membership, and separation from students who were not members (the 'finches'). The most important of these rituals continue today: branding, the salamander ritual (see below), tags bearing a fraternity's colour worn by members. In addition to initiation, the collective and ritualised drinking in German student fraternities points to another important tradition: that of the profaned duel.

In Europe, academics were the third group, besides the nobility and the military, allowed to wear weapons. Until the nineteenth century, duels among students were rare. Historical reasons in that century, in particular the role of students' duelling societies in the democratic fight for freedom, led to a sharp increase in affairs of honour, and to a shift in duelling practices from the use of the sword or sabre to that of the pistol. The Socialist leader Ferdinand Lassalle, the Russian poets, Michail Lermontov and Alexander Pushkin, and the French Mathematician, Evariste Galois, were among the celebrities who died in a duel.

However, in the twentieth century, there were significantly fewer duels, which were largely prohibited by law. Thus, rituals such as challenging another to a beer drinking contest, drinking relays, and other competitive drinking activities offered themselves as a way to settle disputes without bloodshed.

The *Biercomment* (Beer Conduct)

Books with rules and standards around the different beer rituals appeared in print in Göttingen in 1864 and in Leipzig 1891 (Leipziger Senioren-Convent 1891) with many later editions in the following years. The name of this body of rules and regulations is the '*Biercomment*'. *Comment* (in French) means 'how?', 'in what way?' and so this was a guide to behaviour, politeness, and etiquette. The *Biercomment* was also nicknamed the Eleventh Commandment. One regulation was that only beer and wine should be drunk and in a few exceptional cases sparkling wine. Spirits were not allowed. This is an important difference from American fraternities where hard liquor is also consumed. Beer overtook wine only in the nineteenth century amongst the German fraternities.

In the introductions to these *Biercomment* books the need for drinking rules is justified: outsiders often said that because of the drinking rules students would become intoxicated and depraved. But this, it was claimed in the publications, happened quite rarely. The view of those in the fraternities was that these persons were not victims of the *Biercomment*, but rather of too much drinking without rules, following their personal desires, and that most of the cases would have been students who were not fraternity members and did not follow the *Biercomment*. Many rules were and are associated with raising one's glass to somebody or the whole group, usually accompanied by words or phrases of wishing health: for example '*Prost*' (from the Latin *prosit* meaning 'may it be beneficial', from which stems the verb *zuprosten* – to toast each other) or '*Gesundheit*' (health), '*zum Wohlsein*' (to your well-being), etc. Apart from the beer rules there are several 'beer games' described in the *Biercomment* which are still very popular today.

The '*Bierjunge*' (Beer Boy) and Other Rituals and Games

The president of a fraternity can demand that any member of that fraternity drinks a certain amount of beer as a punishment for some misdemeanour. In fact, any full fraternity member can similarly order this of a novice. Then there is the classical drinking competition, called the '*Bierjunge*'. In the case of a dispute or a provocative comment, a fraternity student (not one of the 'foxes') is allowed to challenge the offending student to a drinking contest to 'prove the truth'. The challenger calls out '*Bierjunge*' and the person challenged calls '*Hängt!*' (hanging!, here meaning accepted). The contestants then each seek a second and one referee. If there are seconds, they, not the contestants, ingeniously discuss the reasons for the '*bier-ehrliche Handlung*' (beer-honesty act). Finally the referee gives the order to the two contestants: '*Von dem Boden an den Hoden; von dem Hoden an den Nabel, von dem Nabel an den Schnabel. Sauft's!*' (From the floor to the balls, from the balls to the navel, from the navel to the beak. Swig!). The winner is the contestant who is first to put his empty glass down without making a mess (Figure 11.1). Beer competitions of bigger groups (for example two fraternities drinking against each other) are called *Bierstafette* (beer relays).

One common beer game is called 'Rubbing a Salamander'. The origin of this phrase is unknown. The president of the active members (students) can give the command to drink a 'salamander'. Everybody must empty his glass of beer.

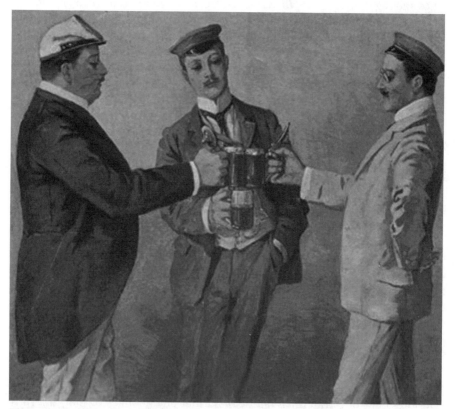

Figure 11.1   The 'Beer-Duel', painted by Georg Mühlberg (1863–1925). Right and left are the contestants; in the middle is the referee.
(Source: http://www.burschenschaftsgeschichte.de/bilder/georg_muehlberg_serie)

Jerome K. Jerome (1914: 189–190; the quotes are verbatim) described the salamander in his novel *Three men on the Bummel*, giving a good description of German university towns before the world wars:

'We will now,' says the chairman, 'a Salamander rub' (*Einen Salamander reiben*). We all rise, and stand like a regiment at attention. 'Is the stuff prepared?' (*Sind die stoffe parat?*) demands the chairman. '*Sunt*', we answer, with one voice. '*Ad excercitium salamandri*,' says the chairman, and we are ready. '*Eins!*' We rub our glasses with a circular motion on the table. '*Zwei!*' Again the glasses growl; also at '*Drei!*' 'Drink!' (*Bibite!*). And with mechanical unison every glass is emptied and held on high. '*Eins!*', says the chairman. The foot of every empty glass twirls upon the table, producing a sound as of the dragging back of a stony beach by a receding wave. '*Zwei!*' The roll swells and sinks again. '*Drei!*' The glasses strike the table with a single crash, and we are in our seats again.'

During the American war of independence, General von Steuben also practised the salamander: 'Instead of wine we had some kind of spirits, with which we made "salamanders"; that is to say, after filling our glasses, we set the liquor on fire and drank it up, flame and all' (Pierre Duponceau, a young French officer, describing the type of game Steuben allowed, in Doyle 1913: 87).

A final detail to mention is that in most fraternity houses there is something called a '*Kotzbecken*' (a puking sink), which in some fraternities is nicknamed the 'pope' in order to offend the Catholic fraternities. It is a practical object reaching roughly chest level with support bars for the user to get hold of to steady himself.

Rituals and Social Cohesion as Social Benefit

Eibl-Eibesfeldt (1979) listed the most important communicative functions of rituals as:

1. Bonding
2. Spacing and competing
3. Appeasing
4. The conquest of fear
5. Rituals to keep 'discipline'.

We can find all of these elements in the drinking rituals of German fraternities as well as in many other cultural contexts. In a study looking at sociological reasons and advantages related to why students generally drink alcohol excessively (Burns and Klawunn 1997), the authors argue that moderate drinking patterns can be modulated by social experience. Regarding the social relevance of drinking alcohol, Brodsky and Peele (1999) write:-

Observational studies consistently describe ritualised sociability in taverns (Fisher 1981, Single and Storm 1985); anthropological research has analyzed the shifting functions and benefits of such public drinking establishments throughout history and across cultures (Heath 1991). At the culture-wide level of cohesion, nations such as Greece, Italy, and Spain 'have acquired a "cultural immunity" to alcohol "problems" based on the ways in which alcohol is interwoven into the matrix of the personal, social, and religious lives of the people of these societies' (Gefou-Madianou 1992, p. 22). There is vast documentation of the moderating influences on drinking and its socialization in general (Blum and Blum 1969, Maloff *et al.* 1982, Peele and Brodsky 1996), and for American subcultures (Greeley *et al.* 1980) such as the Chinese and other Asian groups (Barnett 1955, O'Hare 1995), Jews (Glassner and Berg 1980), and Italians (vs. Irish Americans; Vaillant 1983). Contrasting with these are cultures with proscriptive norms (Akers 1992), where abstinence may not convey the psychosocial disadvantages that it does in cultures where social drinking is the norm (Orcutt 1991, Peele 1999). In addition to moderation or abstinence, however, excessive drinking can increase group coherence, as at binge-drinking weekends in college fraternities (Kuh and Arnold 1993, Wechsler *et al.* 1995).

(Brodsky and Peele 1999: 196)

The Benefit of Social Drinking – An Evolutionary Hypothesis

Peters and Stringham (2006) and Chatterji and De Simone (2006) have shown that drinkers earn more money than non-drinkers. Chatterji and De Simone estimated the relationship between 10th grade binge drinking in 1990 and the labour market outcomes in 2000 among National Educational Longitudinal Survey respondents and concluded: 'For males, negative employment effects and, more strikingly, positive wage effects persist after controlling for achievement as well as background characteristics, educational attainment, and adult binge drinking and family and job characteristics. Accounting for illegal drug use and other problem behaviours in 10th grade eliminates the unemployment effect, but strengthens the wage effect' (Chatterji and De Simone 2006). As the latter cannot be explained by health, income or social capital variables, justifications that are often used for the frequently observed positive correlations between adult alcohol use and earnings, Chatterji and De Simone conjecture that binge drinking conveys unobserved social skills that are rewarded by employers.

In Brodsky and Peele's (1989) comprehensive review, *Psychosocial Benefits of Moderate Alcohol consumption*, their first figure lists the positive effects of alcohol consumption, among which are the improvement of subjective health and of mental health, increased pleasure, reduced stress, increased sociability and social cohesion, increased cognitive and creative performance, increased confidence, bigger income, and social adjustment of young people. The drinking sessions typical for student parties and, even more so for the socially forced, but still ritualised, beer-drinking excesses in fraternities, are a probable example of this last point.

Pape and Hammer (1996) studied young Norwegian males and found indications that those who had first got drunk in their mid-teens tended to have fewer psychological problems later on than did their peers who had had their first experience with drunkenness either earlier or later than their middle adolescence. This finding is puzzling as one might expect that the closer to adulthood the first episode of getting drunk takes place the less serious its repercussions would be in later life.

When Nezlek *et al.* (1994) carried out a study among US college students their results showed that those who said that they had had a few binge-drinking episodes had more social interactions than those students who responded that they had either had none or very many such episodes. Furthermore, the social interactions of the 'moderate' drinkers in their survey were not only more frequent, but also more often intimate. This finding supports the impression one gets at occasions when large quantities of alcohol are consumed, not only in students' dorms but also during traditional feasts in villages and towns and especially during occasions such as the famous Munich Oktoberfest: getting tipsy and moderately drunk enhances social interactions. People who may never have met before and who may come from different parts of the world behave, despite possible language problems, towards each other like friends.

This effect of alcohol is interesting and Grant and MacDonald (2005) discuss whether it is really a loss of inhibition brought about by alcohol or still a form of inhibition. Nezlek et al's (1994) finding in their study of students in US colleges suggests that such limited drunkenness is, as it were, 'prosocial', that is it is something which seems to become a long-lasting social benefit for later life. This leads to the conclusion that there are social and psychological benefits, both immediately and later, in having had a few binge-drinking episodes as a student.

The problem with binge drinking and perhaps more seriously so with consumption of regular, large daily amounts of alcohol, is that a number of those persons exposed to the quite strong social pressure to drink as much as others will suffer health risks and even, as Kaiser *et al.* (this volume) argue, get to the problematic state of socially and psychiatrically relevant alcoholism. Still, one could well argue that getting used to the effects of alcohol relatively early in life may have a protective function. This is particularly evident among those who grow up in a society where alcohol is consumed in a regular, but moderate and mostly controlled fashion, and where it is considered a normal accompaniment of meals and social gatherings, as in Italy, Spain, France and Germany, to name a few (see also Lowe and Foxcroft 1993). In contrast, a number of European countries, especially the Scandinavian ones such as Norway, have, and have long had, a policy which strongly discourages alcohol consumption. The big question is whether this prohibition-type of government control, in which alcohol is usually sold for very high prices, in state-owned premises with their barred counters, which look more like prisons than shops, is having the desired effect in reducing alcohol consumption in general and alcoholism in particular.

Finally, one is tempted to ask why alcohol consumption plays such a big role in so many societies around the world. The detrimental effects of alcoholism (a not too rare risk of regular drinking, see chapter 2) are very obvious. Given the almost global pattern of drinking alcoholic beverages (see also the Introduction) one wonders whether there are some patterns of drinking which may bring with them some advantages. Some studies have shown this, e.g, those which are published by Peele and Grant (1999) in an edited book which focuses on positive aspects of consuming alcohol, and on the fights of some governments to control alcohol production and consumption and on the campaigns trying to get this 'evil' substance banned.

Conclusion

In this chapter the following assumptions have been made and discussed:

1. Excessive drinking has a lot of social psychological functions for younger adults.
2. Important functions are
   (a) initiations (rites de passages) (Leemon 1972),
   (b) rituals of virility ('ability to hold one's drink') due to a not yet consolidated sureness of the masculine role,
   (c) producing closeness, ending in social networks.
3. In the German fraternities there are a great many drinking rituals.
4. Rituals have important anthropological meanings (ranking, etc.)
5. Some of these beer-drinking rituals (drinking competitions) can be understood as profaned forms of duels.
6. Comparable with the duel the function of these drinking competitions is, for example, resolution of conflicts.
7. Strong ritualisation and rules in German fraternities with a long tradition constitute the necessary limiting framework for excessive drinking.
8. In US fraternities without these drinking rules and rituals dangerous situations and mortal cases are observed (Nuwer 1999), almost unknown in Germany, although students have the same age and social background.

Notes

1. See: http://en.wikipedia.org/wiki/Studentenverbindung (accessed 6 October 2009).
2. See ttp://en.wikipedia.org/wiki/Fraternities_and_sororitiesh (accessed 6 October 2009).

References

Akers, R.L. (1992) *Drugs, alcohol and society: Social structure, process and policy*, Wadsworth, Belmont, MA.

Barnett, M.L. (1955) Alcoholism in the Cantonese of New York City: an anthropological study. In Diethelm, O. (ed) *Etiology of chronic alcoholism*, Charles C. Thomas, Springfield, Illinois: 179–227.

Barry, A.E. (2007) Using theory-based constructs to explore the impact of Greek membership on alcohol-related beliefs and behaviors: a systematic literature review, *Journal of American College Health*, 56: 307–315.

Baum-Baicker, C. (1985) The psychological benefits of moderate alcohol consumption: a review of the literature, *Drug and Alcohol Dependence*, 15: 305–322.

Blum, R.H., and Blum, E.M. (1969) A cultural case study. In R.H. Blum and Associates (eds), *Drugs: Vol. 1. Society and drugs*, Jossey-Bass, San Francisco: 188–227.

Brodsky, A. and Peele, S. (1999) Psychosocial benefits of moderate alcohol consumption. Alcohol's role in a broader conception of health and well-being. In Peele S. and Grant, M. (eds) *Alcohol and pleasure: A health perspective*, Brunner/Mazel, Philadelphia: 187–207.

Burns W.D. and Klawunn M. (1998) The web of caring: an approach to accountability in alcohol policy. In US Department of Education (eds) *Designing Alcohol and other Drug Prevention Programs in Higher Education. Bringing theory into practice*, US Department of Education, Newton, Mass: 49–124.

Cashin, J.R., Presley, C.A. and Meilman, P.W. (1998) Alcohol use in the Greek system: follow the leader? *Journal of Studies on Alcohol and Drugs*, 59: 63–70.

Chatterji, P. and De Simone, J. (2006) *High School Alcohol Use and Young Adult Labor Market Outcomes*, National Bureau of Economic Research, NBER Working Paper No. 12529, Cambridge, MA.

De Simone, J. (2007) Fraternity membership and binge drinking, *Journal of Health Economics*, 26: 950–967.

Doyle, J.B. (1913) *Frederick William von Steuben and the American Revolution*, H.C. Cook, Steubenville, OH.

Eibl-Eibesfeldt, I. (1979) Ritual and ritualization from a biological perspective. In von Cranach, M., Foppa, K., Lepenies, W. and Ploog, D. (eds) *Human Ethology. Claims and limits of a new discipline*, Cambridge University Press, Cambridge: 3–55.

Fisher, J.C. (1981). Psychosocial correlates of tavern use: a national probability sample study. In Harford, T.C. and Gaines, L.S. (eds) *Social Drinking Contexts*, NIAAA Research Mongraph No. 7, National Institute on Alcohol Abuse and Alcoholism, Washington, DC.: 34–53.

Gefou-Madianou, D. (ed.) (1992) *Alcohol, Gender and Culture*, Routledge, London.

Glassner, B. and Berg, B. (1980) How Jews avoid alcohol problems, *American Sociological Review*, 45: 647–664.

Grant, N.K. and Macdonald, T.K. (2005) Can alcohol lead to inhibition or disinhibition? Applying alcohol myopia to animal experimentation, *Alcohol Alcohol,* 40(5): 373–378.

Greeley, A.M., McCready, W.C. and Theisen, G. (1980) *Ethnic Drinking Subcultures*, Praeger, New York.

Grossarth-Maticek, R. and Eysenck, H.J. (1995). Self-regulation and mortality from cancer, coronary heart disease, and other causes: a prospective study, *Personality and Individual Differences*, 19: 781–795.

Grossarth-Maticek, R., Eysenck, H.J. and Boyle, G.J. (1995) Alcohol consumption and health: synergistic interaction with personality, *Psychological Reports*, 77: 675–687.

Heath, D.B. (1991) Alcohol studies and anthropology. In Pittman, D.J. and White, H.R. (eds) *Society, Culture, and Drinking Patterns Re-examined*, Rutgers Center of Alcohol Studies, New Brunswick: 87–108.

Jerome, J.K. (1914) *Three Men on the Bummel*, Arrowsmith, Bristol.

Kuh, G.D. and Arnold, J.C. (1993) Liquid bonding: a cultural analysis of the role of alcohol in fraternity pledgeship, *Journal of College Student Development*, 34: 327–334.

Larimer, M.E., Turner, A.P., Mallett, K.A. and Geisner, I.M. (2004) Predicting drinking behavior and alcohol-related problems among fraternity and sorority members: examining the role of descriptive and injunctive norms, *Psychology of Addictive Behaviors*, 18: 203–212.

Lee, H., Gledhill-Hoyt, J., Maenner, G., Dowdall, G.W. and Wechsler, H. (1998) Changes in binge drinking and related problems among American college students between 1993 and 1997, *Journal of American College Health* 47: 57–68.

Leemon, T.A. (1972) *The Rites of Passage in a Student Culture: A study of the dynamics of transition*, Teachers College Press, New York.

Leipziger Senioren-Convent (1891) *Leipziger Biercomment, nebst einem Anhang: Bierspiele. Offizielle Ausgabe des Leiziger SC*, Literarische Anstalt August Schulze, Leipzig.

Lowe, G. and Foxcroft, D.R. (1993) Young people, drinking and family life, *Alcologia*, 5: 205–209.

Maloff, D., Becker, H.S., Fonaroff, A. and Rodin, J. (1982) Informal social controls and their influence on substance use. In Zinberg, N.E. and Harding, W.M. (eds) *Control Over Intoxicant Use*, Human Sciences Press, New York: 53–76.

Midanik, L.T. (1995) Alcohol consumption and social consequences, dependence, and positive benefits in general population surveys. In Holder, H.D. and Edwards, G. (eds) *Alcohol and Public Policy: Evidence and issues*, Oxford University Press, Oxford: 62–81.

Neighbors, C., Lee, C.M., Lewis, M.A., Fossos, N. and Larimer, M.E. (2007) Are social norms the best predictor of outcomes among heavy-drinking college students? *Journal of Studies on Alcohol and Drugs*, 68: 556–565.

Nezlek, J.B., Pilkington, C.J. and Bilbro, K.G. (1994) Moderation in excess: binge drinking and social interaction among college students, *Journal of Studies on Alcohol*, 55: 342–351.

Nuwer H. (1999) *Wrongs of Passage: Fraternities, Sororities, Hazing, and Binge Drinking*, Indiana University Press, Bloomington, cited in O'Hare, T. (1995) differences in Asian and white drinking: consumption level, drinking contexts, and expectancies, *Addictive Behaviors*, 20: 261–266.

O'Hare, T. (1995) Differences in Asian and White drinking consumption level, drinking contexts, and expectancies, *Addictive Behaviors*, 20: 261–266.

Orcutt, J.D. (1991) Beyond the 'exotic and the pathologic': alcohol problems, norm qualities, and sociological theories of deviance. In Roman, P.M. (ed.) *Alcohol: The development of sociological perspectives on use and abuse*, Rutgers Center of Alcohol Studies, New Brunswick: 145–173.

Pape, H. and Hammer, T. (1996) Sober adolescence – predictor of psychological maladjustment in young adulthood? *Scandinavian Journal of Psychology*, 37: 362–377.

Peele, S. (1999) Promoting positive drinking: alcohol, necessary evil or positive good? In Peele, S. and Grant, M. (eds) *Alcohol and pleasure: A health perspective*, Brunner/Mazel, Philadelphia: 375–389.

Peele, S. and Brodsky, A. (1996). *Alcohol and Society: How culture influences the way people drink*, Pamphlet prepared for The Wine Institute, San Francisco: CA, July, 1996.

Peele, S. and Grant, M. (1999) (eds) *Alcohol and Pleasure: a health perspective*, Taylor and Francis, Philadelphia.

Peters, B.L. and Stringham, E. (2006) No booze? You may lose: why drinkers earn more money than nondrinkers, *Journal of Labor Research*, 27: 411–421.

Pittman, D.J. (1996) What do we know about beneficial consequences of moderate alcohol consumption on social and physical well-being? A critical review of the recent literature, *Contemporary Drug Problems*, 23: 389–406.

Poikolainen, K. (1994) The other health benefits of moderate alcohol intake, *Contemporary Drug Problems* 21: 91–99.

Presley, C.A., Meilman, P.W., and Lyerla, R. (1993) *Alcohol and Drugs on American College Campuses: Use, consequences, and perceptions of the campus environment*, Southern Illinois University, Core Institute, Carbondale, Illinois.

Reeves Sanday, P. (1990) *Fraternity Gang Rape: Sex, brotherhood, and privilege on campus*, New York Universities Press, New York.

Reeves Sanday, P. (1996) Rape prone versus rape free campus cultures, *Violence Against Women*, 2: 191–208.

Ryan, B.E., Colthurst, T. and Segars, L. (1994) *College Alcohol Risk Assessment Guide*, University of California at San Diego, Alcohol, Tobacco, and Other Drug Studies, San Diego.

Single, E. and Storm, T. (1985) *Public Drinking and Public Policy*, Addiction Research Foundation, Toronto.

Turrisi, R., Mallett, K.A., Mastroleo, N.R. and Larimer, M.E. (2006) Heavy drinking in college students: who is at risk and what is being done about it? *Journal of General Psychology*, 133: 401–420.

Vaillant, G.E. (1983) *The Natural History of Alcoholism*, Harvard University Press, Cambridge, MA.

Völger, G. and Welck, K. (eds) (1990) *Männerbünde Männerbande. Zur Rolle des Mannes im Kulturvergleich*, 2 volumes, Rautenstrauch-Joest-Museum, Köln.

Wechsler, H., Davenport, A., Dowdall, G., Moeykens, B. and Castillo, S. (1994) Health and behavioral consequences of binge drinking in college: A national survey of students at 140 campuses. *Journal of the American Medical Association* 272(21): 1672–1677.

Wechsler, H., Dowdall, G.W., Davenport, A. and Castillo, S. (1995) Correlates of student binge drinking, *American Journal of Public Health*, 85: 921–926.

Wechsler, H., Dowdall, G.W., Maenner, G., Gledhill-Hoyt, J., Lee, H. (1998) Changes in binge drinking and related problems among American college students between 1993 and 1997, *Journal of American College Health*, 47: 57–68.

Wechsler, H., Kuh, G. and Davenport, A. (1996) Fraternities, sororities and binge drinking: results from a national study of American colleges, *National Association of Student Personnel Administrators*, 33: 260–279.

Wechsler, H., Lee, J.E., Kuo, M., Seibring, M., Nelson, T.F. and Lee, H. (2002) Trends in college binge drinking during a period of increased prevention efforts: findings from 4 Harvard School of Public Health College Alcohol Study Surveys: 1993–2001, *Journal of American College Health*, 50: 203–217.

Weitzman, E.R, Nelson, T.F. and Wechsler H. (2003) Taking up binge drinking in college: the influences of person, social group, and environment, *Journal of Adolescent Health*, 32: 26–35.

CHAPTER 12
RUGBY, RACING AND BEER IN NEW ZEALAND: COLONISING A CONSUMER CULTURE

Nancy J. Pollock

Introduction

Both bread and beer are major cultural icons in the New Zealand lifestyle. They represent manifestations of consumer colonisation of New Zealand and the Pacific. Introduced less than 200 years ago by settlers from Britain, they have very rapidly developed a strong hold over the social scene as well as over the language of consumerism. A crate of beer, or a 'six-pack', is the necessary accompaniment when watching a rugby match or horse racing on television with one's mates. The crate shared with a 'mate' helps to lubricate and intoxicate – and hopefully celebrate! A mate is an especially good friend, a person with whom one shares drinking and other leisure activities. Work mates are usually differentiated from 'weekend mates'. The term *'mates'* used to be used only for males, but now applies to both men and women, usually to same-gender friendships. The term 'guys', or 'blokes', has recently replaced 'mates' in some circles. In Australia, a mate is often termed a *'cobber'*. Sharing a crate of beer is the hallmark of these friendships.

Beer is the staff of life, essential to refresh, whether that is the soul, the beer belly, or the bond with the 'boys'. It is the hallmark of the Kiwi at leisure.[1] We can thus draw the contrast between beer and bread, also the staff of life, essential to feed the working man or woman. But whereas bread is the staff of life for both men and women, boys and girls, beer has been essential to key male forms of recreation: rugby and racing.

A good Kiwi bloke spends his weekends with his mates watching rugby and racing on television with a crate of beer beside them. The beer is the essential element, as without that the game or the race cannot be properly enjoyed. For those physically attending the game, it used to be accepted for each man to take a six pack, or a half gallon jug (explained below) to stoke their enthusiasm. But that has been outlawed recently in the cause of safety and sobriety.

I will outline the background to this development of a beer culture in New Zealand, in order to provide an understanding of the key concepts which are part of everyday Kiwi English (Holmes 1998; see also Hutchins 2009). It will become clear just how gendered beer-drinking culture has become. The place of beer in Kiwi culture is a matter of 'taste' both literally and figuratively (Bourdieu 1984).

I will argue that this unique Kiwi culture associated with beer has developed purposefully. The culture of beer, along with rugby and racing, did not just happen, but has been almost a conscious process in the construction of a new identity in a land far distant from the homeland of the immigrants, the colonisers. Even though the main components, barley and other grains and the hops, had to be transferred from Europe and cultivated, i.e., introduced to a new environment, they succeeded because they were deemed so essential.

My appreciation of the idiosyncrasies of beer drinking has developed as an immigrant '*Pom*'. I arrived from the United States in 1970, to be thrown into a culture that was supposedly genteel British, but in fact was marked by the 'six o'clock swill',[2] and the Friday night 'bashes' at which a group of mates each 'shouted' their round,[3] whether they needed it or not. Women were not welcome, and felt very out of place in a public bar. 'Nice' women did not drink beer in public.

Colonisation by Beer

Bread and beer were introduced by the colonial masters at the beginning of the nineteenth century as essentials to maintain a civilised lifestyle in what was considered a barbaric land – not as bad as places in the Pacific where cannibals were the big threat, but still hardly civilised. New Zealand was reported to be inhabited by Maori running about half naked, wearing frightening tattoos on their faces, and greeting newcomers by poking out their tongues and pressing noses. Beer was available only to the newly arrived as they considered Maori people would not be able to hold their liquor. Today Maori communities are among the largest consumers of beer.

The New Zealand beer culture has thus been developed in another hemisphere using the basic technology imported from 'home',[4] but adapting the product and its usages to new cultural settings. Visitors from Europe can thus recognize enough of the elements of Kiwi beer culture, while also finding it is 'not the same as home'.

Hops were introduced to New Zealand in 1821. Reverend Samuel Marsden, a recently arrived church minister, lists the plants grown at the Kerikeri Mission, which included "one bed devoted to hops, and one to wheat, oats and barley" (Leach 1984:13). Ale and porter were the named brews of the times. We learn that in 1840 a bottle cost two shillings (Burton 1982:17), a not inconsiderable sum. Presumably it was sold to those not lucky enough to grow their own ingredients. Beer was drunk both in the home and at public dinners where it joined wine and champagne as the beverages used to toast the occasion. By 1870 consumption had reached fifteen litres per head per annum. Beer had replaced rum, which had been the main alcoholic beverage available in Sydney, Australia (Simpson 1999: 155).

Prohibition in the second half of the nineteenth century, however, brought about a small decline in alcohol consumption but a marked rise in the consumption of beer. Simpson (1999: 155) attributes this to the surge of migrants who 'freed at last from the constraints of poverty in their new land seized the opportunity to drink deeper than they ever had an opportunity to do before'. They had come from pastoral England and the continent, where water quality was unsuitable for drinking.

In 1873 the first Licensing Act in New Zealand came into effect following English examples. It limited hours of consumption and the number of outlets that could be licensed. Ironically beer consumption increased steadily so that it doubled between 1938 and 1968. From 1970 to 1987 it increased a further 20 per cent (NZ Statistical Yearbook 1999). In the last ten years beer consumption has failed to increase despite a proliferation of boutique breweries. Wine has become the more favoured 'tipple' (meaning beverage).

Restrictions on licensing hours introduced in the 1870s required public drinking houses to close at 6 P.M. and that restriction lasted for over one hundred years. In the 1970s there was great debate in Parliament as to the wisdom of extending the opening hours to 10. It was expected that beer consumption would increase, and thus drunkenness also. But the 'six o'clock closing'[5] had meant that at 5 P.M. men rushed from their place of work in Wellington or Auckland to the pub in order to cram in as many pints as they could before the pubs shut at 6 P.M. – hence the term ' six o'clock swill'. In 1988 a further closing hours bill was passed that allowed certain public houses to stay open until 12 P.M., but they had to apply for a special licence and meet certain conditions.

With six o'clock closing went 'the half gallon jug' – a glass jar with a screw top lid that held a half gallon of beer. Most men leaving the pub at 6 P.M. for home or a mate's place would be seen with one or two jars under their arms. These 'half g's', as they were known, could be refilled at off-licence premises, and were thus a cheaper way of drinking beer. The Half Gallon Jar was immortalised in a book of short word pictures of New Zealand life in the 1950s, which was given just that title (Hori 1963).

Two breweries have dominated the beer drinking scene in New Zealand, D.B. (or Dominion Breweries) and Lion – both legacies of the colonial era, as their labels convey. Today they provide the umbrella companies for many smaller breweries as the marketing arm under a corporate label. Monteiths is one of many small breweries. It is based in Westport on the west coast of the South Island – serving a sparse but very thirsty population that used to be dominated by coal miners and stevedores. 'Coasters'[6] are known for their dedicated drinking habits. They have supported their local brewery faithfully.

Those patrons were outraged when D.B. announced in March 2001 that they were moving the brewery to Auckland in the name of economic efficiency. Coasters were furious, pointing out that the Monteiths label clearly claims that the beer is brewed on the west coast, and thus D.B. would be guilty of mislabelling and subject to challenges under the Fair Trading Act.

A similar argument has arisen over Speights beer, another small brewery. Their bottles bear the label *"Brewed in Dunedin since 1876"*, so their advocates claim that moving the brewery north to Christchurch will not only be another case of mislabelling, but also misleading to the many Speights consumers. Lawyers for Lion, the parent company, suggest that the label can be read in two ways, so that when moving the brewery to Christchurch they are still acknowledging on the label the long time connection with Dunedin. South Island people, largely of Scottish origin in the initial settlement, are known to be fervent addicts to their style of life, which includes their local tipple.

Small breweries are thus associated with different regions of New Zealand. Each has its loyal customers who support their particular brand whether at home, or when travelling beyond the home territory. Speciality beer has thus become a major symbol of regional identity.

The amount of beer consumed in New Zealand has fallen from 400 million litres in 1990 to 300 million litres in 2000. It is the mid-level alcohol beers (2.5–4.35 per cent alcohol content) which are being consumed less, while consumption of high-alcohol beers increased between December 1999 and December 2000 (Alcohol Advisory Council 2001). New Zealand consumption ranked thirteenth in the world in 1999, with the Czech Republic at number 1 and Germany at number 3. New Zealand showed the greatest rate of decline in beer consumption between 1970 and 1999, dropping by 30 per cent over that period. On average the top 5 per cent of male drinkers consumed 63 cans of beer a week in 1995 (Alcohol Advisory Council 2001). Men drink more at pubs, nightclubs, and other people's homes and at sports or racing events. But still 41 per cent of all alcohol is drunk in the home, especially by those in the older age groups.

Most pubs stock six to eight different brands of beer, including a couple of American and Dutch beers. Beer exports have largely relied on the Steinlager label, which has been the 'flagship' beer for New Zealand, and can be found in Asia and Europe.

The boutique beers have increased markedly in the last fifteen years. Specialist brewers have emulated their counterparts in the wine industry to produce a unique brew. These have extended from variations on the regular hop to include light and Ice beers. Recently brewers are trying out new citrus-flavoured beer. Tui, a large brand name, is being marketed for its "malty chocolate aroma with a hint of caramel' whereas Ice lager beer is 'relatively sweet and floral with a short finish'. These labels entice drinkers of both genders, as well as the old and the young, to sample a new twist on their favourite beverage. The consumer is being titillated.

Competition between breweries is formalised in the annual New Zealand Hop Marketing Board Beer awards. A panel of judges tastes upwards of 200 beers over three days looking for winners in nine classes that cover 45 categories. The prizes are keenly sought after as they help to boost sales. In 2001 the Supreme champion was Monk's Millenium, brewed by Cock and Bull, Auckland, with Big John's Special Reserve brewed by Harringtons, Christchurch as Reserve (Burton 2001). The parallel with wine awards is obvious. And it is clear that the small breweries are raising the standard of beers available. These awards are very influential in the consumer world at home and internationally. Beer is joining this marketing ploy. Drinking establishments in New Zealand do not have the aura of the British pub. Just why that was not recreated in the new land by the immigrants is unclear. Instead we have 'booze barns', which are architecturally uninteresting buildings both from the outside as well as the inside. The large open interior space is broken up with small but high circular tables, around which the drinkers cluster either standing, or perched on a stool. Formerly in the centre of the table was a container of water in which smokers doused their cigarettes. The whole ambience was designed for the 'fast and furious' reign of drinkers, the "swill" mentality until the 1970s. Comfort came from the satisfaction in the beer, not in the homely furnishings. The carpeted floor became very odoriferous, so the passer-by could get a strong whiff of the pub's activities in the morning when the windows were open for cleaning.

The public bar was strictly men only. If women wanted to drink in a pub, they had to settle in the Lounge bar, where lower tables and softer chairs were provided. But that separated the men from the girls. Even in 1970 the attitude still existed that female patrons only went to pubs if they were '*asking for trouble*'. Gradually over the last thirty years, women and men have been able to drink together in pubs, and groups of women will gather in a pub on a Friday night, though perhaps at different tables from those where men are drinking. Long wooden tables have replaced the small round perches. And many pubs have introduced a pool table as well as television, so the 'punters' (those who bid on horse racing, and now on rugby games) can watch while drinking. In the early 1980s pubs were encouraged to offer pub food, such as a plate dinner of fish and chips, or ham and chips, in order to moderate the level of drunkenness.

The Language of Beer

Because beer drinking has been such an integral part of Kiwi consumer culture, it has developed a language of its own. Several phrases and words have been referred to above. Those words have their parallels in 'Strine', otherwise known as Australian English, but the same word may take on a slightly different meaning when used 'across the Ditch' (i.e., on the other side of the Tasman sea, in Australia).

Rugby, racing and beer still stand together as a cluster of elements that mark a Kiwi 'religion'. The culture has been changing over the last twenty years, but

many of the phrases remain, and new ones have slipped into everyday par-
lance, particularly as a result of demasculinising the associations of beer.

Friday nights continue to be the busiest pub nights. The TGIF ('Thank God
it's Friday') syndrome is often cited, with a long weekend ahead to sober up, or
drink more, depending on choice. In most family households it is expected that
the men, as well as the younger working women, will be "late home" on a Friday
night, meaning they are going to stop in at the pub with a group of mates.

Beer is still the most common drink at parties, though wine is overtaking it in
some circles. Most parties provide both today. In the 1970s the common invitation to a party was issued as "Ladies a plate, guys a crate". That meant that the
women should bring a plate with some baking on it, to be shared with everyone,
while the men were expected to bring a crate (of pint bottles) of beer to be
shared. This indicated a very marked division of labour based on the expectation
that the lady would be at home baking, i.e., not working, while the man would
pass by the pub to pick up a crate of beer on his way home from work.

Instead of a crate a man could turn up at a party with a couple of half gallon
jars of beer. This was cheaper, and in one sense marked working-class people,
or those on low incomes from those who could afford the commercially bottled
Lion Brown, or D.B., that was more expensive. The 'half g's', as they were
known, contained a rather amorphous brew, and one that lacked any of the
distinguishing characteristics that were coming in as breweries diversified their
product. They were drunk at room temperature.

Home brew has made a major impact on the breweries. Serious beer drinkers buy their plastic tank and the associated equipment, and take pride in
watching the brew manufacture itself in the kitchen or laundry. The consumption of home brew has proliferated to such an extent that shops devoted solely
to these consumers' needs are to be found in all major shopping centres. Home
brew is thus one of the spin-off recreational activities that beer has generated
over time.

The six o'clock swill, referred to above, the habit of drinking at pubs that
closed at 6 P.M., is remembered fondly by older Kiwis. It ended in 1970 when
licensing laws changed to allow pubs to stay open until 10 P.M. It had its negative features, but there was a sense of camaraderie and 'blokism' that drew
those who were desperate for their measure of beer into the safety of the pub.
For those men who had been warned about the 'dangers' of beer by their
womenfolk of the 1920s and 1930s and the temperance days, the six o'clock
swill provided a quick but delicious transition between work and home. It was
a strictly male time; so, few women participated. Even in the 1960s, very few
women were working in New Zealand; so pub culture changed as more women
joined the public service and other branches of the workforce in the 1970s and
1980s. The six o'clock swill is nevertheless looked back on today as part of the
glories of bygone days.

New Zealand has exported this 'pub culture' to its Polynesian neighbours,
but each has developed its own label, e.g., Tongan Royal Beer and Fiji Bitter.
Aid money has been used to build breweries in each of the major centres, both

to provide jobs and to reduce imports of beverages. The drinking culture is less geared to the working day, but has its own local rules and protocols. This marked a major change from the 1960s when, under colonial rule, all forms of alcohol were forbidden to Pacific Island people. The link between rugby and beer in Samoa, Tonga and Fiji is growing, as teams such as Manu Samoa become icons for the marketing of Samoan beer.

Conclusions

Beer drinking is a major consumer activity that has stamped itself on Kiwi culture. It has adjusted from colonial beginnings in Britain to take on clear identifying features on the other side of the world. These include the 'watering holes' that are favoured by the devotees, as well as the language associated with beer drinking.

In earlier times beer was every man's drink. Slowly that has changed as wine making has proliferated so successfully. The cask of wine (3 litres) echoed the image of the half gallon jug of beer. The working class differentiators of the past have been eroded. The price of each is about equivalent, as is their social status. Drink-driving prohibitions have become a major feature today that distinguishes a non-drinker, i.e., the driver, from the drinkers.

We can argue that while beer used to be strictly a male recreational leisured activity, bread making was the female counterpart. Bread making was necessary, and therefore should be classed as 'work', but was not recognised as such. But the gender division that such gastronomic icons represent is a mark of Kiwi society only up to about the 1980s. Strong feminist movements, and concerns for gender balance in all quarters of Kiwi life, brought major changes. In retrospect we can see just how the genders were divided in their work and in their leisure. The pub has changed, just as bread-making has changed, in the last twenty years.

Rugby, racing and beer continue to dominate Kiwi society. They have become markers of Kiwi pride and identity. The competition between beers has become as keen as the competition between wines, and bread makers, and rugby teams. The concept of awards for best breads, jams and other produce that marked the Agricultural and Pastoral shows throughout the country has moved up a technological level, but persists in its new form. Some firms, including faculties of the university, run competitions for the best "home brew" by their staff. It is very democratic, as everyone gets to taste the products.

A large percentage of discretionary spending of the Kiwi dollar goes on rugby, racing and beer. Beer is the essential in that trio. It is the component that is perhaps more visible in the aphorisms quoted above, in the many pubs in both urban and rural settlements, and also in the beer bellies that mark the serious devotee. Beer accounts for a large proportion when accounting for Kiwi tastes.

Notes

1. Kiwi refers to the name commonly applied to those resident in New Zealand, either by choice or by designation.
2. Six o'clock swill refers to the practice of consuming beer at pubs. Since bars closed at 6 P.M. each night, patrons tried to drink as much beer as possible before that time, often within an hour after leaving work.
3. A 'shout', as a noun or verb applies to a round of drinks provided and paid for by a member of the group.
4. Home means Britain here, and frequently does mean Britain.
5. 'Six o'clock closing' refers to the government regulation that all pubs must close by 6 P.M.
6. 'Coasters' – people living on the coast.

References

Alcohol Advisory Council (ALAC) (2001) *Alcohol Effects*, Fact Pack, *www.alac.org.nz* (accessed 19 July 2001).
Bourdieu, P. (1984) *Distinction: A Social Critique of the Judgement of Taste,* Harvard University Press, Cambridge.
Burton, D. (1982) *Two Hundred Years of New Zealand Food and Cookery*, Reed & Co. Ltd., Auckland.
Burton, David (2001) Beers, cheers, *Wellington Evening Post*, 7 April 2001: C 3.
Holmes, Janet (1998) A Kiwi cocktail: current changes in New Zealand English. In Lindquist, H., Klintborg, S., Levin, M. and Estling, M. (eds) *The Major Varieties of English*, Vaxjo University, Vaxjo: 37–48.
Hutchins, Graham (2009) *Your Shout: A toast to drink and drinking in New Zealand*, Hodder Moa, Auckland.
Hori (1963) *The Half Gallon Jar*, A.D. Organ Ltd, Auckland [reprinted from *N.Z. Home Life and Home Companion*].
Leach, H. (1984) *1000 Years of Gardening in New Zealand*, Reed & Co. Ltd., Auckland.
New Zealand Statistical Yearbook (1999), Dept. of Statistics, Wellington.
Simpson, T. (1999) *A Distant Feast: The origins of New Zealand's cuisine*, Random House, Auckland.

CHAPTER 13
BEER, RITUAL AND CONVIVIALITY IN NORTHERN CAMEROON

Igor de Garine

Introduction

Beer drinking is widespread in Africa – and Northern Cameroon appears to be a good area in which to study it, as it is home to six ethnic groups: the Masa, Muzey, Tupuri and Kera, located in the lowland, flooded area of the Logone River; and the Koma and the Duupa, who dwell in the Alantika mountains in North-West Cameroon on the Nigerian border (see figures 13.1, 13.2 and 13.3.)

Figure 13.1 Sorghum beer drinking among the Muzey

Figure 13.2   Sorghum beer drinking among the Masa

Beer can be studied from many perspectives: nutritional, religious, social and economic. I shall say something on each aspect and then develop those aspects which are relevant to its social use, for which I shall focus on the Koma.

Brewing

The raw material is sorghum (*Sorghum*) and pearl millet (*Pennisetum*); each society favours its own specific varieties but mostly *Sorghum caudatum* is used.

There are two main kinds of beer: a gruel-like fermented liquid (*balsa*) and a light, carefully filtered liquid (*bilbil*, a general term used in Northern Cameroon). The Masa and Muzey use a very light gruel (in Masa *suma*, in Muzey *doleyna*), the Duupa only know the thick fermented pap (*bumma*), the Tupuri and the Kera use the light kind (in Tupuri *yi*, in Kera *kumi*). The Koma use both the light beer (*vum*) and the thick one (*balsa*).

Brewing techniques are similar among the different groups. For one litre of the light beer brewed by the Muzey, 0.3 kg of grain is needed, whereas 0.4 kg is used by the Duupa for the thick one.

Brewing is a rather complicated process demanding care in order to avoid failure. The appropriate timing for each step in the process has to be respected (see tables 13.1. and 13.2.).

Table 13.1   Timetable for the preparation of *balsa* (thick beer) among the Koma

Either red sorghum or pearl millet is used.	
The grain is converted into flour. The flour is left in water for two days	2 days
On the third day it is put into a large jar and cooked to become a gruel	1 day
Germinated grain is ground into flour which is mixed with the gruel	1 day
The mixture is left to ferment for one day	1 day
The following day it is filtered and heated. After cooking it is ready to drink	1 day
Total	**6 days**

Figure 13.3   Filtering the thick sorghum beer among the Koma

Table 13.2 Timetable for the preparation of *doleyna* (light beer) among the Muzey

The grain used is mostly sorghum.		

Preparation of the grain:	Pounding to separate the grain from the ear	1 day
Malting:	Soaking	2 days
	Germination of the grain under a basket-work mat or *Calotropis procera* leaves	3 days
	Drying in the sun in thin layers	2 days
Brewing:	Pounding the dry, germinated grain into flour, sieving the flour. The flour is diluted and left to rest in a large earthenware jar for about 6 hours. In the evening, the liquid is decanted into three smaller earthenware vessels where it undergoes its first cooking, (about two hours). The top of the liquid is set aside. The product is poured back into the larger jar and left to cool. The top is mixed with the rest. The earthenware jar is tapped during one night	1 day
	Next morning the beer is tasted. It should be sweet. It is filtered, and the residue is given to the children to eat. The beer is put back into three smaller jars and cooked a second time for 3 hours	1 day
	It is put back into the large jar and left to cool	1 day
	Yeast is added to it, the vessel is tapped and the beer left to ferment	1 night
	The scum is removed, the beer is poured back into the smaller pots and it is ready to drink.	1 day
	Total	**12 days**

Beer is a liquid in which something mysterious – fermentation – has happened. Even in a work on modern beer during the twentieth century, Scriban (1975) mentions that, although beer is made exclusively from natural products (in many countries barley, water, hops, yeast), to the layman's eye its manufacturing characteristically retains a rather mysterious aura.

Nutritional Aspects

Millet and sorghum beer has, like the classic barley beers, some nutritional value. Périssé *et al.* (1959) discuss a traditional beer in Togo which is similar to the lightest ones of Northern Cameroon and they mention nutritional advantages in terms of B-group vitamins but a loss in terms of calories, proteins and calcium. Among the Masa, 100 g of sorghum porridge represent 140 calories, while the same amount of beer contains only 60 calories. The *affouk* beer of Northern Cameroon described by Chevassus-Agnes *et al.* (1976) is similar to the thicker type of beer of the Koma. 100 g of the liquid represents 67 calories and the residue, after filtering, 74 calories. Most of the time the residue is consumed as well (as may have happened in Mesopotamia, which might shed light on the term 'liquid bread').

The Quantities Absorbed Vary According to the Groups

Among the Masa and Muzey, beer is mostly consumed during important religious ceremonies. The same occurs among the Kera and Tupuri but they also enjoy informal beer drinking on market days. Among the Tupuri, Guillard (1965: 487) mentions an average daily consumption of 74 g. The Duupa and the Koma consume all manner of types of beer for all kinds of occasions, both ritual and profane.

Whereas during the dry season (April), the Duupa consume 820 g of thick beer daily, representing 550 kcal. out of the 1431 kcal. of the total intake, in August the consumption is 370 g of beer, representing 248 kcal. of the 1483 kcal. daily intake (see 13. 3).

Table 13.3   Daily nutritional value of the meals and minimal consumption of '*bumma*' beer among the Duupa

	April			August		
	meals	820 g bumma	total	meals	370 g bumma	total
Energy (Kcal)	881.0	550.0	1,431.0	1,235.0	248.0	1,483.0
Protein (g)	20.1	9.8	37.9	42.3	4.4	46.7
Lipids (g)	27.0	2.5	29.5	34.1	1.1	35.2
Glucids (g)	138.4	65.6	204.0	201.4	29.6	230.0
Ca (mg)	288.0	246.0	534.0	387.0	111.0	498.0
Thiamine (mg)	>0.7	0.6	>1.3	1.2	0.3	1.5
Riboflavine (mg)	>0.27	0.3	>0.61	0.7	0.2	0.8
Niacine (mg)	>9.0	4.1	>13.1	15.1	19.0	17.0
Vit. C (mg)	>7.0		>7.0	131.0		131.0

(source: Stappersand Matze. 1991:11)

Among the Duupa, the staple dish (sorghum porridge) may be lacking 30 per cent of the time, but beer is consumed almost daily (Stappers and Matze 1991: 11). Among the Koma, both types of beer are present. They consume a daily average of 615 g, half of the total weight of the daily intake ration. In the lowland village we studied, it reached an average of 823 g per day (Koppert 1991: 48) (see Table 13.4).

In both groups, one third of their energy is obtained from beer.

The populations of Northern Cameroon are aware of the nutritional value of beer and they all use it during field working parties as a fuel to keep the participants in high spirits, also during demanding activities such as weeding. However, one should look beyond the material aspects.

Table 13.4 Per capita consumption in grams and percentage of total weight of the ration in various foods among the Koma.

	Bimlérou village		Bakipa village		All Koma	
Cereals	325	24.1%	394	34.5%	354	28.6%
Tubers	36	2.7%	149	13.0%	89	7.2%
Oil seeds	15	1.1%	27	2.4%	20	1.6%
Pulses	9	0.7%	6	0.5%	7	0.6%
Fruits	17	1.2%	37	3.2%	26	2.1%
Vegetables	56	4.1%	27	2.4%	41	3.3%
Leaves	58	4.3%	73	6.3%	64	5.2%
Meat, fish	6	0.5%	19	1.6%	15	1.2%
Eggs, milk	1	0.1%	0	0.0%	0	0.0%
Drinks (sorghum beer)	**823**	**61.0%**	**409**	**35.8%**	**615**	**49.8%**
Salt	3	0.2%	3	0.2%	3	0.2%
Grass ashes salt	1	0.1%	1	0.1%	1	0.1%
Total	1349	100%	1144	100%	1261	100%
Total per capita	1733 kcal		2045 kcal		1900 kcal	

(source: Koppert 1991:48)

The Mystery

Beer is not an inert matter, it is alive. Anthropomorphic aspects are constantly referred to by North Cameroonian groups. It has a 'head', the top part, which is strong and masculine. So, the first drinker should be a mature individual of sufficient magical strength. The bottom, which is also strong, is female.

The processes at work in brewing are not totally under control. They depend on the technical ability of the brewer but also, according to local belief, on the protection of supernatural beings, who should not be offended while the beer is being prepared. Brewing is a time of expectation when no boisterous actions or noisy conflicts should occur. Among the Koma, sexual intercourse is forbidden after the first cooking. Among the Muzey, members of possession colleges, impersonating the deities, come to sleep in the shed where fermentation occurs to make sure that everything goes well. This is not inconvenient as they themselves are involved in the production process.

Fermentation is the focus. It implies germination and is linked to life and the success of crops which allow human beings to subsist. In many traditional societies, complex physical or chemical processes, such as firing earthenware or smelting, should develop in an atmosphere of social harmony. This is also the case for brewing. Therefore menstruating women, who also undergo a mysterious process, should not interfere or take part in the brewing, or even be present.

Mythology

The main aspect to be emphasised is the spontaneity of fermentation. This explains technically how 'beer' may have first developed from a portion of cereal porridge, accidentally left to ferment, to the current conscious use of yeast, allowing brewing to be planned in terms of time. The groups from Northern Cameroon know about spontaneously fermenting paps [*cufuta* among the Muzey, which is a woman's drink made of sorghum (de Garine, I. 2001: 54)]. Ritually the Kera make a kind of beer without yeast for the sacrifices they hold in honour of twins.

Many of the groups (Kera, Tupuri and Koma) make a distinction between a primitive period when yeast was not used and the present day period of intentional brewing.

Many myths refer to the origin of yeast. According to a Tupuri myth, a woman forgot sorghum pap and, a few days later, some foam appeared on top of it. She collected and dried it, and used it to inseminate other beverages. That woman was a Peve, a group to which the Mundang and Kera also refer. Mythically, yeast was brought by a member of the Peve group, often a person lost in the bush. He acted as a demiurge. For instance, he surreptitiously introduced yeast into the festive beverage of the Tupuri of the Doré clan, bringing them death since they buried the drunk, believing them to be dead (de Garine I. 2001: 59). But, by making sorghum porridge leftovers grow sour, he also caused emancipation from the natural forces at work. If we wish to paraphrase Levi Strauss, yeast represents the success of culture over the natural forces of decay. One may be tempted to refer to the ancient mythology of Mesopotamia in which the primitive humans lived in the wild on crude, raw foods while the gods and socialised man rejoiced in cooked foods and fermented drinks, mostly beer (Glassner 1991: 128).

Time

Being able to obtain beer at will, independently of time, season and place, is a conspicuous feature of this beverage. Wine is dependent on specific harvests, grapes or juicy berries. Beer can be obtained from many carbohydrates: cereals, tubers or starchy fruits like bananas. Brewing determines a specific time span which can, however, occur at any period of the year, according to cultural needs.

Among the Northern Cameroonian populations we are dealing with, the brewing process takes from five to twelve days (Tables 13.1 and 13.2). *Balsa*, thick beer, can be obtained more rapidly than *bilbil*. The Koma, who are inveterate beer drinkers, shorten the preparation time by storing ready-to-use germinated grain in their granaries. Among the Masa and Muzey, the brewing period is fairly constant, around twelve days.

Religion

Among the Masa and the Muzey, beer is consumed mostly during the main religious rituals and, secondarily for profane pleasure. Small family rituals, such as births, do not usually involve consuming beer.

Traditional beer is the beverage of the occult powers and the ancestors. Its consumption usually takes place after the slaughtering of the animals offered to the supernatural beings, and before the communal meal, prepared from the meat of the sacrificial animals and loaves of sorghum or thick millet porridge *(boule)*. There is a special day to denominate this offering *(caraw suma*, which means to pour the beer). Among the Tupuri, Kera, Duupa and especially the Koma, beer drinking may also mark the terminal phase of major rituals. Beer is poured on the various altars, inside the house of the main wife (Tupuri), at the entrance of the compound, on the garbage heap of the Earth Priest, near a shrouded corpse, etc.

Among the Gisey Masa, for the ancestors' festival *(krofta)* the prayer is the following: 'Gisey (Mother Earth), I pour your beer on the ground so that disease doesn't come. Leave our place alone, drink your beer'. Among the Muzey, for the new harvest, after pounding the arrowroot tuber (*Tacca involucrata*), before the main dance, the Earth Priest pours the beer on to the ground in front of the sacred enclosure and enumerates the guardian spirits: 'Come and partake of your beer and also you, the small spirits who come with the Pé clan, drink your beer galore'. Then, at the entrance of his compound: 'My ancestors, drink your beer, last year has been a bad one. Genies, give us a cool earth'.

Social Aspects

The Tupuri and Kera use beer in the same way as the Masa and Muzey but the hedonistic aspect is more developed. The Duupa and especially the Koma drink it at every gathering, almost daily. It is, to quote the appropriate expression of Netting (1964) about the neighbouring Kofyar, 'a focus of value'. Needless to say, such prodigal use of sorghum and millet beer implies a specific cereal-production policy, in which cereals are grown to make beer in order to fuel working parties to till the fields which will, in turn, produce more cereals to fulfil the social ambitions of the owner (Garine, E. 1995, 1996, 2001). During religious and magical occasions beer is not only drunk or poured on the ground, it is a beneficial liquid sprinkled on people and objects for various symbolic reasons. Among the Koma it is used to cleanse the sacred whistles to make them play in tune.

Beer is not only used to please supernatural beings, it helps communication between fellow humans. It is a token of hospitality and friendship, demonstrating affluence, generosity and kindness. Among the Duupa, two friends sitting side by side and holding the same calabash of beer may empty it together in a single gulp, without taking breath.

Among the Koma, going up the various stages of the age grade system implies slaughtering cattle and lavishly offering beer to the elderly and the upper age sets (Garine, E. 1996). At the same time, the religious celebrations are occasions for individuals to display their prestige, gaining consideration and admittance to the upper strata of the age grade society.

The main beer celebrations of one of our Koma informants (Issa) and his elder brother (two compounds), typical over a lifetime, were as follows:

24 March
Light beer for the unearthing of the ancestors' skulls (a periodic thanksgiving ritual): 28 beer jars (each about 8 litres) – 6 to the diggers, 6 to his best friend, the rest to his age set and any others attending.
For the female descendants of the most recently deceased: 15 pots of light beer.
For the male descendants of the skull: 42 pots.
29 March
Drinking at the market place (no record).
4 April
Unearthing of the skull of his own father: 45 pots. His elder brother offered 85 pots. A total of 1720 litres of beer consumed (between 29 March and 4 April)
5 April
Beer was still flowing lavishly until 13th April (no record).
4 and 5 May
Beer for the *Naga napo* (cattle dance), This is the 'good wife festival', thanking her for her work.
Beer from the maternal kin (quantity unrecorded).
For the in-laws living up in the mountains: 25 pots.
For the bull roarer initiates (the age grade society): 47 pots.
For the cow keeper: 1 pot.
For the brothers who distribute the beer: 2 pots.
August and September
Thick beer is consumed every evening for the dance of the masks. It is fuel for those who carry them.

This list does not include minor rituals and informal drinking between villagers and at the surrounding market places.

Pleasure and Business

Beer drinking for pleasure occurs in all groups, mostly on market days, and is a financially profitable venture in all Northern Cameroonian populations (Seignobos 1976). In Tupuri country as well as among the mountain groups, beer may be the main commodity offered at the markets. The Koma are again outstanding in this field.

Dogari (1984: 71), a Nigerian author, insists on the ubiquity of beer in Koma daily life and states that '90% of the population are drunkards. They believe that drunkenness is both socially and culturally good ... good for a person's health.' It cannot be denied that drinking traditional beer brings inebriation and that the strength of the beverage is one of its favoured aspects. In all groups an extensive vocabulary relates to the taste and the quality of beer: sweet, acid, well-fermented, strong, weak, a failure, spoilt.

Socially, unsuccessful brewing is a matter of shame. It demonstrates incompetence but also suggests that there has been a breach of prohibitions during the process. The fact that something went wrong also demonstrates a lack of friendliness from the supernatural beings. In Koma language, the term for spoilt beer is the same as for a miscarriage.

Intoxication

There are many terms to describe the various stages of intoxication: for instance, in Koma: 'being in good shape', 'feeling dizzy', 'beer hits the head', 'being drunk', 'being overcome', 'vomiting', 'feeling weakness in one's joints after drinking'. There are often a number of drunkards and a few inveterate alcoholics crawling from drinking place to drinking place. Being drunk does not appear to be an offence, it is common during social gatherings and dances. Mothers, who carry their newborn babies tightly strapped to their backs in a goatskin, are watched especially closely in order to prevent them from crushing the infant by lying on their backs, falling or simply resting against a wall.

Holding one's drink demonstrates strength and wisdom among mature adults, high in the age grade system. Drinking contests are common, as is bragging about one's capacity to drink. The individuals having reached the antepenultimate rank in the age grade system are entitled not to share their beer pot with others if they do not wish to. They can also defy others to drink from their pot because they fear their magical leverage. Some of these pots are carefully decorated. Their name, 'the disturbing pots', refers to the magical power which may be dormant in each.

Symbolically, beer is considered a 'hot' drink. Those who have had to refrain from using it must be reintroduced to drinking it. Consuming the top of a pot, considered highly alcoholic, is not a harmless act. 'Cutting the head of the beer' should be done by a mature man belonging to the upper age grade.

Merriment

The many social and religious meanings of beer should not convey the idea that it is a solemn beverage. On the contrary, among the Koma its availability creates an excuse for playful behaviour. The following are parts of recordings made during one of the main rituals related to the obtaining of age grade, the *waraga*.

Yengu, the organiser of the ritual, after naming his ancestors and sprinkling the audience with beer: 'Children, sit down, you are about to receive some beer.' (He takes some beer in his mouth and spits on the ground twice. People congratulate themselves.)

A member of the audience: 'The sacrifice is finished, we are going to drink.'

A man: 'Today we are going to drink until we are exhausted.'

Another man: 'If we are to drink like that, where is the necessary beer supply?'

Organiser: 'If you wanted to drink galore, you should have brought me more grain.'

A man: 'This beer is really very good.'

Organiser: 'I am going to drink three calabashes in a row.'

Wife of the organiser: 'You, the men, are greedy and selfish.'

Organiser: 'Good wife, wait until I drink two calabashes. Here is the pot for the women.'

A man: 'It's my turn, begin with me.'

Another man: 'You are weak. Don't take care of him, give me some.'

Another man: 'Give me the bottom of the pot, I will share it with my friend.'

Another man: 'I see that the beer will be sufficient, we already talk very much.'

A woman: 'Don't give too much to the little girls or they'll get drunk.'

A man: 'If they are drunk, they should simply go and sleep.'

A woman: 'Give me more beer, if not it will merely fill my goitre.'

Many people in the audience: 'Give us some more.'

One of the elders: 'Now we're full up. You, the organiser, I thank you.'

The climate is created for relaxed interchanges, jokes and the expression of mock rivalry. Each man maintains a joking relationship with the members of his circumcision group, among whom one is especially dear to his heart. He also has a privileged relationship with one member of his paternal or maternal in-laws, his *zanera*, who often acts as his counsellor in ritual matters and receives the lion's share of the offerings, especially beer.

With his circumcision partners, and especially his best friend, mock fighting and insults are customary. They bring fun to the party. This burlesque bellicosity is not immediately intelligible to the outside ethnographer. Pretending to steal a pot of beer, refusing to give it or to share it, or referring to derisive and intimate deeds of one's partner are constant episodes but, as the social gathering goes on, the tone sometimes changes and loud arguments may take place. They play a cathartic role by allowing small conflicts to be brought forward and solved in a cheerful climate, with little consequence due to loss of face. Making opposing parties confront each other on specific issues, partaking in a drinking party, is a very common outlet used by village chiefs to avoid going to the official law court – always an expensive matter.

Sex

Drinking together also allows people to touch upon sexual matters, to court and, finally, to copulate. During the Koma threshing parties, the participants, who belong to neighbouring villages, are just emerging from a period when illicit sex has been prohibited for fear of symbolically jeopardising the growing crop. Threshing festivals are the starting point for the resumption of sexual life. This is ritually acknowledged by sexual licence during the gatherings, in which beer drinking helps. The participants, who are tipsy with beer but work hard, exchange licentious songs and words. One example will suffice:

A woman begins: 'I am not afraid of men even if their penis is like a tiger fish' (*Hydrocyon* sp).
The men answer: 'I can use a woman if her hole is as open as a door.'
The women: 'We thank those with a penis.'
The men: 'We praise those with a clitoris.'
The men: 'We are insulting you. Please, ladies, forgive us, we are drunk. We came to work but we need beer.'
The women: 'That woman, she says she does not like boys with little penises, she likes them big!'
The men: 'We don't care about what you favour, we just fuck. If you look for big pricks, sometime you will die!'
A man: 'I'm thirsty, our penises are thirsty.'
A man: 'If I put my ring around my penis, I can transfix you up to your throat' ... etc.

A 'Locus of Value'

Much of what Netting (1964: 358) wrote about the Kofyar applies to the Koma. 'Beer is a locus of value and plays the role of a social lubricant.' It increases sociability and relaxation. This aspect was already mentioned in the Mesopotamian tablets. According to the Enôma Elis myth quoted by Glassner (1991: 134): 'the gods participated in their banquet ... they ate bread and drank beer, this mellow and heady beverage ... sniffing this intoxicating beverage, they felt their bodies to be relaxed, without any worries, their soul lighthearted ...'. Jackson (1993), in his *Beer Companion*, writes: 'Beer's greatest use is a sociable relaxant ... a sociable beer must not be too strong'. Beer drinking delineates a time and a spot where behaviour which is different from the day-to-day one is acceptable, allowing for easy interpersonal contacts. This aspect is particularly conspicuous among the Tepehuanes and Tarahumara Indians of the state of Chihuahua in Mexico. Their composure in daily life is quite stern and they fit the stereotype about monosyllabic talk. They need maize beer (*tesguino*) drinking parties and becoming tipsy and drunk, to override rather conspicuously their restrained behaviour.

If we were to draw general conclusions about the social use of beer among the Northern Cameroonian populations, we would say that beer is a rather mild alcoholic beverage (around 3 per cent alcohol by volume), facilitating conviviality and social catharsis and merriment. Social tipsiness, rather than heavy individual intoxication creating stupour, is being sought. Some technical aspects should be mentioned. Brewing takes time, as does getting drunk on a beverage with a low alcoholic content. It leaves space to talk, joke, communicate, and convivially to empty one's bladder. Traditional beer brewing and consumption can delineate at any time of the year a privileged period which generates a convivial climate, favouring socialisation. In this respect, it is distinct from spirit drinking, which is a more individual and aggressive avenue to solving personal stress through rapid intoxication. Should we therefore conclude that, in Northern Cameroon, traditional beer drinking has mostly a positive function? No, because it also provides the raw material for the distillation of the local spirit *(arki)*, with all its physical and mental drawbacks.

Today manufactured beer is increasingly available and abundantly advertised. It is used at will to provide drunkenness and can result in addiction. It retains, however, a number of the features of traditional drinking, displaying generosity and prestige, allowing for animated talks, being used as a token medium to engage in courtship as well as to placate a thirsty policeman.

There is no doubt that the pace of the acculturation process, the increased psychological stress it generates, and contacts with urbanised individuals from Southern Cameroon will tend to favour drinks which provide more rapid intoxication, oblivion of one's low status, and stupour, the syndrome of 'the anxiety drinker' (Ferguson 1968: 160), familiar to alcohol specialists (Haworth 1995; Heath 1995; Marshall 1979). This is the case for the plains populations, Masa, Tupuri and Kera, who are more involved in the cash economy of Cameroon. The day will soon come when the mountain groups of Northern Cameroon will adopt home-distillation of cereals, and indulge in *arki* drinking. This will rapidly bring disruption to their culture and have health consequences, as is already the case for many other Cameroonian populations.

References

Chevassus-Agnes, S., Favier, J.C. and Joseph, A. (1979) *Technologie traditionnelle et valeur nutritive des bières de sorgho du Cameroun*, Cahiers de IONAREST 2(3): 83–112.

Dogari, A. (1984) *The Cultural History of the Koma*, Artz books, Aarhus, Denmark.

Ferguson, F.N. (1968) Navaho drinking: some tentative hypotheses, *Human Organization* 27(2): 159–167.

Garine, E. (1995) *Le Mil et la Bière: le système agraire des Duupa du Massif de Poli (Nord Cameroun)*, Ph.D. Thesis, University of Paris.

Garine, E. (1996) Organisation saisonnière du système de subsistence du Duupa Massif de Poli (Nord Cameroun). In Froment, A., de Garine, I., Binam Bikoi, C. and Loung, J.F. (eds.) *Bien Manger et Bien Vivre. Anthropologie alimentaire et développement en Afrique intertropicale: du biologique au social,* L'Harmattan/ORSTOM, Paris: 211–222.

Garine, E. (2001) An ethnographic account of the many roles of millet beer in the culture of the Duupa agriculturalists (Poli mountains) Northern Cameroon. In de Garine, I. and de Garine, V. (eds) *Drinking: Anthropological approaches,* Berghahn Books, Oxford 191–204.

Garine, I. de (1995) Food and the status quest in five African cultures. In Wiessner, P. and Schiefenhövel, W. (eds) *Food and the Status Quest,* Berghahn Books, Oxford: 193–218.

Garine, I. de (2001) Drinking in Northern Cameroon among the Masa and Muzey. In de Garine, I. and de Garine, V. (eds) *Drinking: Anthropological approaches,* Berghahn Books, Oxford: 51–65.

Glassner, J.S. (1991) Les dieux et les hommes: Le vin et la bière en Mésopotamie ancienne. In Fournier, D. and D'Onofrio, S. (eds) *Le Ferment divin,* Editions de la Maison des Sciences de l'Homme, Paris : 127–146.

Guillard, J. (1965) *Golompui. Analyse des conditions de modernisation d'un village du Nord Cameroun,* Mouton & Co/Ecole Pratique des Hautes Etudes, Paris/La Haye.

Haworth, A. (1995) Zambia. In Heath, D.B. (ed.) *International Handbook on Alcohol and Culture,* Greenwood Press, Westport, C.T./London: 316–327.

Heath, D.B. (ed.) (1995) *International Handbook on Alcohol and Culture,* Greenwood Press, Westport, C.T./London.

Jackson, M. (1993) *Beer Companion,* Mitchell Beazly, London.

Koppert, G.J.A. (1991) *Rapport provisoire des enquêtes alimentaires de l'anthropométrie nutritionnelle des actogrammes et de la dépense énergétique (Yassa, Mvœ de la côte, Mvœ de la forêt, Pygmées Kola, Duupa, Koma, Massa, Mousey, Evodoula).* Projet Anthropologie Alimentaire des Populations Camerounaises. ORSTOM, Yaoundé.

Marshall, M. (ed.) (1979) *Beliefs, Behaviors and Alcoholic Beverages: A cross-cultural survey,* The University of Michigan Press, Ann Arbor.

Netting, R. Mc.C. (1965) *Beer* as a locus of value among the West African Kofyar. *American. Anthropologist* 66(2): 375–384.

Périssé, J., Adrian, J., Rerat, A. and Le Berre, S. (1959) Bilan nutritif de la transformation du sorgho en bière : preparation, composition, consommation d'une bière du Togo, *Annales de Nutrition et Alimentation,* 13(1): 1–15.

Scriban, R. (1975). La fabrication de la bière, *Cahiers de Nutrition et de Dietetique,* Suppl. 4 : 15–24.

Seignobos, C. (1976) La bière de mil dans le Nord Cameroun: un phénomène de mini-économie, *Recherches sur l'Approvisionnement des villes,* CEGET, CNRS, Paris: 1–37.

Stappers, H. and Matze, M. (1991) *Alimentation et mode de vie des Duupa de la Montagne de Poli (Province du Nord, Cameroun),* Université de Wageningen, Centre de Nutrition, IMPM/ISH, Yaoundé.

CHAPTER 14
THE GENDER OF BEER: BEER SYMBOLISM AMONG THE KAPSIKI/HIGI AND THE DOGON

Walter van Beek

Introduction

Throughout Sub-Saharan Africa beer is an important economic enterprise, a vehicle of social relations and also a repository of symbolism (Jolly 2004; Abbink 2002). Here I shall concern myself with the third aspect, symbolism. Usually, beer links up with ancestors, as throughout Africa the consumption, exchange and sharing of beer ties in closely with the lineage system and its local history (e.g., Mueller–Kosack 2003). In this article I want to follow up on this approach, and show that beer symbolism is more dialectic and contradictory than is usually assumed. In fact, beer seems to highlight the arenas between men and women: beer is gendered.

In the following I trace the symbolic aspects of indigenous beer in two African societies, the Kapsiki/Higi of North Cameroon and North Eastern Nigeria (they form in fact one group, bearing different names in either country) and the Dogon of Mali; the data on the two groups stem from my own field research and involvement in both, starting in 1972 for the Kapsiki and in 1979 among the Dogon, both continuing till the present. In these two cultures beer carries specific symbolic connotations, which can be interpreted from its place in the rituals. My general approach is that of a 'controlled comparison': from a comparable setting, differences in symbolism are shown to be consonant with variations in society and religion. Both groups are rural village cultures, based on subsistence cultivation (sorghum and millet), without political centralisation but with a separate blacksmith population, both residing in a mountainous area; they really are quite comparable (for details see van Beek 1994). Yet they show intriguing differences, which surface in the beer, which is an important symbol in both cultures, but with opposite connotations.

Beer and Male Bonding: The Kapsiki of Cameroon

Mogodé, 14 April, 4 A.M.:

> In the afternoon of the first full day of her wedding, Kuve Kwanyé, Zra's
> bride, awaits the 'blessing of the bride'. About 3 p.m., a group of the
> groom's maternal uncles plus some of their friends and the village chief
> gather at the back of the compound, hidden from the eyes of outsiders.
> Zra, the groom, pours beer from his sacrificial jar into the ritual calabash,
> and hands it to the village headman. At last, people fall silent when he
> pronounces a blessing over it: 'She has to bear girls, first one and then
> another one. We libate for the people who are dead. If anybody wants to
> harm, let him be restrained. Let the groom marry more women and all be
> healthy.' He then spills the beer over the floor. The groom fills the cala-
> bash for the second time and hands it over to his uncles. Passing it on,
> each of them spits in the beer. One of them then takes the calabash to the
> nearby hut of the bride. Clothed just in her iron apron, Kuve kneels on
> the doorstep of her hut for the blessing. The uncle takes a mouthful of
> beer and sprinkles it over the kneeling girl: 'You must be healthy, you
> should bear many children and repay the bride price. You have to bear
> children one after the other.' Again he douses the girl with beer, and
> repeats his blessing: 'Please bear your children, not one by one, but one
> after the other.' Then he hands her the calabash: she has to empty it,
> drinking a part, and letting the rest run over her body. When the bride's
> body is wholly washed with beer, the men are satisfied. She is now their
> nephew's. Though much of the ritual is still to follow, from this moment
> Kuve is considered as belonging to the house, truly married to Zra, a wife
> of the lineage (Figure 14.1).

Two kinds of beer dominate Kapsiki brewing, *tè* and *mpedli*. The first, *tè*, is
the ritual beer, the 'red' kind of beer that will be my focus here. *Mpedli*, the
'white' beer, is for market use and immediate consumption. The two represent
polar opposites: the white beer is brewed by women, has no ritual significance,
is made by a quick process and has to be consumed immediately. The brewing
procedure is relatively simple. The white *mpedli* beer is considered a new
variety, adapted to the exigencies of the local market because of its quick
preparation. In recent years the red *tè* beer has increasingly become a sales
commodity for women both at the village markets and in the cities, as it is
generally preferred by the men over *mpeldi*.

However, the red variety is traditionally brewed by men, following a strict
procedure, with numerous prohibitions, and used for ritual purposes.
Symbolism is focused on this beer rather than on the *mpedli*, and it is this beer
that gives the Kapsiki their name: '*Kapsiki*' stems from the verb *pseke*, meaning
to sprout. The recipe for red beer is essentially the same throughout the

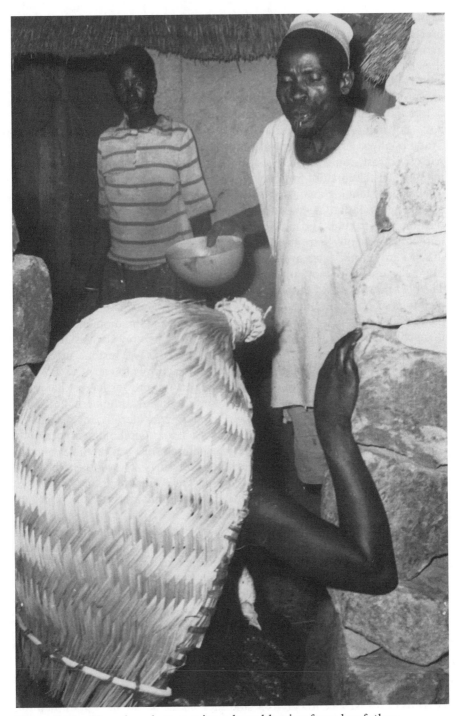

Figure 14.1 Kuve kneels to receive a beer blessing from her father

Cameroonian north. The millet or sorghum grains (the Kapsiki like both but prefer sorghum) are soaked in water for a night and then left on a roof to germinate. This *tè njine* is closely linked to death and danger, in Kapsiki thought. The sprouts are vulnerable to supernatural attack, so they will not be left too long on the roof. If small quantities of beer are to be made, the sprouts are left to dry inside the brewing hut, covered with a cloth. About four days before the event, the blackened dry sprouts are ground, then soaked again for half a day in a full jar of water and cooked for the first time for several hours. Traditionally a large earthenware brewing pot (*wuta*) is used, but also steel barrels or cast-iron cooking pots may serve the same purpose. In the afternoon, when the mixture has cooled down, the clear part is ladled into other smaller jars standing against the brewery wall. The remaining murky part is cooked again until the evening and is then mixed with the rest of the brew in the other jars to cool. The male brewer waits during the night, tasting the brew until it turns slightly sour, then filters it back into the large *wuta*, and lights up the fire around the large *wuta* jar (which is fixed in the earth) or under the drum. A slow fire is kept burning for the whole night until the next afternoon. The beer now turns sweetish (*tè kwarhèni*). In the evening, the man filters the beer for a second time and cautiously pours the brew into a number of narrow-necked beer jars, *rhewelepe tè* (spilling is a bad thing at this moment), and shuts them with a bundle of leaves. The jars are left in the brewery. As no yeast is added, it takes three days for the beer to ferment. The residue used to be thrown away but today is used as garden manure or pig food.

One taboo dominates ritual beer brewing. If the brewer has sexual intercourse, the beer becomes gluey and unfit for drinking. At the end of the second day, the beer may be used for sacrifice. Called *sarerhè* (literally: the blacksmith drinks), blacksmiths do indeed drink it and use it for household sacrifices when officiating. On the third day it is ready to be used for both sacrifices and for the public drinking that accompanies large offerings. The whole process of brewing has been performed in a hut specifically built for brewing *tè*. In Kapsiki architecture, this hut, as a strictly male domain, is usually built into the compound wall, opposite from the entrance.

Any sacrifice involving a goat or a sheep, i.e., any important familial or village sacrifice, calls for red beer. The *tè* is poured out in an oblong sacrificial cup made of blackened earthenware and sprinkled on the altar as one of the final parts of the proceedings. The altar, in fact, is a beer jar, a special one called *melè*. Several types are available, depending on the personal history of the owner. This special jar provides a link between the brewer and his father. Made to order by a woman blacksmith after the death of the brewer's father, the jar, filled with beer, rests on the father's grave for a whole night during the rites of the second funeral. In fact, the whole cycle of death rites ends when the jar is brought back home by the son of the deceased. Addressing the jar, still filled with beer, as 'father', the son puts it in the middle of his compound. He calls in his wives and children, and they all drink, the man first, then the women and finally the children. The jar will remain stored under one of the brewer's granaries, shut with a cow's horn. For each sacrifice it will be filled, together with the normal beer jars. During the sacrifice the *melè* is the centre of attention: some blood, a small piece of liver and cooked mush will be smeared on it '*to have father eat*', and the first beer to be tasted both by the jar and the main officiates is poured from this very *melè*.

Thus, any offering involving *tè* is part of a larger social matrix. The final drinking is quite formal. In the early morning ward members, clansmen and friends gather in the forecourt of the house, responding to the whispered invitation of the evening before. Standing in the entrance to the house, the brewer then starts to explain why he has called them. He conveys his message in elliptical language, just hinting at the real cause: 'I had a dream, and put some grains in the water afterwards'. The dream points to the divination he has sought, often a series of consultations. Grains in the water represent the brewing process. As most already know why he is sacrificing, no further explanation is needed. But his use of encoded speech is a sign of his maturity and '*savoir faire*'.

Beer drinking is the high point of the sacrifice and the most social aspect of the ritual. All the other activities, killing and roasting the goat and cooking the meal, have already been done in strict privacy behind the high compound wall that shields the family from the view of outsiders. Throughout the day of the actual sacrifice, the hut's entrance will be barricaded by a wooden pole to signal that a sacrifice is in process. Anyone entering would do so at his peril for it is dangerous for an outsider, i.e., someone not closely related, to enter the compound during a sacrifice. The drinking guests do not enter; they stay in the forecourt situated outside the compound proper, just in front of the one and only entrance.

This type of sacrifice, immolating a goat, followed by a meal for a small in-group, and beer for a large gathering of outsiders, is standard in Kapsiki culture. Not only households, but also wards, lineages, clans and even the village as a whole follow this sacrificial pattern. Beer is not always brewed for the occasion, but it is always poured on the altar, and in most cases drunk. Attendance at the final drinking session of a village sacrifice, though, is restricted. This particular sacrifice is shrouded in privacy and some secrecy. People are obliged to stay at home and not work in their fields, while the elders of the major clans accompany the village chief and the chief's blacksmith up the mountain to make a sacrifice at the ruins of the ancestral abode of the village.

Beer figures prominently in other rituals besides those involving sacrifice. A crucial one is the ritual to procure rain. Beer is used to 'wash' the sacred objects of rain-making sites. During the rain hunt of Mogodé, several old grinding stones, attributed to rainmakers of old, are washed with *tè*. Where rainmakers still operate, their implements, stones and mortars are washed with beer. Without beer, no rain (of course, the reverse holds as well). Beer in Kapsiki is a central and polyvalent symbol. One clear message of beer is fertility; the bride is washed in beer and the message is one of procreation, the quicker the better, the more the merrier (van Beek 1987). In rain making rituals, rain easily joins fertility as one of the connotations. Beer socializes the private ritual of sacrifice, separates the bride from her parents and joins her with her in-laws. The symbolism attached to beer is definitely male: brewed by men, used in the *melè* which represents the late father, red beer forms the link between the generations of a lineage. Pouring beer expresses the permanence of the agnatic line; the rain–beer link focuses fertility too, but is also a discourse on power relations (van Beek 1997). The brewer is the one who is rooted, bearer of localized power that should produce fertility, rain, crops and children.

Beer and the Power of Women: The Dogon of Mali

In Dogon society beer brewing is women's work (Jolly 2004). As an example we take the central myth of the *sigi* ritual, a spectacular ritual held every sixty years among the Dogon villages of the Bandiagara cliff. The myth recounts how the ritual came about, and ends in elaborate instructions on how to brew beer, i.e., instructions for women. (Contrary to earlier reports, Dogon has no creation myths, van Beek 1992, 2004). We take up the myth halfway: after many peregrinations, the hero Sene Senu enters an elephant in order to be 'instructed':

> The elephant ate Sene Senu, and for three whole years Sene Senu remained in the elephant's belly. Eventually the elephant grew thirsty and went to a waterhole just outside the village. The animal then defecated and out came Sene Senu carrying with him the *dalewa* – a forked *sigi* stool – the oblong calabash and the horse tail. At that moment his sister came along to fetch water. Seeing Sene Senu she tried to speak to him but he had no speech. She ran back into the village and cried out loud: 'Sene Senu is at the pool'. Her father thought she was crazy, as Sene Senu had been eaten three years ago, and all condolences had long passed. 'Look for yourself,' she said, and so he did. At the waterhole, his father asked Sene Senu to come home. Sene Senu started to speak in the language of the *sigi*: 'Go and brew beer, let everyone adorn himself in his finest; if not, I will not be able to return home. So go and receive me.' Sene Senu then gave very detailed instructions on how to sprout millet grains, how to grind them, in short how to brew 'real beer'. When everything had been done as instructed, the elders came to Sene Senu and asked: 'Who shall lead?' Sene Senu then sang one of the 12 *sigi* songs, 'Please forgive me, elders, you are the oldest, but if you do not know the road of the *sigi*, I am the first, and I will turn to the left.' The elders respond: 'Yes, you know the way. Three years is not three days; you have been inside the elephant, you know more than we do.' Thus, Sene Senu came home, and in this way the *sigi* arrived in the villages.

Sene Senu's sister is the first to find her brother, the lost hero, who returned after three years. Thus, she is the first to learn the new knowledge of how to brew beer. The Dogon women brew a lot and they brew well, using sophisticated techniques and recipes.

In Tireli, a village renowned for its women brewers, Yadagi routinely brews her lot to sell every market day (van Beek and Hollyman 2002). She starts brewing three days before the market by soaking 25 kg of millet grains in water. Being an innovative brewer, she adds some sorghum for a fuller taste. The sorghum adds volume and concentration to the beer.

The process itself is remarkably similar to that of the Kapsiki: sprouting the millet and sorghum grains, drying and grinding them, soaking in water, and then the long boil. What is different here, in this Dogon case, is the sophistication of the process. Yadagi uses an ingenious recipe in which some batches are boiled longer, some shorter: the first becomes bitter, past caramelisation stage, the other is still sweet. These will serve as her ingredients in the final test of each brewer, the blending towards the proper taste. So, Yadagi uses three different batches: the main brew, a short boiled sweet one, plus the bitter tasting batch. The main blending is done now with the last one.

After the long and sleepless hours of tending the fire all night long, the stage is set for the final touch. Carefully, Yadagi adds the bitter brew to the main body, tasting it after every few spoonfuls. If necessary, she can use some of the sweet batch to balance the taste. When the main batch is well blended, she pours half of the sweet stuff in the bitter batch, producing the so-called *konyo bonu*, a heavy bitter-sweet brew considered a delicacy by women. This by-product is often presented to the old women of the ward. The rest of the sweet batch is drunk as *konyo wè* or *konyo wâyâ*, by those with a very sweet tooth. Prominent among these are the honey bees that come in with the first sun. For this reason blending is done very early, often while it is still dark. Carefully, with her broom, Yadagi removes these unwanted customers from the brown brew. Pleased with the results of her work, she ladles the light-brownish brew, now called *konyo buruk*, from the jar into four smaller 20-litre *dei no* (drinking jars) used for transportation and selling. Then it is time for the final touch, fermentation. Yadagi puts a small sack, plaited from baobab fibres, with yeasted remains of former brews for a few minutes in each jar to start fermentation. The still-hot brew responds immediately: whitish clouds start billowing up from the pot, giving off a yeasty odour that Yadagi sniffs with satisfaction. She tastes a little: the beer is good, real *konyo* at last.

Women brew (Figure 14.2), but men drink. We saw the myth of the *sigi*, now what happens during the ritual?

Every sixty years, Dogon men during the *sigi* festival follow the road of Sene Senu, their beer-pioneering ancestor (van Beek 1992). The ritual is an ambulatory dance, from the village's waterhole (in each village) where Sene Senu was found, into and through the village. Preparation for this ceremony extends

Figure 14.2   Brewing Dogon beer

over three months during which time the ritual speakers for the village are initiated, i.e., taught the Dogon traditions in the ritual language (*sigi so*). Carefully, they prepare their outfits: long Dogon trousers, the *dalewa* (a Y-shaped stool for sitting on while savouring one's beer), a cowry-bedecked shirt, pennants in their ears, a special white bonnet, the horse's tail and the oblong calabash. With blue paint on their faces the men imitate the female cicatrisation. The other men dress up as well, but with fewer decorations.

In the early morning, the *sigi* line of men is formed at the foot of the scree, strictly according to age with the oldest in front. The smallest toddlers who can just walk come at the end (if they are not carried on the shoulders of others). Accompanied by village drums, the initiates then lead the way, ringing iron bells. The long line of dancing men and boys follows the *sigi* route through the village, passing the major ritual spots, before ending at a dancing area. A long line of beer jars is waiting for the men. The initiates then recite the *sigi* myth (referred to above) in a ritual language recounting how they stayed with their companions in the bush for three months. They offer thanks for the food and beer, adding general admonitions on how to behave towards elders, kinsmen and strangers. Then, with all the men seated comfortably on their stools, the oldest initiate of the assembled young boys puts his horse tail into a jar, swings it around and pointing it in all four cardinal directions, pours some beer on the floor and lets all initiates drink from the calabashes. General drinking follows, from old to young, drinking and passing the calabashes with the left hand. When the beer at the dancing ground is finished, the men return home to drink the beer their women have brewed. Throughout the proceedings the women, dressed in everyday clothes, have been spectators, kept at a distance by the old men who have seen the *sigi* before. Many of these men are too old for active participation, and merely watch and comment on the proceedings.

The *sigi* festival is the apex of drinking, the sum of life: one hour of total fulfilment, drinking beer seated on the symbol of oneself. The *dalewa* stool and the ritual calabash are specially for the beer drunk during that ritual, never to be used again. They will be kept in the granary of the lineage elder, till the death of the owner. Then they will be destroyed.

Beer is present in other rituals as well, but nowhere as central as in the *sigi*. Beer, in most of the large Dogon rituals, is simply consumed rather than used as a symbolic vehicle. For example, the rites of the first harvest (*yugo di* and *yu turu*) feature *punu*, the white millet gruel much more closely associated with ritual sacrifice. Similarly beer appears during the boisterous rituals marking the end of the dry season, when newly acquired wives are being lauded, and women and men praise each other. Funerals require large quantities of food and beer for entertaining guests but the central ritual is a beer-less and bloodless sacrifice preceded and followed by mock battles with guns, dancing and above all singing.

What distinguishes the *sigi* and the use of beer at the *sigi* from other rituals is the lack of sacrifice. Rather, the *sigi* is a ritual of reversal, in which the standard age hierarchy is inverted, in which male and female roles are mixed and in which not the history of the village but the history of a mythical individual is celebrated. So, in the reversal of values, beer comes to the fore.

In Dogon sacrifices, the spoken word is dominant, plus a large array of foodstuffs which are presented at the altar. In principle everybody is welcome. In the evening, the elders of the various lineages come to praise and to bless the altar and the owner of the house and to taste the beer. The food is gone by now, but a few jars of beer still remain to be sipped by the old men, as they pronounce a stream of blessings to one another pouring standard formulas over each other's heads. The speeches are the focus of the occasion.

Why is beer's ritual role – in any ritual but the *sigi* – limited? The Dogon elders are quite clear about it: beer is a woman's thing, brewed by women, incorporating women's creative variations on the basic recipe, and finished during the night when no men are present. One can never be sure that it is ritually clean. If a woman 'does not know the word' and does not respect custom, she might have been cooking the millet ingredients while ritually impure. In other words, she may have been menstruating. Men purify themselves before each and every ritual, but with women there is no certainty. If a menstruating woman even indirectly touched the altar, she would seriously defile it, annihilating whatever benefit could be accrued from the sacrifice. In short, in Dogon society beer is a woman's creation which is indispensable for men but bears a clear risk.

Beer is the vehicle of female impurity, even of female aggression. Poison, so the discourse goes, is administered by women through the beer. Buying at the market one has to be careful. Unless buying from a kinswoman – which normally is the case – a man always will invite the selling woman to taste from the batch first, a seemingly polite gesture, but also a protection against witchcraft, as witchcraft is defined as the proclivity to poison other people (van Beek 1994). So in Dogon symbolism, beer is female stuff drunk by men. The symbolism is quite straightforward: ritual drinking is an extension of social drinking. Amount and taste are more important than ritual and symbolic content and thus blending, filtering and timing of fermentation dominate the attention for beer. Drinking is the aim, not a statement of symbolic virility. But then, drinking in Dogon is a very social act: nobody eats alone, nobody drinks alone. Drinking is speaking, speaking the words of the world, bestowing the blessings of the mouth upon the head of the other. Beer has an intimation of communitas, but then one that is only reached by drinking together, and drinking a lot.

Conclusion: The Gender of Beer

In Kapsiki and Dogon societies beer is an important, flexible and polyvalent symbol. Beer for the Kapsiki is associated with male power, rain and procreation, aspects that easily merge in a context of continuity of the patrilineage. Rain also serves as a discourse on power (van Beek 1997). The interdiction on sex during preparation, though fairly common in Africa, is revealing. Ritual brewing is strictly male, without any female intervention. Kapsiki beer, *tè*, is male bonding: beer secures the transfer of people from one social group to another, or from the living to the realm of the dead.

Dogon beer is a female force. Men, the main drinkers, depend on women for the production of their beer, and they fear that aspect. They fear the impurities of menstruation and the wilfulness and irresponsibility of women who are deemed to lack respect for the order of men. Beer symbolism tells a Dogon story of opposition, lack of control and the gulf between the genders in a society full of overt harmony. However, the symbolic content should not be exaggerated in Dogon religion: beer is in most rituals for drinking, to receive guests, to welcome new adults, to welcome the masks entering the village during the *dama* masquerade. There beer should above all be plentiful.

Yet some commonalities show. In Kapsiki culture beer stipulates lineage structure, the cooperation between the genders. Dogon beer highlights gender differences, men versus women and to some extent village versus bush, but these distinctions are relevant and important in both cultures. Yet, there is more. In both Kapsiki and Dogon, beer symbolism stresses the antithesis of the normal situation. Kapsiki beer seems to express strong lineages, communality between house and village, and a harmonious cooperation between men and women; in short, beer portrays the society as a harmonious whole, just as most Kapsiki ritual tends to do (van Beek 1994). However, reality is different for the individualistic, autarchy-oriented Kapsiki; lineages are not that powerful, private households try to keep the rest of the village at arm's length, and men and women often are at odds. Beer de-problematises problematic relations within Kapsiki society.

In Dogon beer problematises a usually non-problematic relationship, highlights the fragility of interdependency between societal categories. Here, too, the beer symbolism is very dialectic: on the one hand it clearly accentuates structure, but it negates this structure at the same time. Even if drinking may lead to sociability and communal experiences, it is not communitas in itself. Beer, exaggerating gender differences, is essentially divisive in this harmony-oriented society.

In both cultures beer symbolism appears as a structure-oriented discourse, which mediates that very structure by overemphasis: the powerful and permanent lineage system, the sharp gender distinction. This overemphasis runs counter to the main trends in both cultures: the trend towards individualism in Kapsiki, and the tendency to a sometimes stifling harmony-orientation in Dogon. Beer symbolism in both cultures is a gentle exaggeration of cultural norms, a meta-commentary on society itself: beer teaches not to take cultural premises too seriously, a slightly bent mirror for the culture to have a look at itself and to enjoy the distortions.

References

Abbink, J. (2002) Drinking, prestige and power: alcohol and cultural hegemony in Maji, Southern Ethiopia. In Bryceson, D.B. (ed.) *Alcohol in Africa: Mixing business, pleasure and politics*, Heineman, Portsmouth: 161–188.

Beek, W.E.A. van (1987) *The Kapsiki and Higi of the Mandara Mountains*, Waveland Press, Prospect Heights.

Beek, W.E.A. van (1991). Dogon restudied: a field evaluation of the work of Marcel Griaule, *Current Anthropology*, 32(2): 139–167.

Beek, W.E.A. van (1992) Becoming human in Dogon, Mali. In Ajmer, G. (ed.) *Coming into Existence: Birth and metaphors of birth*, IASSA, Göteborg: 47–69.

Beek, W.E.A. van (1994) The innocent sorcerer: coping with evil in two African societies, Kapsiki and Dogon. In Blakely, T., van Beek, W.E.A. and Thomson, D.L. (eds), *Religion in Africa: Experience and expression*, James Currey and Heinemann, Portsmouth, New Hampshire 196–228.

Beek, W.E.A. van (1997) Rain as a discourse of power: rainmaking in Kapsiki. In Jungraithmayer, H., Barreteau, D. and Seibert, U. (eds) *L'Homme et l'Eau dans le Bassin du Lac Chad*, ORSTOM, Paris: 285–297.

Beek, W.E.A. van (2004) Haunting Griaule: experiences from the restudy of the Dogon, *History in Africa*, 31: 43–68.

Beek, W.E.A. van and Hollyman, S. (photographer) (2002) *Africa's People of the Cliffs: The Dogon*, Abrams, New York.

Jolly, E. (2004) *Boire avec esprit. Bière de mil et société Dogon*, Société d'Ethnologie, Nanterre.

Mueller-Kosack, G. (2003) *The Way of the Beer: Ritual re-enactment of history among the Mafa: Terrace farmers of the Mandara mountains (North Cameroon)*, Mandaras, London.

CHAPTER 15
RITUAL USE OF BEER IN SOUTH-WEST TANZANIA[1]

Ruth Kutalek

Introduction

In south-west Tanzania people know two types of traditionally fermented drink. *Ulanzi* is from the sap of a bamboo species which grows in the cooler climates of the mountainous regions. Its harvest is highly seasonal – only during the rainy season do the bamboo sprouts produce enough sweet sap to be collected and fermented. Production and marketing are usually done in small-scale enterprises. Taking care of the bamboo groves and harvest of the sap is the task of women and men alike. The groves are usually owned by individuals who are able to earn, by Tanzanian standards, not inconsiderable amounts of money. Marketing of *ulanzi* is solely in the hands of women who rent small bars to sell this and other traditionally fermented drinks.

The general term for traditionally produced beer is *pombe* (Sw.).[2] It is basically made from cereals or other starchy plants such as cooking bananas or cassava. Depending on its ingredients and stage of fermentation, *pombe* has various names. *Komoni* (from English 'common') is made from maize and finger millet (*ulezi – Eleusine* sp.); *kimbumu* (Be.) contains more millet than maize; *ufuge* (Be.) is made solely from millet; *kindi* (Be.) from unpeeled cassava (*muhogo*); *myakaya* (Be.) contains cassava, maize and millet; and *kangara*, (Sw.) is made from maize and sugar or honey. *Togwa* (Sw.) or *malenga* (Sw.) indicates beer in its early stages of production. Among the Bena in the south-western highlands maize and finger millet[3] are preferably used to produce *pombe*.

Sometimes *mlangali* (Sw., a succulent *Euphorbia* sp.) is mixed into the brew, obviously using its irritating effect on the mucous membrane to make the customer drink more. According to Schultes and Hofmann (1979: 109) in former Tanganyika, *Datura ferox* (a plant of the nightshade family) was added to beer for its inebriating effects.[4] In northern areas it was reportedly used to facilitate robbery.

> In Bukoba it is a seasonal occupation of certain natives of that district to entice travellers to a meal and a convivial bowl of *pombe*. The victims become stupose or at times maniacal and while in this state they are deprived of any possessions which their hosts deem worthy of acquisition. The Medical Officer reported that he had examined victims some time after their illness and found their pupils dilated and markedly inactive to light. (Raymond 1938: 75).

People in the south-western highlands, however, never used *Datura* as an additive to beer.

Production of Beer

The processing and marketing of *pombe* is the responsibility of women (see also Obot 2000).[5] It is produced at home and sold to a local *klabu* (slang from English 'club', Sw. *kilabu*). Sometimes also private homes are converted into bars (see Subbo 2001: 205). This gives the women the possibility of earning some money and makes them, to some extent, independent from male income (Holtzmann 2001). The *pombe* shops are often rented by a woman who also sells the beer. Even small villages have at least one *kilabu*. Beer is sold in plastic containers of about one third of a litre. It is sometimes shared by one or two customers who are closely related (see Garine, E. 2001: 196). The main consumers of beer are men but also women, especially of older age, increasingly drink *pombe*.

As a first step of production, the finger millet and maize are soaked, left to germinate for a few days and then dried in the sun. The sprouted and dried millet can be bought at the market but is often produced at home. The cereals are then pounded, some water is added and the dough is allowed to stand for a while. The sprouted and dried maize is carried to a milling machine where it is processed into fine flour. Nowadays in semi-urban areas it is very rare to find that the maize has been pounded by hand. As a next step, water is boiled in a large oil barrel, then the maize flour is added, the whole mixture is heated again and finally the millet-mixture is added. The liquid is left overnight to rest. In the morning the warm brew is filtered through woven plastic sacks (Figure 15.1) – formerly the sieve was made of plant fibres (see Krauss 1994) – and then it is ready to sell. As far as I was told, no industrial yeast or yeast from previous brewing is added. Sprouted millet contains wild yeast (Raymond 1938) which probably is enough of a source for fermentation. Also the pots and plastic containers used for the production of beer are contaminated with yeast, which seems to be enough to start new fermentation.

Figure 15.1   Beer being transferred into plastic containers, ready to be served.

Consumption

As much as 380 litres of traditional beer per person is consumed annually in rural areas (Krauss 1994). Quite a quantity is needed for person to become intoxicated by beer. The alcoholic content of traditional beer is around 2.5 – 4 per cent (Papas *et al.* 2008; Shayo *et al.* 2000; Tusekwa *et al.* 2000). It is lower in alcohol content and higher in nutrients than most industrially produced beers (King and Burgess 1993). Beer is properly claimed as a food as it is a thick brew (see also Obot 2000). People in the south-west of Tanzania say that *pombe* is 'eaten' not drunk. Most of the solid matter is still left in, even after being filtered once during production and once before consumption. *Pombe*, in comparison to industrially produced beer, is considered a healthy brew which in its early phases of fermentation is given to children, old or sick people and pregnant women. Early fermented beer is high in nutritional properties (Mandishona *et al.* 1999). Generally, fermentation improves food digestion and has several other health benefits (Etkin 2006; Etkin and Ross 2004).[6]

The food aspect of beer is also stressed by one Ngoni boy who in the early 1950s wrote in an essay at school: 'Beer and cattle are the food of the Ngoni. ... If your friend comes and he doesn't get beer and meat, then although he gets porridge, he still says that there was hunger in the house. ... Our life depends on drinking beer.' And, comparing this habit of the Ngoni to another ethnic group, the Cewa, another boy commented: 'The Cewa are just slaves, they merely eat. The Ngoni are like the Whites; they eat little and drink much' (Barnes 1951: 218f.).

Today, beer is, in the first place, consumed as a recreational drink. People come together in a small *klabu* to gossip, to talk about agricultural issues, about family matters and to get a little tipsy. In former times beer also played an important role in rituals concerning all major social events such as birth, marriage, adulthood and death but also in communal work and in warfare.

Beer's Role in History

In former times, beer was important to obtain assistance from neighbours for work (Culwick and Culwick 1935; Dempwolff 1914; McAllister 2004). This was a way to reward the workers. No communal work was thinkable without the provision of beer. When a house was to be built, a roof to be thatched, a harvest to be brought in, beer had to be provided. Especially during the months of greatest agricultural activity beer was highly prized. At such times people could no longer afford to brew beer because they had to ration their food. Barnes comments on the Ngoni: 'Most of the outside assistance that may be required in a garden is raised by means of a beer-party. The man's wife brews beer, and it is made known in the village and around about that on such-and-such a day there will be a party to hoe in their garden. A dozen or so people go to the garden in the morning, and work until the task set by the owner of the garden is completed. They then move to the village and are refreshed with beer' (Barnes 1951: 219).

In times of war beer was brewed to encourage the warriors. The chief 'gives them beer and puts some magical substances into it, which they drink together' (Dempwolff 1914: 111). When returning from the battlefields 'they send a messenger with the news that the troops are on their way home and they should start with brewing beer. When they are at home, now drinking beer, then they talk with enthusiasm' (ibid.: 112). In the south-west beer was important when taking away the bride to meet her groom. When a woman was well advanced in pregnancy she returned to her mother. Beer was brewed and drunk while instructing the mother-to-be. When the child was born and capable of living, beer was brewed and the infant was shown to the community (ibid.). Nigman (1908) reports that in addition to the living, also the ancestors celebrated a newborn baby with beer. A small pot of unfermented beer was put on the roof of the house for the ancestors, in some regions near the door. If the pot was not emptied by the next day – a sign that the offering was not accepted – the ritual had to be done again. In the past among the Bena, the girls had to undergo certain initiation rituals involving also circumcision, in which unfermented beer or *togwa* was served (Culwick and Culwick 1935).

Great amounts of unfermented beer were also prepared for funeral rites. A small amount was poured over the grave as an offering and a pot of it placed at the head of the grave. If the grave was some distance from the house the pot was placed outside the hut and a little beer poured on the grave next morning. It was vital that the spirits approved the offering. If the beer was unspoiled and good, the people could proceed to drink it, but if anything had gone wrong with the brew the spirit expressed his dissatisfaction and the ritual had to be repeated. The funeral rites were also known as *ugimbi ya matapatapa* – the 'beer of causing-to-arrive'. If a man died, the rites were followed by *ugimbi ya mapwere* – the 'beer of inheritance', when the heirs assembled to divide up the property. During the period between the two feasts the closest female relatives wore old and worn clothes, but on the day of *ugimbi ya mapwere* they appeared washed and dressed in new clothes (Culwick and Culwick 1935: 126f.).

Today: Offerings to the Ancestors

Beer is *the* sacrificial food. It has a very high symbolic value (de Garine 2001: 58f.). The offering to the ancestors or *tambiko* is one of the few rituals practised today in which beer is still significant. This ritual traditionally takes place once a year or once every two years but in urgent cases like severe disease, drought or loss of cattle, the *tambiko* may be held any time. The *tambiko* today is a very private affair. As the late Mr. Mtenzi, a Bena elder, once told me: 'There are many clans which are still doing it (the *tambiko*) but they wouldn't like other people to know about it. Like, for instance, now, we go to L. every second year, we wouldn't like other people to know, but we do it, every second year.'

When the meat, beer and flour are offered to the ancestors they show with very clear signs if the offering is accepted or not. Mr. Mtenzi:

> If I go to these ancestors and speak to them, they don't speak, the ancestors themselves, but the actions which are happening outside are the ones that show that they have accepted me or they are angry. For instance we go there with our cows, kill the cows and if this meat is eaten without (us) fighting (with each other), then they have accepted. Sometimes, the animal who you would like to kill runs away. With this they show that they don't like it.

For a *tambiko,* fermented beer is used nowadays, but in the past, unfermented beer or *togwa* was offered. In the evening, pots with beer were placed on the graves and if the beer was still sweet the next morning and did not turn sour, the offering was accepted. If something went wrong, the offering had to be repeated until it was accepted (Culwick and Culwick 1935).

The first *tambiko* I witnessed took place in Ilembula, a small town south of the main Makambako–Mbeya road in November 1997. A traditional healer, Mariam, invited me to participate in this ritual which, as it turned out later, was held because one of her relatives had severe economic problems. Mariam gave last instructions to her family:[7]

We cut pieces of meat to share in the family. Now we begin the process, our guest here will make some photographs. Don't close your eyes; look at the European snapping you. She will record, be careful, speak good words. You, the elder, please start to do it. The European here will snap even the dirty things here. She will be surprised when we do this, because they don't have that there. This meat goes with the liquor, you tell the audience, so that we start drinking. This flour is from maize, as well as the pombe. Now start talking to your ancestors, to your late father and your grandparents.

The first one to begin the offering was the father of the person concerned:

I have now come with this son that he is coming to pray for you and give you something you need. Now take the pieces of meat. Now please, this is the meat I want to give you where you are. These pieces of meat you all should eat, please don't be mean, share it. I told you that all family members must be together where they are. Tell them all that we are doing this. ... Check that the cows and goats are in good order. When I earn money it is lost unknowingly. We need to prove if you received our things here, that everything is going good. If we find that the results are not good, we suspect you to be witches. Always come in our house and talk to us. Now we pour pombe, now you have got to do this, after you eat this meat you have to drink the pombe. Have these bites of meat with it.

After the elders finished their prayers the young man who was responsible for the *tambiko* spoke:

You, grandfather, what I am telling you now, listen to me. As you told me formerly, it's true that I had to prepare this ceremony. Today the ceremony is this one. Please, stand for my problems; I have got so many of them. I don't want to see other troubles arising. If I get more problems I have to think that you are still a witch. I brewed this pombe; the meat is here for you. I still ask you to stand for my problems. What I produce from my farm should be profitable. If you don't stand for me I don't know what you will get next time. I have something to eat so you can eat. Please, the herds should be productive. If you start killing the animals here, what do you think you will get next time? You have to protect them. All the earnings must be prospering, therefore I give you this animal which has blood. Take the blood. As the other member said, don't think we killed a rat, it's for you, drink and feel happy. You must dance accordingly as you were doing while alive. We shall be happy when you receive us. I say thank you.

After everybody in the group offered his share of meat, flour and *pombe* and when they saw that it was accepted by the ancestors, they themselves were then allowed to eat the rest of the meat, drink beer and celebrate.

Traditional concepts of disease not only include physical symptoms but also miserable living conditions, misfortune in business or problems related to the family. To treat a patient adequately it is vital that, besides bodily or mental symptoms, the cause of a disease is detected. In the following case the traditional healer Lutumo (Kutalek 2001), through divination and discussion, reveals that the patient's disease is caused by an evil-wishing ancestor. He consequently suggests that she hold a *tambiko*. Usually these kinds of diseases or conditions are severe or long lasting and concern the whole family.

Lutumo: How many children do you have?
Patient: Three boys, two girls.
L: What do you find them suffering?
P: They are suffering from several things.
L: Is their father present?
P: He died two years ago. Even his brother died, the only who remained is the aunt.
L: Are you a Hehe?
P: Yes.
…
L: Didn't you go to the *waganga* (traditional healers) to ask why these people died?
P: We went a long time ago; we were told that the deceased people were bewitched.
L: When your husband was still alive, did you quarrel with him sometimes? Do you remember it?
P: Yes.
L: You should remember it well. Who started to quarrel?
P: (does not answer)
L: You should remember. That's why these children are suffering.
…
L: Did they build the grave of their father?
P: No. But the grave of my brother-in-law was built by his own children, but the grave of my husband was not built by my children.
L: First you should go and bring the hens to *babu* (grandfather) and *bibi* (grandmother); second, your children and their elder brother should go and build the grave of their own father. While building it, take some of the *pombe*, cook some *ugali* (maize-porridge) and meat and call your own family.

A *tambiko* is also held when the ancestors are severely upset because social or religious rules were not obeyed. Lutumo once told me the following story: Years ago he worked for the Tanzanian Wattle Company, which has large plantations of wattle trees (*Acacia melanoxylon*) around Njombe. The bark of the trees is used for tanning; the wood is needed to supply the wood-factory, the tea estate, the hospital and attached houses with electricity. When the factory was built he was still a young man. As he told me:

> Before building the factory it wouldn't work because the people didn't like a factory here. The (former) owner of the area said that that place was for their *tambiko* (offerings). The white people had to give a cow to remove the ghosts there. They did it. When they installed the electricity they had to do the same thing. This time I was one of them who ate the cow, to do the offerings. When they installed the electricity I was in Dar es Salaam, the machine wouldn't work. ... They had to phone me to come back. When I came back I went there and I made the things (offerings) and the factory went on well.

> I and another three, we ordered one black cow for them. Before slaughtering it we said, 'We can't slaughter the cow before asking the ancestors (*msimwi*)'. [8] Before slaughtering the cow we took some flour and put it there. ... We had some beer. I had to put one bottle to each of the posts for the ancestors to drink. Beer, just local pombe. ... Lastly the white people came to see what we have done. Those white people made pictures of that. Then we had to pour that pombe around the posts. The rest which remained we drank ourselves. The white people asked: 'Can we start now to light the electricity?' 'You should wait. You should stay for three minutes so that we see the ancestors.' After a few minutes I asked: 'Where is your machine?' We went there, it was not working well, doing the opposite, returning back. When we checked the machine we put some finger millet [as an offering]. 'Now start your machine.' It worked. ... I have got big ancestors!

Discussion

Beer is of high social and ritual importance. Men, and in some regions also women, come together in clubs to exchange ideas, to do business or discuss family matters. Beer is used in traditional ceremonies and is especially important when communicating with ancestors. Though half of the grain in Africa is consumed in the form of beer, in few manuals on nutrition in developing countries is beer given the necessary space as an important nutritional factor (Kracht and Schulz 1999; Marchione 1999; Foster 1992). Its method of production allows women to earn money independently from male income, an aspect that up to now has not been given much attention. If women are able to earn money, the nutritious standards of their families increase because women usually give food a higher priority than men do (King and Burgess 1993). Also women are usually more willing than men to spend their income on the education of their children. On the other hand the production of beer can lead to considerable problems within families and communities (Carlson 1992). Women, especially if they become prosperous, often put their reputation at stake when brewing beer (Subbo 2001). Men who are frequent customers of *pombe* shops can spend considerable amounts of money there – money that is often better spent on more vital things. Furthermore, in beer production, cereals or other starchy plants are consumed almost only by adults and rarely by children. Although public drinking is accepted and drunkenness in many societies even has a prestigious image (de Garine 2001: 63), it is also often seen as a sign of social decline.

Problems in Tanzania are especially evident with the production of a spirit called *gongo* which is often made of beer. *Gongo* is also produced by women who, in need of money for their family, are driven to crime because the private distilling of alcohol in Tanzania is forbidden by law. Almost every day newspapers report on the illegal distillation of alcohol which is mentioned in the same breath as homicide and rape. In fact, especially if alcohol is distilled in modern vessels that do not permit the methylalcohol to evaporate, as the traditional vessels do, many victims die of poisoning or go blind through the consumption of contaminated alcohol. In the production of distilled alcohol, important nutrition factors are taken out of the circle, thus enhancing food insecurity. Consumption of distilled alcohol is becoming an increasing social, economic and public health problem in many parts of Africa (Luginaah and Dakubo 2003).

Notes

1. An earlier version of this paper has been published in *Viennese Ethnomedicine Newsletter* 8(1) (2005), 16–24, who have given permission for publication of this version.
2. The yeast *Schizosaccharomyces pombe* is named after the traditional Swahili term for beer. The abbreviations, Sw. means Swahili, Be. Bena.
3. The ability of finger millet to convert starch into sugars is only surpassed by barley (Anonymous 1996).
4. In Ethiopia *geisho, Rhamnus prinoides*, is added to flavour the local beer and probably also to enhance its intoxicating effect (Vetter 1997).
5. Among the Duupa in Northern Cameroon, for example, beer brewing is done by men (de Garine 2001: 194).
6. Potentially harmful mycotoxins can be present in traditionally brewed beer as is the case with other cereal preparations. It is, however, reported that for beer brewing often mouldy cereals are used (Shephard *et al.* 2005).
7. It is fairly unusual that a woman leads a *tambiko*. However, this might be due to her status as a traditional healer.
8. Slang of the Swahili word *mzimu* (Pl.: *misimu*); ancestors.

References

Anonymous (1996) *Lost Crops of Africa*, Vol. 1: *Grains*, National Academy Press, Washington.

Barnes, J.A. (1951) The Fort Jameson Ngoni. In Colson, E. and Gluckman, M. (eds) *Seven Tribes of British Central Africa*, Manchester University Press, Manchester: 194–252.

Carlson, R.G. (1992) Symbolic mediation and commoditization: a critical examination of alcohol use among the Haya of Bukoba, Tanzania, *Medical Anthropology*, 15: 41–62.

Colson, E. and Gluckman, M. (eds) (1951) *Seven Tribes of British Central Africa*, Manchester University Press, Manchester.

Culwick, A.T. and Culwick, G.M. (1935) *Ubena of the Rivers*, Allen and Unwin, London.

Dempwolff, O. (1914) Beiträge zur Volksbeschreibung der Hehe, *Baessler Archiv*, 4: 87–163.

Etkin, N. (2006) *Edible Medicines: An ethnopharmacology of food*, University of Arizona Press, Tucson.

Etkin, N. and Ross, P. (2004) (Ethno)pharmacology of foraging, phytofoods, and fermantation, *Viennese Ethnomedicine Newsletter*, 6(2): 4–8.

Foster, P. (1992) *The World Food Problem: Tackling the causes of undernutrition in the Third World*, Lynne Rienner Publishers, Boulder.

Garine, E. (2001) An ethnographic account of the many roles of millet beer in the culture of the Duupa agriculturalists, (Poli Mountains) Northern Cameroon. In Garine, I. de and V. de (eds) *Drinking: Anthropological approaches*, Berghahn Books, Oxford: 191–204.

Garine, I. de (2001) Drinking in Northern Cameroon among the Masa and Muzey. In Garine, I. de and Garine, V. de (eds) *Drinking: Anthropological approaches*, Berghahn Books, Oxford: 51–65.

Holtzman, J. (2001) The food of elders, the 'ration' of women: brewing, gender, and domestic process among the Samburu of Northern Kenya, *American Anthropologist*, 103(4): 1041–1058.

King, F.S. and Burgess, A. (1993) *Nutrition for Developing Countries*, Oxford University Press, Oxford.

Kracht, U and Schulz, M. (eds) (1999) *Food Security and Nutrition*, LIT, New York.

Krauss, I. (1994) *'Heute back' ich, morgen brau' ich ...' Zur Kulturgeschichte von Brot und Bier*, Eiselen Siftung, Ulm.

Kutalek, R. (2001) *Steven Lihonama Lutumo. Leben und Arbeit eines traditionellen Heilers der Bena Südwest-Tansanias. Ein Beitrag zur biographischen Forschung in der Ethnomedizin*, VWB Verlag, Berlin.

Luginaah, I. and Dakubo, C. (2003) Consumption and impacts of local brewed alcohol (akpeteshie) in the upper west region of Ghana: a public health tragedy, *Social Science and Medicine*, 57(9): 1747–1760.

Mandishona, E.M., Moyo, V.M., Gordeuk, V.R., Khumalo, H., Saungweme, T., Gangaidzo, I.T., Gomo, Z.A., Rouault, T., MacPhail, A.P. (1999) A traditional beverage prevents iron deficiency in African women of child bearing age, *European Journal of Clinical Nutrition*, 53(9): 722–725.

Marchione, T.J. (1999) *Scaling Up, Scaling Down: Overcoming malnutrition in developing countries*, Gordon and Breach, Amsterdam.

McAllister, P. (2004) Labor and beer in the Transkei, South Africa: Xhosa work parties in historical and contemporary perspective, *Human Organization*, 63(1): 100–111.

Nigmann, E. (1908) *Die Wahehe. Ihre Geschichte, Kult-, Rechts-, Kriegs- und Jagdgebräuche*, Berlin (no publisher given).

Obot, I.S. (2000) The measurement of drinking patterns and alcohol problems in Nigeria. *Journal of Substance Abuse*, 12: 169–181.

Papas, R.K., Sidle J.E., Wamalwa, E.S., Okumu, T.O., Bryant, K.L., Goulet, J.L., Maisto, S.A., Braithwaite, R.S., and Justice, A.C. (2008) Estimating alcohol content of traditional brew in Western Kenya using culturally relevant methods: the case for cost over volume, *AIDS and* Behavio, 14(4): 836–844.

Raymond, W.D. (1938) Native Materia Medica. III. The Deliriants, *Tanganyika Notes and Records*, 5: 72–75.

Schultes, R.E. and Hofmann, A. (1979) *Plants of the Gods: Origins of hallucinogenic use*, McGraw Hill, New York.

Shayo, N.B. Kamala, A. Gidamis, A.B. and Nnko, S.A.M. (2000) Aspects of manufacture, composition and safety of orubisi: a traditional alcoholic beverage in the northwestern region of Tanzania, *International Journal of Food Sciences and Nutrition*, 51(5): 395–402.

Shephard, G.S., van der Westhuizen, L., Gatyeni, P.M., Somdyala, N.I.M., Burger, H. and Marasas, W.F.O. (2005) Fumonisin mycotoxins in traditional Xhosa maize beer in South Africa, *Journal of Agricultural and Food Chemistry*, 53(24): 9634–9637.

Subbo, Wilfred K. (2001) Socio-economic and cultural implications of alcoholic beverages among the Abagusii of Western Kenya. In Garine, I. de and Garine, V. de *Drinking: Anthropological approaches*, Berghahn Books, Oxford: 205–211.

Tusekwa, A.B., Mosha, T.C.E., Laswai, H.S. and Towo, E.E. (2000) Traditional alcoholic beverages of Tanzania: production, quality and changes in quality attributes during storage, *International Journal of Food Sciences and Nutrition*, 51(2): 135–143.

Vetter, S. (1997) *Geisho: Its uses, production potential and problems in Northern Tigray, Ethiopia*, FARM Africa, Institute for Sustainable Development, Axum, Addis Ababa.

CHAPTER 16
BREWING SORGHUM BEER IN BURKINA FASO: A STUDY IN FOOD TECHNOLOGY FROM THE PERSPECTIVE OF ANTHROPOLOGICAL LINGUISTICS

François Belliard

Introduction

Sorghum beer is the traditional beverage of many savannah populations throughout Africa, whereas forest populations often drink palm wine. Beer can also be made with millet or corn, depending on the region. It appeared in Ancient Egypt and is still consumed, even where occidental beers are sold.

In a short first part I shall give some information about the consumption of beer among the *gyóòhé* ethnic group of Burkina Faso. The data for this article have been collected during three fieldwork trips in 1998–2000 in the Yantenga village (Diabo rural municipality, Gourma province), 210 km east from capital town Ouagadougou, Burkina Faso, West Africa. The few thousands *gyóòhé* people are mostly farmers. They speak *gyóòré*,[1] which is closely related to *mòoré* (five million speakers), one of the major languages of Burkina.

I will then present a detailed description of their brewing technique from an anthropological linguistics point of view. This means that the analysis is based on what people say (on what is lexicalized), thus using texts in the local language. This approach enables one to understand how people conceptualise this preparation, without being mistaken by the occidental categorisations and the approximation of translations into Indo-European languages.

Consumption: The Role of Beer in Society

In general, we can say that an important social aspect of beer drinking is that it brings the *gyóòhé* together; people rarely drink alone. Beer is drunk at any time of the day and night; the occasions and places are multiple (Lestrange 1981).

It is common for men to drink beer during the old men's meetings, when problems of the village are discussed. A strict hierarchy is then respected, and drinking rules are observed. The youngest person serves the others. He holds the jar containing beer with his right hand and the calabash in his left. Beer is commonly drunk from calabashes. The oldest man is the first to be served, then the other men are served from the oldest to the youngest.

People drink beer during important events like funerals, birth celebrations, weddings, etc. Litres of beer are brought and drunk by participants all night long, while everybody dances and sings.

Beer can also be drunk to symbolise reconciliation between persons who had had problems one with each other. It is common to pour a few drops of beer on the floor before drinking, to give a part symbolically to the ancestors (beer brings human beings and ancestors together).

Sweet beer (not fermented yet) is often used in rituals; it is then poured on a fetish (a sacred rock or tree, etc.). Fermented beer cannot be used as it would 'agitate' genies.

People can also drink while working in the fields. Invitations to cultivate are common. Twenty or thirty persons work together and have a break each hour to drink beer that has been brought to them by women. According to the *gyóòhé*, beer gives force and strength and is very helpful for working faster. Motivation is also given by music played on horns or drums.

Nowadays, beer is commonly sold and drunk in the 'court' *zàkká* of the woman who did the brewing, which is called a 'cabaret' *ráa dùuú* (beer / house) for this occasion. Customers arrive at six in the morning and buy beer. It's a really convivial time and social status can, at least for a moment, be forgotten. Men, women and adolescents drink in a friendly atmosphere.

There are also cases where beer can bring trouble. Drunkenness can make people malicious or even make people fight. The *gyóòhé* are very aware of that negative effect, and therefore they try to control their consumption of beer. As they say, beer can bring the best (understanding and a clear vision of life) or the worst, depending on the temperament of the person who drinks.

Beer Making

In *gyóòré*, there are three ways to express the preparation of 'beer' *ráã* ,[2] all of these being related to cooking:

ráã kɔ̀gbɔ́	(beer / preparing [food])
ráã rǎmmrè	(beer / stirring a boiling liquid)
ráã dɔ̀gbɔ̀	(beer / cooking)

The *gyóòhé* generally conceptualise beer brewing as a procedure involving heating.

There are two main processes involved:

- malting, which consists of immersing grain in water (germination), and then of drying it (about two weeks)
- brewing, which is composed of successive cooking and filtering operations and is terminated by the fermentation of the liquid with yeast (two days)

This presentation must be understood as a synthesis of the preparations I observed, rather than a recipe which would be the same for every woman (men never brew beer). Each woman has her personal 'touch' which makes her beer taste specific.

Malting

Malting lasts at least twelve days. The goal of this process is to obtain malt by germination and drying of the 'grain' *ká* or *kí* (see figure 16.1). One can use grain from 'red sorghum' *ká-ráàá*, 'white sorghum' *bá-níŋŋá* or 'millet' *ká-z'e*.

Germination
The first phase is the 'soaking' *súub'u*.[3] One puts the grain in an 'earthenware jar' *v̀ǎŋŋ zóoré* (soil / jar) full of 'water' *kʊ́ʔǎ̃*. The grain will stay there for two or three days. The aim is to lay the grain in an aquatic environment, in order to get the germination started.

Then comes the 'draining' *yʋ̀abɔ́*:[4] one scoops the grains out of the water with a 'calabash' *wǎnnɛ* and puts it in a drainer (a simple 'basket' *bòdgó*) with another jar below. The liquid which drips out, i.e., the 'straining' *gǎh wèeá* (bitter, unpleasant / bush) is either thrown away or given as food to chickens.

Once drained, the grain is put to rest in an empty jar for two days: this is the 'resting' *gíʔlb'ɔ*.[5] One takes care to cover the jar with a lid and to 'sprinkle the grain with water' *zǎghbɔ́*. If it's too dry, it doesn't germinate, if it's too wet the grain dies. The aim is once more to stimulate germination, but this time by placing the grain in contact with water and especially air.

At the end of these two days, the grain has begun to 'germinate' *búlí*, and one 'soaks it again' *tĩ́lbú* in a jar of water for two days. It's interesting to see that the term for the first soaking (*súub'u*) is different from the term used for the second soaking. This word, *tĩ́lbú*, is specific; it can't be used in another context. It shows that this action is conceptualised independently (depending on the consistency of the grain) from the first soaking, even if the action is physically the same. A white 'foam' *púh púurì* (bursting, emanation / annoyance) appears at the surface of the water during this second soaking.

Finally, the grain must be drained one more time (second 'draining' *yʋ̀abɔ́*) and put to rest for two days (this second 'resting' *gíʔlb'ɔ* can take place either in a jar or in a house, with a plastic bag covering the grain). The grain has now totally germinated, and it can be dried.

Drying

'Drying' *kʷèehbó* consists of two processes: 'agglomerating' *píʔbú* and 'crumbling-laying out' *láhbɔ̀*.

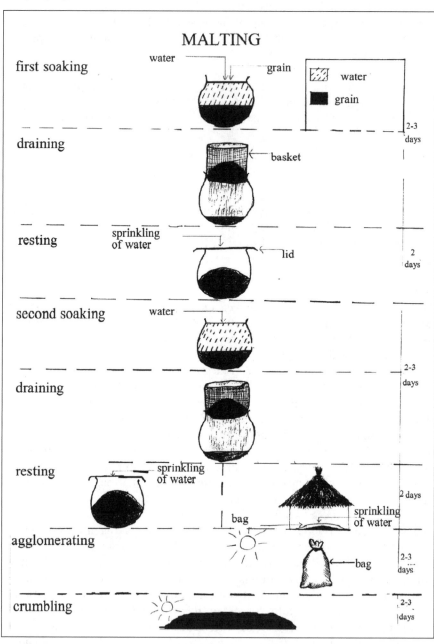

Figure 16.1   Malting.   (Diagram drawn by the author in the field.)

For agglomerating one packs the grain down in a 100 kg bag (or in a 'filter' *tʷákká*) and puts it outside under the sun. Two or three days later, the grain has swollen and forms a homogeneous paste.

For crumbling one removes the grain from the bag, crumbles the grains attached together by the sprouts, and lays it out on a plastic bag, on a rock, or on the soil. It lasts two or three days, depending on the weather (sun, temperature, etc.). The goal is to stop germination. Once dry, the grain has become malt, ready to be used for brewing.

Synthesis

The *gyóòhé* give great importance to malting: they say that if it is not done correctly, the beer won't taste good. That may be the reason why the first three steps (soaking, draining and resting) occur twice, while in other West African populations it usually occurs only once. Of first importance is the good management of the physical conditions: water (soaking), air (resting), sun and heat (agglomerating, crumbling). Table 16.1 gives an account of the importance of these natural elements during the process and of the consistency of the grain.

Table 16.1   Relative importance of natural elements on the consistency of the grain[6]

stages		water	air	heat	consistency of the grain
first soaking	súub'u	+++	-	*	soaked malt flour
resting	gíʔlb'ɔ	++	++	*	first germination (sprouts)
second soaking	tĩĩlbú	+++	-	*	swollen germinated grain
resting	gíʔlb'ɔ	++	++	*	second germination (plant)
agglomeration	píʔbú	+	+	++	fluid mass
crumbling-laying out	láhbɔ	-	+++	+++	crumbled mass and then dry malt

Brewing

Brewing lasts two days (see figures 16.2 and 16.3); one can drink beer in the morning of the third day. Women always use two pairs of jars for the brewing; generally one pair contains a particular fluid, the other one contains another fluid.

The First Day

'Milling' *yárbɔ*

'Malt' *kấmá* must be milled. This used to be done exclusively on a 'millstone' *níɾɛ*, but nowadays it's also made with a 'mechanical mill' *màsín dùuú* (machine / house). It then becomes 'malt flour' *kấm zwá*.

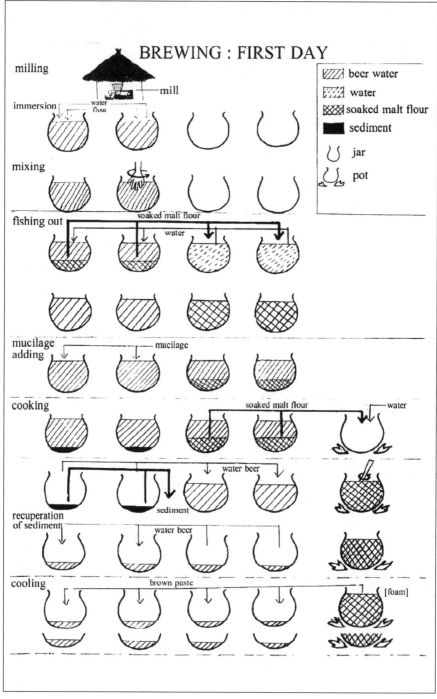

Figure 16.2 Brewing – first day. (Diagram drawn by the author in the field.)

'Immersion' *síĩbù*
This flour needs to be immersed in jars of water.

'Mixing' *síanbɔ*
Then one has to mix flour and water with the arm ('mixing' *síanbɔ*).

'Fishing out' *yàabɔ*
Once mixed, one waits until the flour settles down in the jars. This 'soaked malt flour' *kắm cágrè* needs to be fished out, separated from 'beer water' *rắ kúʔằ* which is much more liquid: this is the 'fishing out' *yàabɔ*. Soaked malt flour is fished out with a calabash, put in other jars of water and some of this water is added to the two first jars containing beer water. At the end of this sequence we have two jars full of beer water and two jars full of soaked malt flour. At this moment, 'floating residues' *kắm-súgdú* must be removed from the jars with a little strainer, in order not to have a bitter beer.

'Mucilage adding'*sálbɔ*
Then one adds a 'mucilaginous vegetal ingredient' *sánnɔ* into the jars containing beer water. It can be for example leaves or barks of *Hibiscus esculentus* (Malvaceae), *Bombax costatum* (Bombacaceae), *Andansonia digitata* (Bombacaceae), or *Piliostigma thonningii* (Caesalpiniaceae). Mucilage is a sticky fluid which settles thick particles at the bottom of the jars.

'Cooking' *rúgbɔ*
During this time, soaked malt flour has settled down in the jars. The beer water at the surface is removed and kept in a basin. Soaked malt flour is then cooked in one (or two) 'pot(s), metallic jar(s)' *búgmí zóoré* (fire / jar) during two or three hours.

'Recuperation of sediment' *zóobó*[7]
While the flour is being cooked, one removes beer water from the two first jars and pours it into the other jars. At the bottom of the first jars there is the 'sediment settled by mucilage' *pèennó*. One gathers this sediment with a calabash, strains it and dries it. It will be used later to prepare meals and sauces. The remaining beer water is shared between the four jars.

'Cooling' *yéeb'o*
When the soaked malt flour is cooked, white 'foam' *púh púurì* appears. It means the soaked malt flour has transformed into 'brown paste' *kɔ̃gré*. One must remove it from the pot and put it in the jars containing beer water, in order to cool it until the second day.

The second day
The second day begins when the liquid in the jars is clear and when it tastes sour. There are four main stages: separation of the layers, cooling, recuperation of sediment and fermentation.

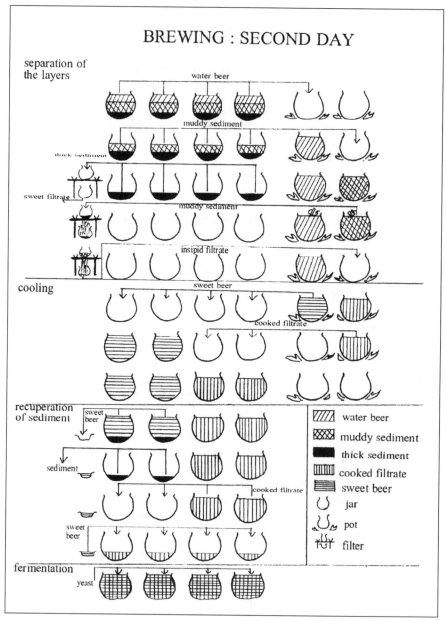

Figure 16.3   Brewing – second day.   (Diagram drawn by the author in the field.)

'Separation of the layers' *zʷàlgbɔ́*

This phase groups together three actions: 'separation of the layers' *zʷàlgbɔ́* properly speaking, 'cooking' *rúgbɔ̀* and 'filtering' *tʷàglbɔ́*.

Three layers of different nature then settle in the jars during the night. One takes off these three layers consecutively with a calabash, taking care not to make the liquid cloudy. The first layer (beer water) is clear, liquid and orange coloured. The second ('muddy sediment' *kʷɑ̃́ŋ kʷáré*) is beige and thick. These two first layers are cooked for several hours in separate pots. The last one ('thick sediment' *bíhì*) is brown and very thick. It is filtered in the 'filter' *tʷákká*, which is made up of two jars, one above the other, the upper one being pierced by little holes. Once filtered, one gets the 'sweet filtrate' *bʷálgá* which is red and creamy. Children are used to drinking this filtrate. Muddy sediments are also filtered (after about thirty minutes of cooking) to give the 'insipid filtrate' *tʷákk kúʔɑ̃́ sàbhgá* which is very clear. This filtrate is also cooked for five hours. Once cooked, it becomes the 'cooked filtrate' *sídgà*.

'Cooling' *yéeb'o*

Once cooked, the beer water (first layer) has become 'sweet beer' *rɑ̃́ núʔdɔ̀* which is red and sweet. One removes it from the pot and pours it into two jars. Cooked filtrate is also poured into two jars. The aim is to cool these two liquids.

'Recuperation of sediment' *zóobó*

Once cooled, sweet beer is put in a basin. At the bottom of the jar there is the 'sweet beer's sediment' *kɔ̃́ūdɔ̀* which would be drunk by children. After this operation, sweet beer and cooked filtrate are mixed together.

'Fermentation' *kùlgbɔ́*

When the liquid is cooled, one will put 'yeast' *rá béllè* in it. The liquid must not be too warm because it would kill the yeast. Four to six hours later, alcohol has developed and one can drink the beer.

Synthesis

One important fact that has been shown by this study is that the *gyóòhé* give great importance to the taste (sour, sweet) and to the consistency (thick, clear) of the fluids manipulated. They also have many terms for these fluids at each stage of the preparation. Table 16.2 sums up this process of brewing.

Table 16.2   Different treatments of the fluids

Fluids	consistency	color	taste	obtained from separation from	cooking to filtrate	filtrated	cooling	edible
beer water *rǎ-kʊ́ʔà*	liquid	light orange	~	~	6h	~	~	~	~
sediment settled by mucilage *pèennó*	sediment	grey	~	beer water	~	~	~	~	to eat dry
soaked malt flour *kǎm-cágrè*	sediment	grey	~	beer water	3h	~	~	~	~
brown paste *kɔ́grè*	sediment	brown	~	~	already cooked	~	~	yes	~
muddy sediment *kʷǎŋ-kʷáré*	sediment	beige	~	beer water	30 min	+	~	~	~
thick sediment *bíhì*	sediment	brown	~	muddy sediment	~	+	~	~	for pigs
sweet filtrate *bʷálgá*	liquid	red	sweet	~	~	~	+	~	to drink
insipid filtrate *tʷákk-kʊ́ʔǎ-sàbhgá*	liquid	light orange	~	~	4 h	~	+	~	~
cooked filtrate *síɗgà*	liquid	orange	~	~	already cooked	~	+	yes	~
sweet beer's sediment *kʊ́ʊ̃dɔ*	sediment	blurred dark red	sweet	sweet beer	~	~	~	~	to drink / for pigs
sweet beer *rǎ-nʊ́ʔdɔ*	liquid	red	sweet	~	already cooked	~	~	yes	to drink
beer *rǎǎ*	liquid	orange	alcohol	~	~	~	~	~	to drink

My presentation from the anthropological linguistics perspective shows the ideas the *gyóòhé* have about the different stages of the process and how they divide it into several steps. For example, some previous studies on other populations (Gentil 1944; Jolly 1996) put the malting and the milling of the grain together, whereas in my study milling is grouped with brewing. Some studies consider fermentation as an independent step, whereas I consider it as a part of the brewing. These are some of the many differences which exemplify the variety of concepts of beer and beer brewing in different cultures.

Notes

1. About the notation of the language: /ɪ, ĩ, ʊ, ʊ̃/ are lax vowels opposed to tensed vowels /i, e, u, o/; / ́/ and / ̀/ represent respectively high and low tones, [́] is a downstep; words in *gyóòré* are given in italics, translations between '…' quotation marks or (…) brackets (for composed items). / ̃/ *is used for nasal vowels.* /ʔ/ is a glottal consonant.

2. Traditional beer is called 'dolo' in local French.
3. Generically, *súub'u* refers to the 'filling of something in large quantities'.
4. Generically, *yòabɔ́* refers to 'choosing, sorting'.
5. Generically, *gíʔlb'ɔ* refers to 'lying down'.
6. The relative presence of the elements is symbolised by {+, ++, etc.}; absence of an element is noted {-}; a non-considered element is noted {*}.
7. Generically, *zóobó* refers to 'carving', especially wood.

References

Gentil, P. (1944) Fabrication du dolo (méthode Lobi), *Notes Africaines*, 23: 16–17.
Jolly, E. (1996) *La bière de mil dans la société dogon*, Thèse de doctorat, Université Paris X-Nanterre.
Lestrange, M.T. (1981) La consommation de bière de mil à Etyolo, village bassari du Sénégal oriental, *Objets et mondes*, XXI (3): 107–114.

CHAPTER 17
RICE BEER AND SOCIAL COHESION IN THE KELABIT HIGHLANDS, SARAWAK

Monica Janowski

> The etiquette of drinking is considerable ... the women are usually allowed to lead off, singing in high falsetto a song of welcome in which every few lines the audience, consisting of the entire house, repeats the last line or two as a chorus, allowing the singer a 'breather' and to think what she is going to say next, although some songs are of more or less permanent repetition. Having carried on like this for as much as five minutes, the glass is presented and the whole house joins in a deep ueh, rising in tone as the glass is tilted, and dying away as the glass is lowered again. (Banks 1937: 4)

While I was living in the Kelabit community of Pa' Dalih in the late 1980s and early 1990s, the etiquette described above accompanied the drinking of tea and coffee at *irau* feasts in the Kelabit Highlands in Sarawak, Malaysia.[1] Until the 1960s, it was part of the ceremony accompanying the drinking of *borak* – rice beer. The Kelabit were, in the past, famous for the quantities of *borak* which they made and drank. Now, though, they no longer make rice beer. Here I want to look at *borak*-drinking in the past, at the reasons for the abandonment of borak, and at the social world which has replaced the old borak-focused cosmos.

The plateau on which the group now known as the Kelabit[2] live, in the interior of Sarawak at the headwaters of the Baram River, is not the most obvious place to grow rice; the ecology is sub-montane tropical forest. However, the Kelabit of the Highlands are very successful rice-growers and this has meant that they are able not only to eat rice at every meal but have also, in the past, been able to make large quantities of rice beer. Tom Harrisson, the colourful character who, based in the Kelabit Highlands, directed the resistance movement against the Japanese code-named 'Operation Ants' during the Second World War, and who later became Curator of the Sarawak Museum (Heimann 1997), had this to say about Kelabit rice growing and *borak*-drinking:

> The Kelabits grow much more rice than they need to eat. They may drink almost as much again. Every sort of event – especially the only too frequent death feast – is an excuse for alcoholism ... A common excuse for alcoholism is the arrival of any distinguished visitor ... For the guest, the bombardment of rice beer is hard to take .... The stuff can be prepared in five days, unfortunately, since quantities can be prepared at news of your approach – which will always be at least a week ahead of you. The consequent 'party' may involve anything up to sixty tall Chinese jars of beer. (Harrisson 1949: 145–46)

Kelabit society and economy revolved at that time around the growing of rice, and indeed the same is true now. Success in rice-growing meant, and still means, social status. One of the most important ways in which this was expressed, until the 1960s, was through the brewing of rice beer to be shared with others. Beer was made by boiling rice, sprinkling it with a starter yeast, *lamud*, making the rice into balls (Figure 17.1), putting these balls of *penapa* into a large *bu'an* basket covered with banana leaves for a few days, and then transferring the balls of rice and yeast into jars where it would ferment for days or weeks. The alcohol which was generated through fermentation, called *pa pade* (rice water), was often put aside for consumption by smaller groups; water was then added to the penapa, and this was drunk as borak (Figure 17.1).

Other grains were also used to make borak. The small amounts of other grains such as Job's tears (*kului*) and millet (*bua' lenamud*) – still being grown in the late 1980s in Pa' Dalih but more rarely by 2009 – were grown primarily to make borak. However, borak was usually made of rice.

The essence of status, and the point of making rice beer, was providing for others. The Kelabit system of status hinges on a differentiation between people who are *doo* (good), and those who are *da'at* (bad). Being *doo* means being good at everything, such that you are able to host others as lavishly as possible; being *da'at* means the opposite, in other words always being dependent on others rather than having others dependent on you. You can provide for others through food and drink, mainly through the rice meal and, in the past, through providing rice beer. The prestige associated with making borak is underlined by the fact that it was made in valuable ceramic jars, including, at *irau* feasts (see below) in Chinese dragon jars (*belanai*); belanai were only owned by those of high status, leaders of longhouses and groups of longhouses.

For the Kelabit, consuming rice is a fundamental attribute of being a fully civilised human – as indeed is the case among most people in South East Asia, whether urban or upriver. I have argued that, for the Kelabit, feeding the rice meal to dependants is the basis of both kinship and of status (Janowski 2007).

Figure 17.1   Shaping partially dehusked and boiled rice mixed with starter yeast (*lamud*) into balls to be made into borak. These will be placed in *bu'an* baskets for a few days to begin to ferment. Mariam Lutup Ulun, September 1962. Photographer possibly Zunaidi bin Bolhassan or Tom Harrisson. Copyright Sarawak Museum. (Printed with permission of the Sarawak Museum).

Kelabit children are introduced to rice as early as possible. This is, nowadays, through the medium of thin rice porridge. In the past it was through borak; it would appear that in the past borak was considered an alternative, perhaps even a better, food for babies than rice porridge, as is reflected in what Cutfield, District Officer for Limbang and Lawas, wrote after his visit to a Kelabit house in the Limbang in 1936:

'I went and examined … [a sick child at the Kelabit leader Balang Imat's house], which looked anaemic, and found that its mother was dead. I enquired what they were feeding it on, and to my surprise they replied – '*burak*'. I asked if they were not giving it rice or water or *bubor* [rice gruel] or *krebang*, but they replied, 'No, only *burak*.' (Cutfield 1936: 116)

With the coming of Christianity from the 1950s onwards, the Kelabit gradually began to abandon the making and consumption of borak. The cessation of borak-making was seen as an important symbol of the transition to Christianity by the missionaries of the Borneo Evangelical Mission, who converted the Kelabit (Lees 1979). The Kelabit now belong to its successor church, the Sidang Injil Borneo (SIB). Many continue to believe that alcohol consumption is un-Christian.

Borak and Fertility

The drinking of borak was also associated with bringing men and women together sexually, and hence has associations with fertility. Rice in general brings men and women together; as I have discussed elsewhere, it is grown by the married couple as a unit, gradually bonding them as they establish a lasting marriage (Janowski 1995).

Although borak appears to have been drunk rather more by men than women, women were apparently willing drinkers too: 'The (Kelabit) women join in and neither dislike nor fear too much drink' (Banks 1937: 5). As older people in Pa' Dalih told me, drinking a dish of borak together was what united a couple in marriage before the Kelabit became Christian. At feasts young people took the opportunity to meet youngsters from other longhouses, and many unions were made at these events, lubricated by borak consumption. In the version of the Tukad Rini story told by Ngamung Raja of Long Dano to Carole Rubenstein in 1972, Tukad Rini's brother Iya' Utul Aling Bulan is wooed by Aruring Salud Bulan of the Moon through her offering of borak to him before coming to join him in the sleeping compartment in her longhouse (Rubenstein 1973).

Borak was brewed by women. Rice as crop and as food at the rice meal, and not only in the form of borak, is associated with women (Janowski 1995). In the story of Tukad Rini as told by Ngamung Raja, Aruring Salud Bulan sings a song of power (*nadadir*) telling of her making of borak before offering it to Iya' Utul Aling Bulan (ibid). This is parallel to the *nadadir* recited by Tukad Rini, Iya' Utul Aling Bulan and other male heroes in the story, which is about making war and killing enemies. Thus there was a parallel between borak-making for women and war-making for men, and both were associated with accessing, processing and possession of potency or power (*lalud*). Rice beer is associated more generally in South East Asia with a life-giving force, a force also associated with the valuable dragon jars (*belanai*) in which it is brewed,[3] and which are believed by the Kelabit to be animate. These jars are, among the Kelabit, passed down the male line, and are thus associated with men. In the brewing of rice beer in belanai jars, male and female were brought together, something which is associated with the generation of potent centres in the region (Fox 1980).

Borak and Social Cohesion

The rice meal, *kuman nuba*, literally 'eating rice' – although it consists of both rice and side dishes (described as 'that which is eaten with [rice]', *nok pengu-man*) – is a thrice-daily event at the level of the individual household or hearth-group, and is the main means of delineating and defining this unit (Janowski 1995). It is also eaten together by larger groups of people, but only at *irau* feasts and other special occasions.

Borak, on the other hand, was properly shared with members of other hearth-groups. It was not considered appropriate to drink alone. Until the 1960s/1970s, when they became Christian and abandoned borak-making, the Kelabit consumed borak frequently and in a variety of contexts, all social: in the rice fields at cooperative work groups, in the longhouse in the evenings, whenever there were any guests in the longhouse, and particularly at irau feasts, which were in fact usually simply described as borak, emphasising the fact that the defining feature of the whole occasion was the consumption of vast quantities of borak. This is what Edward Banks, Curator of the Sarawak Museum in the 1930s, tells us about the kind of context in which borak was drunk:

> [I]f he hasn't got any visitors handy [a Kelabit] will send out and invite his friends from the next house. Without some such incentive many do not drink at all, and those that do only occasionally and to such a small extent that it scarcely matters. (Banks 1937: 5)

While the rice meal is an ordered, controlled event, borak-drinking was far from controlled. However, it did not, from the reports of observers, generate disagreements, rivalries or quarrels, but rather tended to generate a strong sense of cohesion. This was despite the fact that Borneo rice beer was quite potent – about 20 per cent alcohol by volume according to Banks (Banks 1937: 4). Banks again:

> I do not suppose a week passes but that [a Kelabit house has] one or two cheerful nights. ... [T]heir rice crops are large and frequent, seldom failing, and by this means they are able to supply themselves with plenty of food and with about an equal sufficiency left over from which to brew drink ... Nothing much can be done in a Kelabit house without them having this preliminary drinking bout ... Considering the amount and

frequency of their potations, quarrels are scarce ... less than a hundred
people will finish up 300 gallons or more of rice spirit [probably rice beer
is meant here] in two nights and a day. (Banks 1937: 5–6)

The 'two days and a night' mentioned here are almost certainly a reference to
a secondary burial feast. The most ostentatious consumption of borak was at
such feasts, which were often simply referred to as borak, although they could
also be described as *irau* or *tseraad*. They were held by high-status individuals
(*lun doo*, literally 'good people'), for the honour of their deceased relatives
(and themselves). Such feasts brought together huge groups of people, and
vast quantities of rice were needed to feed them and provide them with adequate rice beer. Being able to do this, and to make possible such a level of
social activity, was associated with high status. At these events, very large
amounts of borak were consumed, interspersed with rice meals at which the
only accompaniment to rice was meat from domestic animals – buffaloes, pigs
and deer. Twenty to thirty Chinese dragon jars (*belanai*) full of borak were
commonly drunk at one of these feasts. The longer the feast went on the better
– two or three days was usual and four or five days was not out of the ordinary.
As part of the festivities, a mark on the landscape was made – a stone erected,
a notch cut in a mountainside, or an oxbow lake created by diverting a small
river. This was a permanent mark which inscribed in the landscape the prestige
of the individual who had died and of his heirs, who had proved their ability
to bring large numbers of people together, bonded through the consumption
of borak. This bonding was emphasised by the settling of all debts prior to the
commencement of drinking on the part of guests. Thus, all guests were allies
and friends. Feasts were a means of settling social tensions and clearly deline-
ated the social universe within which there should be peace.

   The Kelabit used to recite what can best be described as sagas about the
travels and adventures of mythical ancestors, and the holding of borak feasts
was also associated with status and success in war in such stories. The most
prominent of Kelabit heroic ancestors is Tukad Rini, who, with his kinsmen,
is said to have travelled beyond the sky and to the moon to do battle with other
peoples. Each time he was victorious – always after very long and strenuous
battles – this victory is described as being celebrated by the holding of a borak
feast. This cemented the relationship between the allies who had been fighting
together and made clear the distinction between them and their foes, who did
not drink with them. Thus again we see the generation of cohesion through
the co-consumption of borak.

Borak and Social Hierarchy

Although the making and drinking of borak was associated with a statement of
social hierarchy through the generation of status, the unstructured nature of
borak-drinking events actually led, through gradual inebriation, to an egalitarian

form of cohesion, contrasted to the hierarchical nature of the controlled event which is the rice meal, then and now. Edward Banks had this to say about borak-drinking bouts he had witnessed in the 1930s: 'The scene is almost indescribable ... all authority of their Chief has long since faded away for the moment' (Banks 1937: 5–6). Tom Harrisson found the same in the 1940s and 1950s:

> The socially senior person is served first; the distinguished visitor has dish after dish pressed upon him. The lower classes sit out on the perimeter, until gradually all barriers break down and people are serving each other in all directions, amidst an indescribable babble of conversation and that loud laughter beloved of the Kelabit. (Harrisson 1949: 146)

Robert Lian-Saging has pointed out that his grandfather, Semera Langit, a high-status leader, made a point of brewing special jars of the strongest form of borak, *abpa pade*, especially for drinking with his 'common' guests, telling these guests: 'I can drink with my peers but that is common, you are all my special guests so let's have a drink to that, I can join my peers later for they will not leave the *belanai* till I join them' (email from Robert Lian-Saging, 1 September 2009). In doing this he was clearly emphasising an egalitarianism associated with consumption of borak.

Thus, although borak was provided by one hearth-group, which derived status from this, borak-drinking itself was not associated with the clear construction of a social hierarchy between the provider of the borak and those provided for. This is in contrast to what happens in the provision of food for others through the rice meal; as I have discussed elsewhere, this generates social differentiation (Janowski 1995, 2007). It seems likely that the regular dissolution of differences and emphasis which came out of regular informal drinking bouts contributed to a sense of community which was less structured than the hierarchical relations between people established through feeding or being fed a rice meal.

'New Life' and the Abandonment of Borak

The Kelabit are devout Christians. They became Christian through their own volition, inviting missionaries in, encouraging them and supporting them. All are now Christian apart from a small number who are Muslim through marriage to Muslims, and one unusual individual who led his family into Islam. For the Kelabit, Christianity is a way of providing them with a means of effectively accessing the power (*lalud*) of God. They see their Christianity as the basis of their success in the modern world. This has been considerable, with many Kelabit holding prominent posts in Malaysian society.

   The abandonment of borak is seen not only by the missionaries but also by the Kelabit themselves as emblematic of their adoption of Christianity, of their 'break with the past', of their adoption of a 'new life' (*ulun bru*) (Lian-Saging

1976/77) and of their ability to take on new things and to innovate. Like adherence, before Christianity, to the bird omens which dictated that people should stay home from the fields many days of the year, drinking was seen as having impeded economic performance in the past. Therefore it was felt that giving it up was sensible, and would allow them to be more rapidly successful in the modern world. Tom Harrisson noted the Kelabit inclination to innovate and the link between this and Christianity:

> [T]hen, in 1945, still living strictly in their own Kelabit way of life, they were experimentalists, constantly, and of themselves, trying new ideas ... Always ready to try something else, go somewhere new, do things ... No one from outside told them to do anything they had not evolved for themselves ... Now, in 1958, a new order is coming in. The dead are buried with wooden crosses. The great irau feasts, some of which fed and drank 500 guests for four or five days, are now Christian meetings and festivals at Easter and Christmas ... Some villages are now 100 per cent non-drinking, non-smoking, non-swearing, non-dancing and sabbatarian. (Harrisson 1958: 190–91).

Sweetened tea and coffee have now taken the place of borak in the social contexts when borak would have been drunk in the past. A significant amount of the ritual surrounding drinking has been maintained in relation to drinking tea and coffee. Thus, I witnessed people being encouraged to drink tea and coffee with drinking songs in the late 1980s and early 1990s; tea and coffee being forced down the drinker's throat; and, in Pa' Dalih in the late 1980s, tea and coffee being dispensed at *irau* feasts (now of course no longer called borak feasts) in the same way as was usual in the past when distributing borak (see Figure 17.2). The drinking event still takes place, then; but it is radically different since the drink has no inebriating effect on the drinker.

Prayer may be seen as a partial substitute for drink in leading to an altered state of consciousness and a sense of egalitarian cohesion. The Kelabit are Pentecostalist Christians and individuals sometimes go into altered states of consciousness and 'speak in tongues', communicating the words of God to other believers through translators. Through prayer, it is believed that the *lalud*[4] – the power – of the Holy Spirit enters into people. This leads to an altered consciousness which has some parallels with the state of inebriation through alcohol.

Economic and Social Changes and the Abandonment of Borak

Greater interaction with the outside world has led to radical social and economic changes. The Kelabit have been successful in education and many now have very good jobs in the town environment; but of course many have more

Figure 17.2 Balang Telian dispensing sweet tea at the *irau* for Paran To'oh and Sinah Paran To'oh on 13 April 1987. Copyright Kaz and Monica Janowski.

menial jobs. Differential access to cash and to success in the outside world has created divisions among the Kelabit, since it has led to differences in lifestyle and social environment. There is an increasingly less cohesive social environment both in the highlands and in town. The 'sharing' society which was characteristic of the Kelabit Highlands before the Second World War has gradually been replaced by a more individually oriented, more competitive and divided society. While in the past leaders derived their roles from achievements within Kelabit society, and were accepted widely (if their position was no longer accepted, people would vote with their feet and follow a new leader to establish a new longhouse), nowadays a leader's position derives from a combination of material wealth, which is sometimes resented, and from holding posts which are allocated by the government for political reasons – longhouse leader (*ketua kampong*) or overall chief (*penghulu*).

These changes are reflected and underlined in the switch from making excess rice into borak to selling rice to town. Borak was something in which all partook equally and which did not differentiate individuals in a practical, long-term sense by generating different styles of living. The making of borak meant, in fact, the regular elimination of much of the accumulated difference in wealth between households, although some of this was also converted into prestige possessions (beads, gongs and jars). However, it became possible in 1962, when a regular air service from Bario to the coast began, for those living in the Bario area to send rice to town for sale. Individuals working in town also began to send cash up to their relatives. Some cash is used to pay for sugar, tea and coffee to be offered to participants in cooperative work parties and at feasts, and to buy gifts for guests at *irau*; but much of it is used in ways which fossilise differences between individuals and between hearth-groups – to purchase material possessions made outside the highlands and to generate different styles of living. The sale of excess rice rather than its consumption as borak is arguably divisive and socially differentiating. It is associated with the reduction in a 'sharing' lifestyle among the Kelabit which is linked to the greater presence of cash.

Many Kelabit would argue that the abandonment of borak has led to their society being more ordered and peaceable. However, although there is no doubt that alcohol can fuel quarrels, this depends on the context in which it is drunk. Borak-drinking does not appear to have commonly led to quarrels among the Kelabit, and this was undoubtedly due to the fact that it was drunk within a context in which there was a heavy emphasis on social cohesion and censure of fighting.

Borak-drinking has also been associated by missionaries with social disintegration. It would appear that among the closely related Murut people of the Limbang and Trusan rivers high levels of borak consumption were indeed linked to social anomie:

> In language and customs Muruts and Kelabits are very closely allied but I think it is fair to say the drink has got the former down ... One may see a man come home from his farm and after food settle down to his own jar until he falls over sideways to sleep without going to bed, and wakes where he fell to stagger off to work next morning .... their fertility is declining, their physique fails early, and the generally indescribably filthy conditions under which they live is telling and has told on them for so long that the race is declining. (Banks 1937: 6)

There are, however, good reasons for arguing that the consumption of borak is less strongly associated with social anomie than is the consumption of town-bought alcohol. During the 1980s and 1990s industrially processed alcohol was rarely consumed by Kelabit, and when it was this was compound brandy purchased in sachets in town, consumed in secret. In 2009, there is an increasing level of alcohol consumption in the Kelabit Highlands. Although borak is occasionally made, most alcohol consumed is beer brought in from town.

Alcohol is nowadays consumed in a much less structured and controlled context than was borak in the past. Since it has to be bought, it is also associated with a lack of sharing with others. Most alcohol is now consumed by men, individually or in small groups. It is sometimes associated with uncontrolled male aggression and violence. The consumption of town-bought beer now appears to have the function of bonding small groups of men engaged in male activities rather than, as in the consumption of borak in the past at feasts, the whole of society. The consumption of town-bought beer in 2009 is still undoubtedly associated with sexual desire, but without the ordered gender complementarity which was linked to borak making and consumption in the past, when women made borak, offered it to men, and drank it with them.

Conclusion

The story of borak in the Kelabit Highlands reflects the changes which have taken place in Kelabit society over the past fifty years. Borak in many ways stands for the old way of life. The abandonment of borak stood for a move to enter a new world, a 'new life', associated with Christianity. The Kelabit have been eager to succeed in this new world. However, they have not wanted to entirely abandon the old world, which is at the core of their identity on both an individual and a group level. Borak is a difficult symbol, since it is a strong symbol both of what they see as bad and what they see as good in the old world. It represents the old beliefs and practices, and stands in opposition to Christianity; but it also represents the old sharing way of life, a way of life which bonded people together.

While in the late 1980s it seemed clear to all Kelabit with whom I spoke that the abandonment of borak was a positive move, people seemed less sure about this by the early twenty-first century. Many people expressed, by this time, a certain amount of regret about the fact that it is not made any more, and some women openly made it again. It seems likely that it is not a coincidence that, at the same time, people also express a regret that among the Kelabit there is less sharing, more individualism, and less of an emphasis on social cohesion than in the past.

The story of borak can be seen as an illustration of the complex social significance of alcohol and its potential to be on the one hand dangerous and negative and on the other hand unifying and positive (see papers in Gefou-Madianou 1992; Wilson 2004). Due to its power to alter behaviour and consciousness, alcohol perhaps always teeters on the verge, always carrying the potential of both negative and positive. Among the Kelabit, with the advent of Christianity, borak swung from its position on the positive side of the verge right over to the negative side, but is now in a rather anomalous position, representing both the bad and the good in the old world as well as the bad in the new world. As the contributions to the collection edited by Wilson in particular emphasise, alcohol is often associated with constructions of identity. While borak was associated with constructions of common identity among those who considered themselves kin, town-bought beer is associated with a process of constructing a new identity or identities, particularly among young men. These are individualistic, exclusive, male-only and sometimes associated with uncontrolled aggression. Although Kelabit are generally positive about the 'break with the past' and the new world in which they increasingly live (Lian-Saging 1976/77), they appear to be increasingly negative about some aspects of this, in particular the loss of a strong social cohesion. Town-bought beer can perhaps be seen as standing for this, while there is a sense of some nostalgia about the social cohesion associated with the consumption of borak.

Notes

1. My fieldwork among the Kelabit began with my Ph.D. fieldwork in 1986–88, supported by the UK Economic and Social Research Council. Further periods of fieldwork since then have been supported by the British Academy and the UK Arts and Humanities Research Council, the latter through the project 'The Cultured Rainforest' (2007–2010). Thanks are due to these funders, and to the people of the community of Pa' Dalih.
2. The term Kelabit was not originally one used by the people now known by this term to describe themselves, but has now been accepted as a label which is meaningful (Lian-Saging 1976/77: 4–12).
3. 'In his book *The Golden Germ*, the archaeologist F.D.K. Bosch gives numerous examples of this symbol (the jar) in the art of India and of the Southeast Asian regions which have undergone Indian influence. It frequently assumes the form of a vase containing a liquid which holds the "life-giving, regenerating, health, opulence and fertility-bestowing" essence, from which one or more flowers – often lotuses – protrude' (de Josselin de Jong 1964–5. 288–9).
4. Sometimes the Malay translation of this term, *kuasa*, is used.

References

Banks, E. (1937) Drink, *Sarawak Gazette*, 67: 3–6.
Cutfield, H.E. (1936) Visit to the Kelabit of the Ulu Medihit, *Sarawak Gazette*, 68: 115–116.
Fox, J.J. (1980) *The Flow of Life: Essays on Eastern Indonesia*, Harvard University Press, Cambridge, Massachusetts.
Gefou-Madianou, D. (ed.) (1992). *Alcohol, Gender and Culture*, Routledge, London.
Harrisson, T. (1949) Explorations in Central Borneo, *The Geographical Journal*, CXIV(4–6): 129–150.
Harrisson, T. (1958). The Peoples of Sarawak VII and VIII: The Kelabits and Muruts, *Sarawak Gazette*, 84(1208): 187–191.
Heimann, J.M. (1997) *The Most Offending Soul Alive: Tom Harrisson and his remarkable life*, University of Hawai'i Press, Honolulu.

Janowski, M. (1995). The hearth-group, the conjugal couple and the symbolism of the rice meal among the Kelabit of Sarawak. In Carsten, J. and Hugh-Jones, S. *About the House: Levi-Strauss and beyond*, Cambridge University Press, Cambridge: 84–104.

Janowski, M. (2007). Being 'big', being 'good': feeding, kinship, potency and status among the Kelabit of Sarawak. In Janowski, M. and Kerlogue, F. *Kinship and Food in Southeast Asia*, NIAS Press, Copenhagen: 93–120.

Lees, S. (1979) *Drunk before Dawn*, Overseas Missionary Fellowship, Sevenoaks, Kent.

Lian-Saging, R. (1976/77) *An ethno-history of the Kelabit tribe of Sarawak. A brief look at the Kelabit tribe before World War II and after*, Graduation Exercise submitted in partial fulfilment of the requirements for the Degree of Bachelor of Arts, Hons., Jabatan Sejarah, University of Malaya, Kuala Lumpur.

Rubenstein, C. (1973) Poems of indigenous peoples of Sarawak – some of the songs and chants: Part II, *Sarawak Museum Journal*, XXI(12): 723–1127.

Wilson, T.M. (ed.) (2004) *Drinking Cultures: Alcohol and identity*, Berg, Oxford.

CHAPTER 18
TRADITION AND CHANGE: BEER CONSUMPTION IN NORTHEAST LUZON, PHILIPPINES

Dante M. Aquino and *Gerard A. Persoon*

Introduction

A few years ago the government of the Philippines launched a campaign to strengthen their national identity by popularising various national symbols, as throughout its history since independence the lack of national identity has been the concern of many politicians and nationalist authors. In addition to the common national symbols like the flag, the national anthem and the national heroes, other national symbols were widely publicised. Among these are a national bird (the Philippine eagle, *Pithecophaga jefferyi*), a national tree (*narra*, *Pterocarpus indicus*), a national animal (water buffalo, *Bubalus bubalis*), a national dance (the bamboo dance called *tinikling*), a national house (*nipa* hut), and a national costume for men and women. These were popularised through postage stamps aimed at strengthening the feeling of unity and common identity among the Filipino people. Ironically there was no national drink. Beer would easily have qualified for that distinction and the San Miguel Corporation, as by far the biggest supplier, could have been chosen as the national brewery. That neither of these was added to the list is probably due both to the fact that neither is indigenous to the country, and to the fact that they are also connected to what many people consider to be a national vice. Drinking in this predominantly Catholic country is also associated with drunkenness, gambling, household unrest, and politicians behaving badly.

In this paper we shall describe the use of alcoholic drinks in the Philippines. First of all we shall describe a number of traditional drinks and continue with a discussion about how many of these were replaced by products from commercial breweries because of changes in land-use patterns, improved infrastructure and increased wealth. We will focus on the Cagayan Valley in north-east Luzon and on the way in which drinking is incorporated into the social life of people. We will pay special attention to logging operations and their impact on some forest-dwelling peoples.

Indigenous Alcoholic Drinks in the Philippines

Various kinds of traditional alcoholic drinks can be found in the Philippines. Many of the different ethnic groups in this country used to produce particular kinds of drinks and they had done so long before the country was 'discovered' by Ferdinand Magellan in 1521. In an interesting book on pre-colonial conditions in the country, Scott (1997) mentioned indigenous drinks and described, based on historical records, how these were made in various parts of the archipelago. That the inhabitants prepared their own drinks and were big drinkers was what the Spaniards discovered when they landed in the Visayas, the group of islands in the central Philippines.

In those days, welcoming and entertaining guests were marked by the drinking of beverages. Beverages also played a very important role in sealing the bonds of friendship. The historic 'Blood Compact', made between Rajah Sikatuna and Miguel Lopez de Legazpi on 16 March 1565, is commemorated through a big monument in Barrio Bool on Bohol island (Cortes *et al.* 2000: 30–31). This marker shows their statues drinking from one wine cup in which each have supplied drops of their own blood.

Traditional Drinks in Northern Luzon

We shall describe the more common drinks produced in Northern Luzon, basing our information both on published accounts and on our personal experiences in the area.

Tapuy

Tapuy is a beverage made from rice. It is always prepared within the home and only in limited quantities, seldom for commercial purposes. People from the Southern Cordillera, the Ifugaos, Bontocs and Kankanays in the provinces of Ifugao, Benguet and Nueva Vizcaya used to have this rice wine stored in a dark, cold corner of the house while ageing. It is readily offered when important visitors are in the house or during special occasions. It is prepared by first cooking the rice. After the cooked rice has cooled, yeast is added to it and mixed thoroughly. The mixture is then placed in earthen jars and stored for the ageing process. It is usually prepared after the harvest season. Since, because of irrigation, the locals can easily produce two crops per year, *tapuy* is prepared twice a year. A batch is ready around the next harvesting period just in time for drinks at the end of a harvest day. At this time the mixture is moist or watery. The liquid is extracted from the very soft blend and strained. The concoction is then stored in the same earthen jar or in big bottles, ready for drinking from then on.

Binubudan

Binubudan is an Ilocano and Pangasinense delicacy – eaten as 'alcoholic' rice. It is prepared in the same manner as the *tapuy*. After five to seven days the mixture is ready for consumption. It is served on plates instead of glasses and the moist 'cake' is eaten. The effect on the consumers is the same as an alcoholic beverage. When too much is consumed, one gets drunk and later has a hangover. The preparation of *binubudan* is limited to the household and is only occasional. The quantity is limited to an amount that can be consumed within one to, at most, five days. Beyond this the alcohol content becomes so strong that its 'palatability' is reduced until it is hardly edible.

Basi

Basi is a dark coloured (reddish black) beverage made from sugar cane. It is an Ilocano beverage but known to be produced by other ethnic groups too. It was a common beverage in the Cagayan Valley region before the 1970s, when there were vast lands devoted to permanent dry farming, a great portion of which was planted with sugar cane. *Basi* was then commercially available in the market. When various portions of the region were irrigated in the 1970s, the production of many permanent dry crops was discontinued. And so was the production of *basi*, because *basi* is a by-product of the processing of sugar cane.

After cutting, the canes are taken to a press for the sugar juice to be extracted. The juice is then placed in a big metal vat. The raw juice is boiled in an underground kiln to turn it into syrup and finally into lumps of sugar. The juice extraction process takes almost the whole night, and the cooking/ boiling process takes most of the following day. At certain points in the long boiling process, an amount is taken from the boiling solution and placed in containers. Fruits from a tree locally called *samak* or *binunga* (*Mallotus philippinensis*) are added for seasoning, colour and aroma. Around two months later, a sweetish *basi* is ready but it is at its best at around the sixth month.

Tuba and lambanog

Tuba is a beverage extracted from various palm species, most notably the coconut and the *nipa*. Extracting *tuba* may start the moment a palm tree starts to fruit. *Tuba* is tapped by cutting the pedicel (the stalk connecting the bunch of fruits to the trunk or stem) thus detaching the young fruits. To obtain the most extract, it is best to do this when the coconuts are about knuckle size or when the pedicel is fully developed. A siphon is attached to the cut part and connected to a covered receptacle. The accumulated sap extract is collected every morning. *Tuba* is best consumed the same day it is collected. The day after that it becomes sour and unpalatable.

Lambanog is distilled *tuba*. It is produced particularly in the province of Batangas. It is a very strong colourless drink. It is usually smoothed by adding resins and/or chopped apples. Through this process, its aroma is also improved and a little colour is added.

Recent Developments

The development of the Philippines in the last quarter of the twentieth century has been based on agriculture. Priority was given to the development of potential rice production areas by building roads for accessibility and by the construction of dams for irrigation. As a result of this thrust for development by the government, vast areas previously devoted to permanent dry agriculture were converted to irrigated rice farms planted with the high yielding varieties. With improved accessibility through the construction of all-weather roads and numerous bridges, new commodity items came from the urban centres. The logging companies even hastened accessibility to forest areas. This exposed everyone to the invasion of readily available consumer goods, which displaced the local and traditional ones. Furthermore, the onslaught was further facilitated and bolstered by improved communication through radio and television.

The local home-made beverages in north-east Luzon were replaced by commercially brewed and distilled products because of two forces: the replacement of the crops previously used as raw materials by rice; and the influx of readily available substitute products. All this was promoted by the advance of communication technology and fuelled by aggressive commercials.

San Miguel Beer and Ginebra San Miguel: The Replacements

With its seven big subsidiary companies, the San Miguel Corporation is the biggest beverage company in the Philippines. In 1999, it controlled 84 per cent of the domestic beer market. It had expanded operations in Asia with breweries in Hong Kong targeting the mainland China market, and in Jakarta. It is also the largest liquor manufacturer in the Philippines producing eleven gin, brandy and whisky brands (www.ginebrasanmiguel.com.ph). Although the main products of the San Miguel Corporation are beer and gin, it has diversified to bottled water, ready-to-drink juice, food (meat, processed meat, dairy products, animal feeds) and packaging. Its San Miguel Brewery subsidiary produces the country's most popular beer – San Miguel Pale Pilsen and seven other well-known beer brands (www.sanmiguelbrewery.com.ph).

All-out Advertising

The electrification of the Philippines started in the 1970s at the same time as the construction of the Maharlika Highway which links the whole of Luzon to the Visayas and Mindanao. All-out promotion of beer and liquor products has been pursued through radio and television advertisements touching on the weaknesses of the male Filipino: i.e., his concepts of 'manhood', 'machismo', and 'virility'. Examples of some jingles and quotes: *'Inumin ng tunay na lalaki!'* (The drink of the real man!); *'Atin ito!'* (This is ours!); *'Sarap mag-San Miguel Beer!'* (So delicious to have San Miguel Beer!); *'Barangay Ginebra!'* (The Village Gin!). These advertisements feature the most popular movie actors and sportsmen, usually with a popular and sexy actress in the background. These have significant effects on the *macho* Filipino, who usually idolises popular movie and sports personalities, many of whom enter politics and go on to win national and local elections by a landslide.

The Cagayan Valley

The Cagayan Valley in north-east Luzon is bounded by three mountain ranges, to the east the Sierra Madre, to the west the Cordillera and to the south the Caraballo Mountains. To the north lies the Babuyan Channel, beyond which is the South China Sea. The area has a total land mass of over 26,000 square kilometres. The regional capital is Tuguegarao, about 485 km from Manila along the Maharlika Highway. The climate is a typical tropical monsoon climate. During the wet season the area is often struck by destructive typhoons.

In 2000 the population of the region was just over 2.8 million (NEDA 2005: 20) with an annual growth of 1.8 per cent from 1980 onwards. Regional population density is less than half that of the national average. This makes the Cagayan Valley one of the least densely populated areas in the country. The population is predominantly rural and lives in the countryside in villages and hamlets. It is ethnically highly diverse. In addition to the local groups (Gaddang, Ybanag, Ytawes and Yogad) there has been a large immigration of Ilocano from north-west Luzon and of mountain tribes from the Cordillera. Capital towns and the major commercial centres are all located along the national highway which runs parallel to the Cagayan River. This situation still reflects events from its colonial history (Persoon *et al.* 2009). The Spanish rulers had established commercial, administrative and religious centres in the flood plains which were opened up mainly for the cultivation of tobacco. It is only recently that a number of boom towns based on large-scale logging activities have developed in the foothills of the Sierra Madre.

Social Events and Drinking along the Cagayan River

In the towns along the Maharlika Highway the habit of drinking is closely connected with certain ceremonies, types of activities and gatherings, predominantly of males. It is very rare for Filipino women to drink in public; it is *'just not done'*.

Celebrations

The Philippines is predominantly a Catholic country, a legacy of Spanish colonisation. Once a year, people celebrate the feast day of the patron saints of their towns or *barangays* (villages), as well as the foundation days of these communities. Pompous celebrations are prepared for various other occasions: baptisms, weddings, anniversaries, graduations, debut celebrations, reunions, *despedidas* (trip send offs) like those for overseas workers, and *bienvenidas* (welcomes after a trip) especially for the numerous overseas workers. All these and more are celebrated by a feast of food and drinks. No celebration is complete, at least for the men, without alcoholic beverages. In these feasts, a special place is devoted to drinking with a complete set of the 'necessities', such as table(s) with surrounding chairs and cooling facilities. A significant portion of the budget for these occasions goes on alcohol.

Fiestas (patronal feasts or town-foundation feasts) of towns are celebrated usually for a period of three to five days of merry making. Celebrations, sometimes graced by national government officials, local politicians and celebrities, last day and night. During the nights, with sectoral (religious, veterans, village leaders, women's club, public school teachers, etc.) sponsors, activities such as ballroom dancing and performances by various groups are accompanied by live bands or a simple sound system. On the last night a beauty contest is held to crown a Fiesta Queen who will be paraded around the town the following day, a fitting culmination of the fiesta. Day activities include ground demonstrations (folk and modern dances, ball games, etc.) from various agencies for public viewing. Sports or athletic competitions are sometimes held, the prizes for which are usually awarded during the last night of celebration.

Cockfights

One of the biggest events, in terms of money and crowds, during the fiesta is the cock fight derby. This is a very special event for big-time cockfight *aficionados* and gamblers. During fiestas, the cock fight is an exceptional affair and a big event. Instead of the regular matches by pairs of cocks, a cock fight derby (multiple cock entries from a number of gamblers) is held. Each cock entry will fight (to the death) with others' entries until the champion cock will emerge. In a derby, a participant must 'enter' his best cocks and he has to pay a fixed amount (which will be his bet) for the 'pot money'. From the pot money, a 'jackpot' is set aside for the overall champion. The overall winner, the entry with the most wins, gets the jackpot at the end. Jackpot prizes in derbies may range from US$2,500 to US$12,500 during fiestas of larger towns. For city and national derbies (e.g., the World Slasher Cup 8-Cock Derby periodically held at the Araneta Coliseum, Quezon City) these can reach enormous amounts of money (www.sabong.net.ph/forum/forum).

Whenever and wherever there is a big crowd, especially of men as in a cock fight, drinking sessions are common. Stalls selling drinks and food abound. Some generous winners may decide to spend part of their winnings on buying food and drinks (called 'blow-out') for their friends and friends' acquaintances or on giving cash dole-outs to others (called *balato*). While the cock fighting is going on, winners of earlier matches may already be providing a 'blow-out' outside treating other people with liquor or beer and food. It is not unusual if after some rounds of beer, the drinking session may be extended, as the winner may buy more, or other winners may buy another round. In such instances, the cock fight winners eventually end up as losers, while the beer and liquor sellers will be the winners at the end of the day.

Work

Just a few decades ago, drinking was a usual consequence of any group work undertaken by men. People then had closer social relationships and neighbours and acquaintances were involved in each other's activities. In those days, house construction was usually done by neighbours, with one among them being a 'master' carpenter. On particular days, when the task needed more people, adult male neighbours would be invited to join the *bayanihan* (free group work). Aside from lunch and two snacks (one in mid-morning and another in the afternoon) that the host provided, he also offered gin or beer at the end of the day, before each participant went home for dinner. Activities that could not be done by the household were usually accomplished with the cooperation of others. All activities on the farm that required the participation of others, e.g., ploughing, planting, weeding, and harvesting, usually terminated with a round of gin or beer drinking at the end of the day.

These kinds of drinking, however, are not that common any more, particularly in the areas with highly intensive agriculture along the banks of the Cagayan River. Most tasks related to the household whether in the house or on the farm today involve specially skilled workers and activities are carried out for a price, through a contract. On the farm for example, everything can be contracted to skilled workers, who will do the job more efficiently and faster than unskilled neighbours. Transactions now have become strictly business-like, without the round of drinks at the end of the day.

Also in the past, liquor was used as part of some of the ceremonies related to the work undertaken. For example, before the first house was laid for the so-called ground breaking ceremony, the foundation was sprinkled with gin and animal blood, allegedly to make the building foundation sturdier and to appease the deities therein, so that the household would be left in peace. With building contractors having taken over building houses nowadays, the house is ready for occupancy when turned over to the owner and so the ceremonies are no longer practiced.

'For the Boys'

Filipino men socialise with their peers usually over a round of drinks either in one of their homes or in restaurants, or in the beer houses that abound along the roads. Such occasions are just 'for the boys'. Among young men alcoholic drinks are a way to peer acceptance. Just about anything can instantly become a cause for celebration, and this usually means sharing a bottle of gin or a case of beer.

Men's gin drinking sessions, wherever they may be, are usually tests of strength and stamina. Only one glass is used and a *tangero* (person in charge of pouring gin in the glass) is assigned. He pours the same amount in the glass and passes it around, everyone drinking, with no one spared. The *tagay* ('shot') may be immediately followed by another shot of a 'chaser' (water or Coca Cola, also a product of the San Miguel Corporation). This goes on in rotation until the supply ends or drinkers surrender or are 'dead drunk', whichever comes first. A 'survivor' is established as *tomador* (strong drinker). Drinking sessions may sometimes last through the night.

A necessary ingredient in drinking sessions is the *pulutan* (finger food) which is eaten as the session goes on. This may range from peanuts to fish, canned sardines or meat, the last being the most usual. This is the reason why many beer houses (which also sell gin) are equipped with a *turo-turo* (a cooked-food stall) because orders usually come in pairs (drinks and *pulutan*). Special delicacies for *pulutan* in the Philippines are goat meat and various fish recipes (raw to roasted), but for northern Luzon it used to be dog meat, at least before the dog-ban law was promulgated in the late 1990s. It was then common to see an *azucena* (a restaurant selling 'ready-to-eat' recipes from dog meat) at strategic locations along national roads and in towns. Even during community feasts, dog meat was always a delicacy served with other dishes on the table. These days, as a result of protests by dog lovers, dog meat is no longer consumed 'in public'. It is however still considered a delicacy among certain groups.

San Mariano: The Town where Beer Flowed

San Mariano is a town in the central part of the Cagayan Valley within the foothills of the Sierra Madre mountain ranges. It is about 40 km from the provincial capital town of Ilagan. As it is situated in mountainous terrain with only some narrow alluvial flood plains along its rivers, before the 1970s the status of San Mariano had lagged behind that of other towns found within the wide plains in central Isabela Province (Aquino 1995).

Things started to change in the 1970s when large-scale, mechanised logging came into the town. A great portion of the western slopes of the Sierra Madre is within the jurisdiction of the town. In these areas, timber licence agreements were awarded to big concessionaries. Large automated sawmills were established in the town. These attracted job-seekers from near and far; so, migrants flocked to the town. San Mariano instantly became 'progressive', full of restaurants and beer houses. There was even a so-called 'red light district' within the town. During this period of plenty, the freight haulers of San Miguel Beer could hardly cope with the demand from the town. From a fourth-class municipality, San Mariano was upgraded to first-class and maintained this status during the logging years of the 1970s and 1980s.

Everything ended just as suddenly as it started when the logging moratorium was declared in 1992. San Mariano became a 'ghost' town of sorts. As the 'easy money' was gone, commercial activity was much reduced. Although many migrants opted to stay, the population was greatly dissipated to its current 40,000. There still remains a demand for beer, liquor and gin but it is far lower than 'during those days'.

Logging and Alcohol

Logging is men's work. When there is logging in a town, there is increased activity due to the presence of outsiders like loggers (chainsaw operators, truck drivers, bulldozer operators, helpers, tree markers, log scalers and sawmill operators), and even the families of some of them. There is, therefore, higher commercial activity in the logging and timber processing area, among the most visible of which are the beer houses along the roads. Sometimes, enterprising owners bring in female 'entertainers' for the 'lonely boys' away from home. In Santiago, a city with the highest number of lumber hardware stores in the region of Northeast Luzon, one of these beer-houses-cum-cabaret-and-night-clubs is called the *Lonely Boys' Club* (LBC).

Within the forest, in the logging camps, the log ponds, the check points, or wherever there is logging activity, alcoholic drinks are available, brought either by the workers themselves or by enterprising local businessmen. Logging is partly fuelled by alcoholic beverages.

Conclusion

The drinking of alcohol has long been embedded in Philippine society. However, post-colonisation, changes occurred and the new format of drinking found its way into almost all sectors of the male population. The combination of the dominant Catholic religion with no formalised restrictions on the use of alcohol, and the ideology of macho behaviour among the male population provided the right context for the habit of drinking to become widespread. More recently, infrastructural improvements and the opening up of vast formerly forested areas have brought this habit to all corners of the country. The availability of commercially brewed alcoholic drinks throughout the year has in many cases wiped out all the traditionally and locally produced drinks. It is gradually becoming obvious that drinking commercial alcoholic beverages has become more than a social function. It has become very much part of the public culture of the country or at least of the male part of it. Its relative low price makes it possible for a large number of people to participate in this kind of 'social drinking'. Alcoholic drinks are often also used as 'payment in kind' between the Negrito Agta in the Sierra Madre and outside groups (migrants, loggers) for services provided. The fact that no less a person than a former President of the country is a known drunkard has highlighted the point that this has become a way of life. With the general growth of wealth, alcoholic consumption is likely to continue to increase in the near future.

Interestingly, the consumption of alcoholic drinks in the Philippines has hardly been a topic for anthropological research. Very few studies actually focus on this aspect of community life even though it is mentioned in all ethnographic studies. Use and misuse of alcohol is mainly mentioned in terms of social problems, either in itself (as a threat to health) or as a cause behind family and other types of problems.

Could a deeper look into Filipino drinking help in the identification of the ever-elusive national identity? Translating the words of Ambeth Ocampo, a contemporary Filipino historian, who writes a regular column in the most popular Filipino newspaper *Philippine Daily Inquirer*, we end our paper with the following quotation:

> *Why do we have to look into what people drink and how they are prepared? Maybe, one way to catch that elusive thing called national identity is let people realise that they truly are what they drink.* (Ocampo 2001)

References

Aquino, M.N. (1995) *Socio-economic Impact of the Logging Moratorium in Isabela*, Thesis submitted for Master of Management, Isabela State University, Philippines.

Cortes, R.M., Boncan, C.P. and Jose, R.T. (2000) *The Filipino Saga: History as social change*, New Day Publishers, Quezon City.

Early, J.D. and Headland, Th.N. (1998) *Population Dynamics of a Philippine Rain Forest People: The San Ildefonso Agta*, University Press of Florida, Gainesville.

Headland, Th.N. and Headland, J.D. (1997) Limitation of human rights, land exclusion, and tribal extinction: the Agta Negritos of the Philippines, *Human Organization*, 56(1): 79–90.

National Economic and Development Authority (NEDA) (2005) *Cagayan Valley Regional Physical Framework Plan (2001–2030)*, NEDA R02, Tuguegarao City.

Ocampo, A.R. (2001) Culture and history in food, *Inquirer Op-Ed*, http://www.inq7.net (4 May 2001).

Persoon, G.A., Masipiqueña, A., van der Ploeg, J., Masipiqueña, M. and van Weerd, M. (eds) (2009) *Crossing Boundaries: Celebrating 20 years of environmental research in Cagayan Valley and Sierra Madre*, CVPED, Cabagan.

Rosaldo, M.Z. (1980) *Knowledge and Passion: Ilongot notions of self and social life*, Cambridge University Press, Cambridge.

Rosaldo, R.I. (1980) *Ilongot Headhunting: 1883–1974: A study in society and history*, Stanford University Press, Stanford.

Scott, W.H. (1997) *Barangay: Sixteenth-century Philippine culture and society*, Ateneo de Manila University Press, Quezon City.

Van den Top, G.M. (1998) *The Social Dynamics of Deforestation in the Sierra Madre, Philippines*, Ph.D. thesis, Leiden.

Vanoverbergh, M. (1937–1938) Negritos of eastern Luzon, *Anthropos*, 32: 905–928 and 33: 119–164.

Websites

http://www.ginebrasanmiguel.com.ph
http://www.sabong.net.ph/forum/forum
http://www.sanmiguelbrewery.com.ph

CHAPTER 19
CULTURE, MARKET AND BEER CONSUMPTION

Mabel Gracia Arnaiz

Introduction

This paper analyses the types of messages used by the Spanish beer industry in recent decades to promote its product. Not only has beer consumption consolidated since the 1980s but the type of product, its associated representations and its use have changed. First, I shall consider the role that advertising has played in this change, and then I shall highlight the ideas used by advertisers to guarantee and strengthen the ties between the industry and beer on the one hand and the broad range of consumers on the other.

Advertising Commercials: Practice and Discourse

The food and agriculture industry has been modernised in an attempt to satisfy the specific needs which have been emerging in Western countries (Goody 1984: 251–57) and to improve productivity. Production is now as varied as possible for the capitalist market. The demands of the population were at the margin, or even independent, of this process. The economic system, however, depends on consumption and sufficient expectation must be created to ensure that this consumption is adequate. In this context, publicity is more indispensable today than ever before. As a promotional tool, together with other procedures of marketing, it tries to maintain the constant relationship between the production and the acquisition of goods (Sánchez Guzman 1979, 1982; Briz 1990; Qualter 1994).

For the food industry, advertising in the mass media is costly. Even so, judging from the fact that it is being used more and more, it seems to be profitable,[1] particularly when it comes to giving an outlet for great quantities of articles destined for a socially heterogeneous public. If not through such publicity, how else can such similar merchandise and trade marks be differentiated from one another and personalised in a market which is characterised by fierce competition? How does the food and agriculture industry ensure that its produce reaches such a large number of heterogeneous people? How does it manage to convert them into consumers of the new products that constantly appear in the market? The raison d'être of marketing and advertising is precisely to respond to these questions: that is to say, it must get the products into the shops and ensure that they are purchased. Sales specialists constantly struggle to assure and tighten the links between the industry and its merchandise on the one hand, and the diffuse categories of consumers on the other. This continuous effort requires training, knowledge and specific technology so that specialists can turn merchandise, events, places and people, which are often foreign and distant, into concepts that are close and familiar. In any commercial department, marketing is simply a form of knowledge, a recognised social and cultural ability to interpret and use the information in such a way that it can be recognised as unique and useful (Giddens 1991: 18).[2] Marketing is, then, the knowledge of 'how to' (Lien 1997: 21).

Not only is advertising a communicative practice, but a discourse, insofar as it presents and promotes ideas that go beyond the objective characteristics and functional attributes of the product advertised. It spreads a specific ideology not only about its function, use and benefits, but about how consumers should behave in response to such issues as work, the family, gender, free time, education, the body and health, to give just some examples. So it is true that the main aim of advertising is to circulate and spread news about things and facts and, in this sense, inform. Yet it must do so by persuading in such a way that it attracts the target public or those that can influence purchasing decisions (Spang 1982; Briz 1990; Qualter 1994). Advertising attempts to sell goods, by appealing to consumers through gender identity, celebrity endorsement, romantic imagery, notions of achieving happiness or contentment, and other cultural dimensions not tangibly related to the advertised product or service. At the same time, advertising is not only about social communication, but also about the various networks of cooperative social, personal and financial arrangements among suppliers, clients, advertising personnel, consumers, etc., that are essential to its operation (Malefyt and Moeran 2003). This means that the advertising network promotes its principal objective – to motivate consumption – and also favours operations of an ideological and symbolic nature which legitimate the use of the merchandise and its attributes for reasons that go beyond their material functions (Douglas and Isherwood 1979; McCracken 1988). To consume means to become a carrier and generator of meanings, through a language which expresses values and specific behaviour. Being a consumer means not only acquiring, but also replacing and substituting, goods and services. In this way, people reveal a way of life, a standard of living and even how they understand life itself.

In advertisements for food and drink, this process is evident. The 'how' in food advertising depends on selecting the appropriate media for the messages to reach the target public, while taking particular care about what is communicated and promoted (Barthes 1961). To denominate, classify and identify as consumable industrially produced foods is one of the main tasks of marketing publicity today. Thus, by providing a context, advertising is an indispensable part in the process of converting the transformed and scarcely identifiable foods into entities consider edible.

The Evolution of Beer Consumption in Spain

Beer advertising in Spain clearly emphasises the relationship that exists between the brewing business and culture, in such a way that its analysis provides an account of the evolution of this product in the Spanish food and drinks industry on the one hand, and the discursive associations that have been built up around this alcoholic drink on the other. In this section, I shall briefly consider the first point. The Spanish are greater producers of beer than consumers, and changes in publicity reflect, above all, the power of the beer sector to stimulate national consumption. While Spain in 2003 occupied the ninth position in the ranking of the world's beer producers (Brewers of Europe 2004) and its production has continued to increase (Table 19.1), consumption per capita is much lower, namely: nineteenth in the world, fourteenth in Europe, tenth in the EU and first in the Mediterranean region (see also Chapter 7). It should be noted, however, that some regions in Spain consume more than others. In general, southern, central and eastern regions are the principal consumers, rather than the north and north-western regions. As a result, while Murcia, Madrid and Andalusia consume the most beer, with levels approaching the average consumption of some of the world's principal consumer countries (e.g., Murcia consumes 120 litres per inhabitant and the Netherlands 120.8), Galicia, Navarra, La Rioja and Asturias consume only half this amount per inhabitant.

Table 19.1 Evolution of total beer production in Spain (1000 hl)

2000	2001	2002	2003	2008
26.4	27.7	27.8	30.6	33.4

Source: *Brewers of Europe 2004 and 2009*

The progressive increase in advertising investment within the beer sector (Table 19.2) reveals two important aspects. First, it reveals a change within the Spanish beer industry itself, which, until the 1980s was characterised by its rather modest investment in advertising, owing to strong growth in domestic consumption which made investment in advertising unnecessary. The increase is significant, going from the equivalent of nearly 3 million euros in 1985 to 13 million in 1995 and 80 million in 2005 (Table 19.2).

Table 19.2 Advertising investment for beer in Spain (euros)

1985	1995	2005
2,863,145	13,277,310	79,765,833

Secondly, the increase in advertising investment reveals variations in internal demand which, from 1990, began to stagnate and even fall until 1999.[3] Several reasons have been used to explain the stagnation and decrease recorded from 1990 until 1999. Highlighted among these are the general fall in the consumption of alcoholic drinks, with consumers showing a greater preference for alcohol-free and low calorie drinks; the decline in tourism; and the economic recession. Institutional anti-alcohol campaigns, laws restricting the sale of alcohol and growing concern about appearance and health have undoubtedly contributed to this fall.[4]

However, it is necessary to be cautious in interpreting the data, since they vary according to sources consulted. During the last decade, beer consumption has fluctuated between 52 and 58 litres per capita (Cerveceros de España 2008) registering again a stalemate since 2001–2. Thus, despite the temporary decline during the previous decade, beer has become one of the most frequently consumed drinks by Spaniards (Martin Cerdeño 2008), associated, in quantitative terms, with the increasing demands for mineral water, soft drinks and beer. For example, beer is well placed among alcoholic drinks, placed even higher than wine. According to data for 2007, whereas Spaniards consume 58 litres of beer per capita, the figure for wine is only 22. However, the evolution of per capita household expenditure has increased greatly during this period (Table 19.3).

Table 19.3 Evolution of beer expenditure and consumption

	1987	2007
Household expenditure per capita (euros)	7.6	17.3
Beer consumption per capita (litres)	66.0	58.0

Source: Martin Cerdeño (2008)

This trend has also been reflected in the increase in level of competition among the leading companies and in the advertising budgets of the main brewers. For example, advertising investment by these groups increased from 71,461,990 euros in 2004 to 79,765,833 in 2005, which represents an increase of 11.6 per cent (Marketing News 2006). In this sense, advertising pressure has been used by companies to try to maintain their market shares.

Stabilisation in consumption is the main reason why Spanish brewers have continued to increase their advertising budgets over recent decades, forecasting increased competition among Spanish producers on the one hand and in order to counteract the sharp rise in imports, on the other. In fact, the high investment in advertising was considered to be one of the Spanish beer industry's strong points for strengthening the barriers to entry of new foreign brewers, which have mostly had to enter Spain by buying out or buying into well-established Spanish breweries (Cruzcampo, El Aguila, Damm, Mahou, San Miguel or Unión Cervecera). The incorporation of Spain into the EU and the foreign interest in the Spanish market caused a concentration of brewers and an internationalisation of the sector. Although there is still a prevalence towards strong regionalisation of consumption, together with persistent brand loyalty, imported beers have gradually found their place in the Spanish market. This is confirmed by the strong growth in imports, principally originating in the EU (Germany, Holland and United Kingdom), but also from the United States and Mexico. In 2003, the Spanish demand for imported beers exceeded 8 per cent of total domestic demand. In general, this warm reception owes itself to the image of quality which has been built around these beers and advertising has played a key role in this.

If brand advertising is analysed from the 1960s until the present day, one can observe the following trends: some brands have gradually lost their presence in the advertising spectrum, whereas other brands, often imported ones, have become added to the increasingly wide spectrum of beers. Advertising reflects the diversification of production, with the result that each group offers a considerable number of different types of beer, leaving behind the traditional dichotomy of 'light/dark', so characteristic of the 1960s. Nowadays, beer may be special, draught, Pilsner, normal, extra, dark, dry, smooth, alcohol-free, light, lager, ale or stout, or with lemon, tea or apple, among other things. In spite of such diversification, the preferences of Spanish consumers still centre on the consumption of normal and special beers (normal beer 42 per cent and special beer 50 per cent).

The apparent diversity of types of beer is achieved within the process of industrial concentration in production, with the result that the same brewery may cover many brands and types of beer. Furthermore, brands which compete seemingly with each other, may in reality belong to brewing groups with common financial interests. After the recession of the 1990s, the outlook seemed brighter for the brewing sector, favoured by the policy of economic stability implemented by the central government, the economic upturn and then the rise in tourism. How the economic problems of 2008 and 2009 have effected this has yet to be seen.

The relative consolidation of consumption also coincided with a change in situations associated with beer consumption. In the late 1990s, for the first time, beer was considered a drink for evenings, similar to mixers or other alcoholic drinks. One slogan is an eloquent example: *Sumérgete en el sabor de la noche* (Immerse yourself in the flavour of the night).

However much there is a seasonality in beer consumption, with greater consumption in the hottest months of the year, it is now promoted as a social drink which is suitable for any situation and any time: at lunchtime, during the aperitif, going out at night, celebrations and between meals. In the same vein, in 2009 the group DAMM launched 'Estrella Damm Inedit', a beer supported by Ferran Adrià, specially designed to accompany all types of recipes and meals. It has a blend of malted barley and wheat, flavoured with spices (coriander, orange peel and licorice) and its target market is to compete directly with wine. Moreover, beer not only is promoted as a drink to accompany meals, but also as a central ingredient in the preparation of recipes.

Also beer continues to be drunk in greater proportions outside the home (see also chapter 8) and particularly in metropolitan areas, where the number of establishments specialising in beers has grown, and a more knowledgeable type of consumer has appeared. Similarly, drinking beer has gained in status and now has a more diverse range of consumers. Associated previously with the popular classes and consumed mainly by men, beer has gained an increasingly diversified public that includes women, young people and adults of all social classes, particularly among the middle strata of metropolitan areas and in reduced family households, where the housewife is usually younger than 35 and has paid employment outside of the home (Ministerio de Agricultura, Pesca y Alimentación 2001).

Furthermore, given the growing influence of the medical discourse on the dangers of alcohol for health and slim body shape, and the legal pressure exerted on people who drive drunk, it could be said that the main competition facing beer today is from alcohol-free and low-calorie drinks. The alcohol-free and light beers[5] have proved to be a positive alternative for the brewing industry, judging by the growth in consumption. In the 1990s consumption of this type of beer grew by almost 50 per cent, with 2008 consumption accounting for approximately 10 per cent of the total figure. Spain is the country with the largest share of alcohol-free beer consumption across the European Union. This demonstrates the social penetration of such cultural values, the need to find a new type of beer that will attract consumers concerned about their figure or their health. Furthermore, Damm first launched a gluten-free beer suitable for coeliacs in Spain in 2006 and later in other countries.

I shall now consider how these characteristics and/or needs of the brewing industry have been formulated in advertising.

Discourses used in Beer Advertising

As mentioned above, the consumption of food and drink is socially validated by the characteristics of the products themselves. Advertising communication, the specific function of which is to motivate the message receiver, resorts to different mechanisms of persuasion. It can provide information about the product: e.g., the price, the value and nutritional content, the ingredients, the applications and the forms of use, etc. However, only a small amount of food and drink advertising is purely informative. The great majority uses ornamental elements to retain the interest of the consumer and supplies little or no objective information about the product, particularly in those cases where the article is already familiar to the consumer. This type of advertising was termed *puffery* or superficial by Leet and Driggers (1990). The ornamental elements include all those concepts which help reaffirm the product's status, and their materialistic and symbolic values are introduced discursively.[6] In recent years, beer has been advertised by a combination of at least four predominant discourses: tradition and identity, the aesthetic, the hedonist and social differentiation.[7] Although their arguments differ, they have a common method; they collect everything that is significant for the receivers and then transmit information about consumption practices and food values to show that beer is consumed for what the advertisement says it is.

Tradition and Identity

The discourse based on tradition and social identity has an important role. I understand tradition to be a broad concept referring to the words and images which link food to country craftsmen and the earth, and which identify the rural with values such as nature, authenticity and purity. In this discourse, the myth of all that is rural is exalted, which in turn negates all that is urban and industrial. Passage of time acquires value. In this way the tasks identified as traditional become synonymous with handicraft, craftsmanship and effort in contrast to artificiality, manipulation, and the technology of industry. Lastly, it also makes reference to popular customs in matters of guests, table manners, festive celebrations and rituals, as well as the values that refer us to the collective identity. Defined thus, the discourse of tradition, nature and identity has an important role in beer publicity. Examples are:

- (Damm 1976) *Since 1876. One of the best beers in Europe. It was good 100 years ago.*
- (Estrella Dorada, Damm 1976) *The beer of our land.*
- (El Aguila 1982) *Traditional flavour.*
- (Cervezas Cruzcampo 1991) *Our land, our seeds and Nature: This is the beginning: Enjoying the flavour of one of the best beers: Cruzcampo. This is the ultimate.*

Denomination, origin, name, country and soil are aspects which transmit, at least in part, a certain cultural identity, and reaffirm a position in the market. The nationalist Spain of the Franco era has been replaced by the pluralist Spain of the democracy, which promotes the consumption of local products and even the export of these abroad. Consequently, this gives rise to the concept of a pro-European and international Spain, attempting to reposition its beers in the Spanish market against the pressures of competition from foreign brands and in the international market:

- (San Miguel 1970) *You can drink this beer anywhere in Spain and in much of the rest of the world.*

- (Carlsberg 1988) *Probably the best lager in the world.*
- (San Miguel 1990) *San Miguel, the beer from here that is drunk most frequently in Europe. A leader in exports.*
- (San Miguel 2004) *San Miguel, the beer from here that is widely known across the world.*

For their part, beers of foreign countries also highlight their origin, with a high level of acceptance and positive positioning of such brands among the Spanish public. Damm points out that its beer, A.K. Damm, 'is made with hops from the German region of Hallertau and represents the pure, smooth Alsatian character' (Damm 2001). Other examples are:

- (Heineken 1982) *Dutch and very cool.*
- (Henninger 1987) *A full-bodied German.*

The Discourse of Aestheticism

One relationship between the natural/traditional and health which appears on numerous occasions in food advertising, but is seldom used in beer advertising, if at all, is the nutritional discourse. The reason for its absence lies in the difficulty nowadays of establishing a relationship between alcohol consumption and health. However, some alcohol-free brands of beer are associated with such values and may indirectly reinforce such values, despite the fact that, until recently, such drinks contained small quantities of alcohol. The most significant examples of this are Malz Bier, Cruzcampo Sport and San Miguel Sin Alcohol, which use advertising linked to sport, perfect physique, social and professional success or healthy living , in such a way that places central importance on looking after your body. Consequently, the aesthetic discourse is also something associated with this type of drink. Light or alcohol-free beer is promoted as a beer that will allow you to obtain or maintain a youthful and slim body, owing to its low calorific value, without affecting its flavour whatsoever:

- (Malz Bier, Damm 1990) *I am not prepared to sacrifice the real lager taste. Marta Gil. 23 years old. Student of biology. She enjoys music and sport. She plays jazz three days a week. MALZ BIER SIN. And don't sacrifice the real taste of lager.*
- (Cruzcampo 1990) *Fewer calories. More sport. Low-alcohol lager is becoming the favourite drink of people throughout the world. Cruzcampo Sport has 40% fewer calories than a traditional lager but maintains the full flavour of careful and thorough brewing.*
- (San Miguel 2007) *Your body is asking for a real 0.0%.*

Concern about the consumption of alcohol and its effect on health and physique continues to grow. It is not surprising, therefore, that, since the technology exists to produce a beer without alcohol, in other words, without 'risk', this benefit would be highlighted in its advertising. The campaign for San Miguel Sin Alcohol alcohol-free beer reinforces this idea, using three eloquent sequences, all of which advise avoiding consumption of alcohol during pregnancy, when driving and in the workplace. Thus San Miguel shows us the figure 0.0 (the alcoholic strength of its beer in degrees) by using the stomachs of two women in an advanced state of pregnancy, the two illuminated headlights of a car travelling at night, and the safety helmets of two construction workers.

Beer consumption is paradoxical. Beer, as an alcoholic drink, shares social use with other alcoholic drinks, although its lower alcohol content and different composition places it in a different position from spirits, as beer not only contains less alcohol, but is also easier to drink and contains nutrients. The latter characteristic was already being highlighted in the 1960s, when beer was advertised as 'the drink that nourishes' (Gracia 1998). At this time, wine was also a 'national, popular and healthy' drink. Neither was there any hesitation in systematically associating alcohol consumption with escape, enjoyment, pleasure, personal achievement and sex. Nowadays, however, no advertiser would dare use the concepts of health-nutrition or alcohol as bases of their campaigns, first of all because beer is not drunk for its nutritional value and above all because it remains an alcoholic drink and as such shares, albeit to a lesser extent, the stigma associated with the excessive consumption of alcohol.[8] Not even light beers are openly promoted as being healthy. This is only done once the 'risk', in other words the alcohol, has been technologically removed.

Hedonism

Recently, the call for responsible consumption of alcohol is required in all advertisements. So, the beer industry has entered this message into their marketing strategies. However, in spite of this, appeals to a discourse of hedonism remain a recurring phenomenon. Specific argumentative bases are constructed around this type of discourse. Such commercials refer to the desire to obtain physical or psychological pleasure through the consumption of the proposed product. On the one hand, there are the commercials that refer to flavour and satisfying the taste sense. This issue has been a more or less constant one over several decades; in spite of the fact that tastes are highly variable on social or individual bases, flavour and organoleptic elements have been a constant factor in beer advertising. Examples are:

- (Skol 1960) *Skol is for you. A lively, bubbly beer.*
- (San Miguel 1960) *Because its transparency, flavour and aroma are incomparable.*

However, in my view, of more interest is the other side of the hedonistic argument, which is less related to flavour than to other types of senses and values associated with food and drink: well-being, pleasure and success. While arguments related to flavour are being maintained, more abstract notions related to obtaining pleasure and feeling good and happy, are on the increase:

- (Ambar 1988) *The beer that makes you feel good.*
- (Henninger 1988) *It gives you a good body.*

This hedonistic element has now increasingly been identified with obtaining pleasure through the use of more sensual comparisons in relation to products of capricious consumption. For this reason, beer is often related to moments of leisure and rest which, in Spain, given beer's seasonal nature, translates to trips to the beach or the country in the summer. Examples are:

- (San Miguel 1966) *Days in the country or on the beach. Those cheerful gatherings out in the country or by the sea. Excursions and spontaneous parties.*

By questioning this notion of seasonality and noting a significant change in the uses and situations associated with its consumption, attempts are now being made to promote beer as an all-year-round drink, for any time of day or night and for all occasions, particularly those involving company and sociability:

- (San Miguel 1973) *There are beers for the summer and San Miguel for the whole year round.*
- (Damm 1987) *Drink Woll-Damm. Pub drink by day. Club drink by night.*
- (Adlerbrau 1987) *So special that it has to be shared.*
- (San Miguel 2009) *It´s not a quick beer.*

Another aspect linking alcoholic drinks with hedonism is the allusion to sexual pleasure, more evident in some cases than in others, and usually highlighting male enjoyment (see also chapter 20). Examples of sexism are abundant in this type of commercial. Epidor/Moritz in the 1970s compared beer with women and their physical aspects, giving the man the option of choosing between them, or of simply enjoying both:

- (Moritz 1972) *A blonde and a brunette are waiting for you in the bar. They'll take your thirst away.*

Some commercials in recent years have continued to stress similar ideas, although now the woman may also appear as a consumer. However, women frequently appear in images as mere sexual objects and providers of primary pleasures:

- (Cruzcampo 1987) *It's so original. With that special touch. Are you looking for something? Shandy. What you were looking for.*

The Discourse of Differentiation

Finally, I also include in this classification the discourse of differentiation. This discourse refers to factors that differentiate beers in respect of issues such as origin, prestige, status, exclusiveness or know-how. In respect of this discourse, which appears with relative frequency, I would like to emphasise the paradoxical value of the selectivity contained within it. And I say paradoxical because, as mentioned in the previous section, beer is a mass consumption product aimed at the majority of the population, excepting children. The product is sometimes identified with a particular origin, because this origin is a prestigious one. They can also use French, English or German languages to highlight this difference: for example, *Coupe d'or du bon goût français. Awarded to San Miguel for the high quality of their beer* (San Miguel 1966).

Other commercials attempt to link such products to elites or great cuisines. On other occasions, only one superlative value is stressed, such as unique, best or best-selling:

- (Skol 1980) *Very seldom in life do you discover something extra. Munich is the new extra lager from Skol. Authentically extra.*
- (Mahou 5 Estrellas 1986) *Five-star taste.*

There is no need to mention the quality of the products being advertised: when this is not explicitly stated, it is assumed. However, many do insist on stating it, emphasising the quality associated with the brand and the product, adding an attribute of specific personality and guarantee. This argument aims to inform target consumers that the producers always use the best ingredients and apply the best techniques in order to obtain the best products:

- (San Miguel 1960) *Quality and worldwide fame.*
- (San Miguel 1981) *High-fidelity beer.*
- (Alderbrau 1987) *The quality Spanish beer.*

Some brands allude to their prestigious origin or to the awards they have obtained, while others claim to have been prepared by true gourmets, and some are metaphorically associated with symbols of prestige in our culture, such as works of art and jewels.

Conclusion

Advertising messages are no more than the sum of ideological discourses attractively arranged and with no apparent contradiction, so that once the marketing strategy has been implemented, the specialists strive to reconstruct these discourses and place them in the multimedia plane, choosing the most appropriate channels to diffuse their ideas. In this way, the advertising language – dense, aesthetic, non-grammatical, rhetorical – becomes the means through which announcers and consumers finally meet. Beer advertising in recent years has tended to interrelate different themes – tradition, identity, hedonism, differentiation, health and responsibility – within commercials, which confirms the notion that, increasingly, advertising messages are the union of discourses that undoubtedly absorb all that is contemporary or structurally significant for consumers and for the interests of the beer market. Beers which are light, alcohol-free, extra, special or dark, are all the sum of perfections – high quality, traditional, natural, exquisite, refreshing, stimulating, healthy – and, in the end, they all end up being for consumers just what the commercials say they are.

Notes

1. In just fifteen years, advertising investment in Spain increased from 132,200 million pesetas invested in 1981 to 1,226,441 in 1995 (J. Walter Thompson).
2. For Giddens (1991: 18) marketing is an expert system, a de-regionalising mechanism which, influenced by the liberal ideologies of the US and Western Europe, groups time and space together by deploying forms of technical knowledge with customers that make use of this.
3. A significant proportion of the data on the Spanish beer market referred to in this article have been taken from the report *Estudio sobre la posición competitiva del sector de alimentación y de bebidas en España. Sector de la cerveza y malta de cerveza*, Ministerio de Agricultura, Pesca y Alimentación, Madrid, 1993, Consumption Panels from the Ministerio de Agricultura, Pesca y Alimentación (1995, 1998 and 2000) and the report *Informe Económico 2003. Datos del sector. Cerveceros de España.*
4. Since 1995, the brewing industry established an agreement to self-monitor its advertising. In this regard, all communications should promote responsible and moderate beer consumption habits.
5. So-called 'alcohol-free' beer, or 'fizzy malt' beer (according to Spanish legislation) was first marketed in Spain in the early 80s. This type of beer is mainly characterised as having a greater carbohydrate content and 50 per cent fewer calories, together with only 1 per cent alcohol by volume.
6. Barthes (1961), Chârmet (1976), King (1980) and Fieldhouse (1996) have established different typologies of the principal themes used in food and drink advertising.
7. The data presented here form part of a study undertaken based on a representative sample of Spanish food and drink advertising between 1960 and 1990 and include the analysis of over 500 commercials for various categories of food and drink, in addition to 100 commercials, corresponding to the period 1991–2000, a third of which were for alcoholic drinks. In this study, advertising is considered a source of ethnographic analysis (Gracia 1998).
8. The fact that it is not openly promoted as a healthy drink does not mean that it is not one, however: recent scientific research has shown that consumed in moderate amounts, beer can have positive effects on one's health, increasingly so in older age and in respect of illnesses related to the body's circulation aparatus: González-Gross, Lebrón y Marcos (2000) Revisión bilbiográfica sobre los efectos del consumo moderado de cerveza sobre la salud (online), http: //www.cerveza y salud.org, (see also chapter 2).

References

Atkinson, P. (1980) The symbolic significance of health foods. In Turner, M.R. (ed.) *Nutrition and Lifestyles*, Applied Science Publishers, London.

Barthes, R. (1961) Pour une psycho-sociologie de l'alimentation contemporaine, *Annales*, 16: 977–86.

Bonnain-Moerdyck, R. (1972) Sur la cuisine traditionelle comme culte culinaire du passé, *Ethnologie Française*, 2: 3–4.

Brewers of Europe (2004) *Beer Facts 2003* (online), http://www.brewersofeurope.org/docs/publications/beerfacts2003.pdf, (accessed 11 September 2009).

Briz, J. (1990) La publicidad en un mercado competitivo: caso del sistema agroindustrial. In Briz, J. (ed.) *Publicidad en el sistema agroalimentario. Un análisis comparativo internacional*, Mundi-Prensa, Madrid: 15–37.

Cerveceros de España. (2004) Informe Económico 2003. Datos del sector (online), http://www.cerveceros.org/ingles/pdf/dossiercerveceros.pdf (accessed 11 September 2009).

Cerveceros de España and Ministerio de Medio Ambiente y Medio Rural y Marino. (2008) Informe socioeconómico 2008 del sector de la cerveza en España, http://www.cerveceros.org/pdf/dossiercerveceros08.pdf (accessed 11 September 2009).

Charmet, P.H. (1976) Le publicité et les media comme facteurs de modification du comportement alimentaire, *Annales de la Nutrition et de l'Alimentation*, 30: 481–90.

Douglas, M. and Isherwood, B. (1979) *The World of Goods. Towards an anthropology of consumption*, W.W. Norton, New York.

Fieldhouse, P. (1996) *Food and Nutrition: Customs and cultures*, Chapman and Hall, London.

Giddens, A. (1991) *Modernity and Self-Identity*, Polity Press, Cambridge.

Goody, J. (1984) *Cuisines, cuisine et classes*, Centre Georges Pompidou, Paris.

Gracia, M. (1998) *La transformación de la cultura alimentaria. Cambios y permanencias en un contexto urbano (Barcelona, 1960–1990)*, Ministerio de Cultura, Madrid.

King, S. (1980) Presentation and the choice of food. In Turner, M.R. (ed.) *Nutrition and Lifestyles*, Applied Science Publishers, London.

Leet, R.D. and Driggers, J. (1990) *Economic Decisions for Consumers*, MacMillan Publishing Company, New York.

Lien, M.E. (1997) *Marketing and Modernity*, Berg, Oxford.

McCracken, G. (1988) *Culture and Consumption*, Indiana University Press, Indianapolis.

MarketingNews (2006) *Los estudios son para el verano (I): Inversión publicitaria por sectores de anunciantes* (online), http://www.marketingnews.es/Varios/20060801001, (accessed 11 September 2009).

Malefyt, T.D. and Moeran, B. (eds.) (2003) *Advertising Cultures*, Berg, Oxford.

Martín Cerdeño, V. (2008) 1987–2007: Dos décadas de Panel de Consumo Alimentario, *Distribución y Consumo*, July–August: 208–39.

Ministerio de Agricultura, Pesca y Alimentación (1999) *La alimentación en España*, Ministerio de Agricultura, Pesca y Alimentación, Madrid.

Ministerio de Agricultura, Pesca y Alimentación (2001) *La alimentación en España*, Ministerio de Agricultura, Pesca y Alimentación, Madrid.

Ministerio de Agricultura, Pesca y Alimentación (2003) *Estudio sobre la posición competitiva del sabor de alimentación y bebida en España: Sector de la cerveza y malta de cerveza*, Ministerio de Agricultura, Pesca y Alimentación, Madrid.

Qualter, T.H. (1994) *Publicidad y democracia en la sociedad de masas*, Paidós, Barcelona.

Sahlins, M. (1976) *Culture and Practical Reason*, University of Chicago Press, Chicago.

Sánchez Guzmán, J.R. (1979) *Introducción a la teoría de la publicidad*, Tecnos, Madrid.

Sánchez Guzmán, J.R. (1982) *Breve historia de la publicidad*, Forja, Madrid.

Spang, K. (1982) *Fundamentos de Retórica*, Pamplona, Universidad de Navarra, Pamplona.

CHAPTER 20
BEER AND EUROPEAN MEDIA: GLOBAL VS. LOCAL

Luis Cantarero and *Monica Stacconi*

Introduction

Eating and drinking are physiological needs which can be approached by the researcher from various perspectives. Today, in Europe, in order to comprehend food behaviour it is necessary to consider the relationship between the two apparently opposite poles of functionality and pleasure (Flandrin and Montanari 1996: 863). It is worthwhile wondering what role beer plays within this modern food system. Without ignoring its physiological function, we believe that beer belongs at the pleasure pole, which derives from conviviality. In the past however, depending on the historical period and on the culture, the motivations for beer consumption were not confined to the continuum functionality/pleasure.

Duboe-Laurence and Berger (1988) contend that beer, from its birth in Mesopotamia (4000 BC), was used for paying labourers, curing the sick, honouring the gods, etc. By the Babylonians, beer was considered a nutritious food. Later on, in Egypt, it was used as a ceremonial drink for the cult of the dead and, towards 2100 BC, it was converted into the drink of hospitality, currency and wage. In barbarian Europe it was a drink for warriors and heroes, a trophy, a symbol of prosperity, a treatment for scurvy. It was also spilled during libations and was an ethnic marker: it differentiated barbarian culture from that of the Romans (see Montanari 1993).

During the Middle Ages monasteries made beer production a source of income. Soon the diuretic qualities of beer were discovered by the monks, although they despised its 'power to give ideas' (Toussaint-Samat 1991: 154). The same author explains that beer mixed with hydromel and scented with juniper acquired such popularity during the eighteenth century, as a source of lust, that it was prohibited by the ecclesiastical power. However, during this period beer also had virtues. Under the reign of Henry III of England (1216–1272), beer was 'good' because it filled one's belly and immunised against epidemics. For this reason later on Saint Arnulfo would be proclaimed the patron saint of beer drinkers. During a bout of cholera, he realised that beer drinkers suffered from colic less than those who drank water and he extended the consumption of this alcoholic drink to the rest of the population (Toussaint-Samat 1991: 151). Beer also indicated one's position within the religious order: The *prima melior* (i.e. the 'best' beer reserved for honoured guests and senior members of monasteries in the Middle Ages) of fathers was, of course, of better quality, and brothers had to make do with *potio fortis* (strong drink; i.e., strong beer intended for the monks). As for *cervisia debilis* (weak beer), it was for visitors – nuns, novices, poor pilgrims, etc. – the name alone is very telling in this respect (Toussaint-Samat 1991: 151). This author quotes another example of the usage of beer as a social marker during the Middle Ages: outside the Mediterranean area, the choice of drink was made out of class consciousness. Beer was the drink of the poor, wine that of the rich.

Years later, in the eighteenth century, English people drank beer because it quenched their thirst, was a caloric complement to daily diet, had therapeutic virtues and also had a 'ludic side' since it favoured escapism and social congregation (Montanari 1993: 121). Along with the development of the beer industry in the eighteenth and nineteenth centuries, big producer families make their appearance: Guinness, Kronenbourg, Stella Artois, Heineken, Carlsberg, etc.

Thanks to industrialisation, urbanisation, transportation development, etc., these beers widened their market scope and slowly spread all around the world. As a result, at least in Europe, today the above mentioned brands are available to the whole population. Consumers may purchase them in supermarkets and corner shops, in bars and pubs, at filling stations, railway and bus stations and airports. Due to this globalising process, beer in itself loses its ability to create meaning and it is its different brand names that have come to denote distinctions. Beer drinkers, increasingly often, do not ask for a beer but for a San Miguel, a Coronita, a Heineken, and so on – a choice that is determined by the global and the local markets and the meanings associated with such brands. The analysis of the commercials of one local beer brand from Bavaria (Franziskaner) and of one global brand (Carslberg) will allow us to elucidate such attached meanings. Before discussing our analysis of these brands, however, we will briefly describe the globalisation process and its influence on food.

Global versus Local

Globalisation is the political, economic and sociocultural process which gained strength thanks to the fall of the Berlin wall in 1989 and to the dissolution of the Soviet Union in 1991. As Ramonet argues, the overwhelming victory of the West in the cold war, and that of capitalism over Soviet communism, favoured an inexorable expansion of neoliberal politicies and of the dynamics of globalisation. Until the mid 1990s such policies triumphed almost without encountering any resistance at all (Ramonet 2001: 11). According to Ramonet, a first stage of protest against globalisation took place in 1994 with the appearance of Sub-Commander Marcos and the *Zapatista* movement and, in 1995, with José Bové and the French social movement. The protests concerned the perspectives of those who rule the planet and worldwide capitalism, symbolised for many by the World Economic Forum, which, since 1971, has been held every year in Davos (Switzerland). As Cazorla observes, this meeting gathers together representatives of the two thousand largest companies in the world, which finance the private institution behind the Forum (Cazorla 2001: 11). During the last two years of the twentieth century other anti-globalisation protests have taken place and opposed the Forum: in Seattle, Washington, Prague, Okinawa and Nice. In January 2001 the World Social Forum was held in Porto Alegre, with the intention of overcoming the attitude of protest which had characterised the previous meetings. A proposal was made for a method which should be constructive and might provide for the possible idea of another kind of globalisation, rather than simply adopting an anti-globalisation position (Cazorla 2001: 11).

During this whole period the food system has not remained unscathed by the globalising impulse. In fact, 'McDonalds' has been converted into a symbol of globalisation and has become one of the targets of the anti-globalisation movement. The reason for such attacks is the perception that almost all social sectors (for example, education, sports, politics and religion) have been applying McDonalds' principles to their own practices (Ritzer 1999: 10). According to Ritzer, there are four basic features that characterise world '*McDonaldisation*'. Firstly, the obsession with efficiency, that is to say, for the choice of the best possible means towards the achievement of a given goal. Such means are, among others, simplicity, speed, comfort and the saving of time, money and energy. Secondly, the emphasis on quantification, that is, quantity as synonymous with quality. Stress is put on elements that may be calculated, counted, quantified. Thirdly, prediction is achieved through order, systematisation, routine and lack of surprise: in other words, that people may predict what is going to happen. Fourthly and lastly, control on human beings is increased through the use of technology, by replacing people with machines in the production process.

Thus, globalisation can be said to be one of the main factors conditioning food today (Millán 2000). Industrialisation and the interests of big producers govern the human food system. This results in the production of serial products, the homogenisation, the homologation, the universalisation of food behaviour and thus, as a consequence, the loss of food's cultural meanings. The principles that rule mass food consumption are functionalism, comfort, hygiene, effectiveness, calculation, prediction and control. However, in the food field and along with this globalising process there is a 'localising process'. As Flandrin and Montanari argue (1996: 876), sometimes modernity favours, rather than excludes, the formation of local specifications, due to the fact that such an oppositional food system is used by contemporary consumers as a marker of their cultural identity and of others' *'otherness'*.

The values that condition the consumption of more specialised, local food products are the nostalgia for the past, cultural identity, peculiarity, authenticity, tradition, taste, familiarity, the link with territory, the wish for diversity, etc. This process is, nonetheless, not wholly virtuous either. The local is converted into a pride which, on some occasions, results in a generalised chauvinism. The subsequent ethnocentrism creates a kind of public opinion which goes beyond food facts and certain behaviours become radical. Local fundamentalism feeds on ideological and political discourses of the nationalist-patriotic kind and it recalls past history. As Marchamalo argues (1996: 59), the last big advertising topic after the Spanish civil war, and a consequence of the extreme nationalism promoted by the government, is that of 'Spanishness'. Traders and producers still join in this fashion of using the 'Spanish' as an inexcusable advertising argument. Furthermore, this same author goes on to say that the right to represent the home country becomes a bone of contention among the various companies, which appeal to the brand name tradition (ibid.: 61).

We do not believe, of course, that things are totally global or local and it is worthwhile going beyond monolithic definitions and looking for intermediate positions. The following analysis of two beer commercials, broadcast on different European TV channels, is an attempt to reflect on how this mixed process of globalisation/localisation works in the advertising field. Our main contention in this respect is that this process becomes patent through the brand and not through the beer.

Planet Carlsberg

Among all the commercials we have seen on Spanish channels we have chosen that of Carlsberg because it is the one which best represents globalisation. This commercial made its appearance on Spanish TV in March 2001, and was broadcast in the evening around 10 p.m. The broadcasting time implies that the targeted audience is basically made up of people over 14–15 years of age, although, as shall be seen, this particular commercial seems to be addressing viewers whose age is considered to be between thirty and forty.

The first shot is a close up of two young men in their thirties. They face the camera and are dressed in leisure clothes of short-sleeved shirts. Behind them, crystal-clear sea water can be seen. The first iconic elements of the commercial, on the one hand, have clear connotations of 'relaxation', 'free time', 'summer' and 'holidays'. On the other, the men's clothing suggests that they occupy a certain position in the social structure. They are not wearing t-shirts, and so they look like people who have a university degree and a job related to their studies. Another visual element to take into account as we consider this frame is that both people look bored (one's eyes are lost staring at some point beyond the camera). At this point one of the young men starts talking and the following dialogue ensues:

Carls: Listen Berg …
Berg: Yes, Carls?
Carls: Did you know that Carlsberg is consumed in more than 130 countries around the world?

This dialogue, by introducing the characters of Carls and Berg, shift the viewer's attention from the couple as real – thus as a source of engagement for those who recognise themselves as that kind of people and project on them their desire for holidays, seaside, etc. – to their fictional status. The two young holidaymakers become, in fact, the 'flesh-and-blood' halves that make up the 'identity' of the brand name itself and evoke at the same time many other fictional 'couples' of jokes, of films and, more traditionally, of stories. This strategy allows play with the visual and verbal registers so as to mix images that are recognised as real and are associated with everybody's experience of summer holidays, with a dialogue that projects one into the world of children's tales. In any case, from the beginning, both through images and words, the commercial proposes an association of beer with social functions such as friendship and amusement.

The tale that the viewer is now ready to listen to is soon told: Carls informs Berg that Carlsberg beer is drunk all over the world, a statement that is an evident praise of the cosmopolitan quality of the drink. Carl's assertion is endorsed visually by the image of a bottle of Carlsberg 'launched' rocket-like from the Earth to outer space. The next verbal comment on this image is that of a voice off, announcing 'Planet Carlsberg'. The following images show this planet to be made up of beautiful and alluring women belonging to various ethnic groups. The first woman has oriental looks, long straight hair and is elegantly dressed. Her suggested personality is that of a sensual, feminine and tender girl. The next shot shows three women: the one in the foreground looks like the stereotypical US aggressive woman. She wears clothes that imitate leopard fur; she has got big breasts and looks more overtly sexually provocative than her oriental counterpart. The third woman is black and her outfit, while evoking her African roots, is at the same time very elegant and sophisticated. More women come out of a car which parks by a nightclub: a black girl (more Americanised than the previous one), and two white ones. As they walk into the nightclub the camera lingers on their back: the black woman's bottom is evidently the protagonist of this shot, given that its shape is clearly visible due to the tight trousers she is wearing. Inside the nightclub there are more women of different looks, ages and ethnic groups. All of them, like the previous ones, have a bottle of Carlsberg in their hand (which they, nevertheless, never drink).

It is evident, from the images so far described, that the 'Planet Carlsberg' of the commercial is viewed from (and offered to) a male perspective; after all, a male voice over and a male 'narrator' (Carls) are those who are telling the story of this 'world'. The women who appear in the commercial seem to comply with a patriarchal society, offering themselves as objects of the male view and desire. They are classical, modern, a mixture of the dichotomy virgin/whore that is at the base of patriarchal representation of the female. Carlsberg, no doubt, is proposing the idea of a global world in which people are linked by what they drink. Yet this globalisation is presented through an androcentric view: global is made to coincide with the universality of male dominance.

This is even clearer if one takes into account the words of the voice-over which accompanies the above mentioned images:

230 million square kilometres inhabited by 2,500 million women crowding more than 3,000 million bars. At a ratio of 2.3 bartenders per bar, we have 7 million barmen, or rather, barwomen, ready to give us a Carlsberg ...

The male voice-over seems to be thinking of the world in terms of the quantity of women available, and establishes a direct link between their availability, which is satisfying men's desires, and the beer. The gallery of women is completed, in fact, by four barwomen offering a Carlsberg 'to the viewer' (they look straight into the camera). The journey to Planet Carlsberg, a male fantasy about a promised land, ends when Carls retorts: 'If we weren't lost here!'

The viewer now realises that Carls and Berg are on a deserted beach by an apparently abandoned hut. The miracle is, however, possible with Carlsberg; the provocative 'leopard' woman arises from behind the hut's bar and offers the men a Carlsberg. All of a sudden, the hut becomes the core of a party and the deserted beach is populated by young people dancing and having fun. The camera finally zooms off the place and off the Earth, revealing that this particular place was somewhere in the Mediterranean area. The word 'Carlsberg', divided into 'Carls' and 'Berg' becomes one again, as the letters shift into place together.

To conclude, the global planet proposed by Carlsberg is a world of joy, parties, friendship, in which social relationships are motivated by the search for (heterosexual) sexual pleasure. The variety of ethnic groups in this commercial, more than advocating multicultural values, points to the market-like ideology of quantity plus quality and proposes the association 'women-as-product'. The iconographic discourses of this commercial uphold classic gender roles: men look whereas women are looked at and allure.[1] Those sections of the audience who identify themselves with such traditional (patriarchal) roles are the target of the Carlsberg message. When, at the end of the commercial, Carls and Berg unite to form the word 'Carlsberg', to restore the brand's 'identity' (that for narrative reasons had been 'split' into two characters), the commercial is subtly suggesting that the audience also assert their identity by taking up that of Carlsberg, with all the women, parties and ideology that go with it.

To put it in Eco's words, this commercial is characterised, as almost any other, by a redundant ideology which the semiotician terms 'global' and consists of 'economic-erotic-mundane success in life' (Eco 1978: 305). As to the strategies used in order to sell this ideology this commercial makes use of a 'historical' codification (Eco 1978: 299) that is, of patriarchal connotations of women that have existed for ages.

Franziskaner: *Das Frische an Bayern*

This commercial for Franziskaner beer was broadcast during Christmas 2000 on the German channel DSF. It is characterised by transmitting values that can be considered local, if compared to those conveyed by brands which present themselves as 'international'. This is done in relatively few shots, if one bears in mind the larger montage of the Carlsberg brand.

In the first shot the camera zooms to a big glass of beer within snowed, alpine peaks. The Franziskaner logo, a monk drinking beer, is clearly visible on the front of the glass. At the top, abundant beer froth transforms into snowy ski slopes as the camera zooms up. By the happy sound of Tyrolean-like music a couple of people ski down the slopes. The following shots show a beautiful woman smiling as she leaves her skis in order to take a break at a table with three glasses of Franziskaner beer against the background of the snowy peaks. Three hands raise the glasses and make a toast, letting the glasses clink. The last frame includes the snowy mountains again and the inevitable glass of Franziskaner. The only verbal intervention in the commercial is at the end, when a voice-off reads aloud the legend *'Franziskaner Weissbier, das Frische an Bayern'* ('Franziskaner wheat beer, the freshness of Bavaria').

This commercial, as others, suggests from the beginning the association of beer with holidays, more specifically in relation with winter. The setting which is in the foreground in the commercial is that of alpine peaks, probably familiar to many German viewers used to spending their free time at ski resorts. The music and the logo make it clear that the place in question is meant to evoke, more specifically, Bavarian winter landscapes. Once this context is established the attention is drawn to the beer head. The froth is a typical advertising device, which Eco terms a 'gastronomic icon', one characterised by a strong emotional value. This manifests itself when an object stimulates the viewer's wish on account of the icon's 'violent' representation. For this reason, Eco goes on to say, the frozen film on the glass of beer, the buttery consistence of a sauce, cannot be taken simply as icons denoting 'freeze' and 'sauce' (Eco 1978: 299).

The abundant beer head of our commercial, besides simply denoting the presence of beer, actually causes the viewer's wish to drink such a palatable object. Yet the specific connotations of the froth of Franziskaner beer have to do not only with taste, but also with territory, both as sources of pleasure. The link of the beer to the (familiar) territory is performed, as could be seen, in such a quick way that it appears to be very natural to the spectator. As soon as the camera zooming movement finishes, the froth, by virtue of an overlapping of images, turns into the above-mentioned ski slopes (and by extension, the mountains and Bavaria as a whole). Localising the product in a specific territory, as Caldentay and Gomez point out (1996: 60), amounts to emphasising the importance of the local over the global, the rural over the urban, the personal over the anonymous and the hand-made over the industrially made. To sum up, the physical and psychological satisfaction triggered by taste and territory stem from the represented icon: the froth.

The other obvious feature emerging from the analogy of the white beer froth with the snow is that of purity, a quality that the brand boasts of in the very label of the beer bottle with a sentence that reads: '*Brewed in full accordance with the Bavarian "Purity Law" of 1516*'. Purity is associated here with the naturalness of the method and thus with the lack of artificial ingredients, as well as with other possible meanings related to its being healthy, hygienic, etc. This nostalgia for past purity is not stated with words in the commercial, but visually, with the snowy froth and also with the ever-present image of the monk of the logo. The monk, while hinting at another kind of 'purity', that concerning the religious order (spiritual loftiness for example), is also a reminder of ancient tradition in that he evokes the remote pre-industrial past of the brewing process. The beer label on the one hand, and the emblem of the monk in the commercial on the other, locate the product in a specific time, a past that goes back as far as 1363, the date of the foundation of this Munich brewery near the Franciscan monastery which inspired the brand emblem.[2] Furthermore, the beer is also located in a specific place, Bavaria. These two strategies, locating the product in a set time and space, allow association of the beer with the value of tradition.

As for the beer connotations related to the present time, the commercial avoids the representation of the woman as a sexual icon and stresses, instead, the value of friendship. The beer is associated first with a couple skiing at the same rhythm, then to the relaxed and smiling face of the woman, and lastly to the three glasses of beer held by, supposedly, three friends. Hand in hand with the emphasis on friendship is the connection with sport, in this case skiing, with the obvious related value of health. It is worth commenting, at this point, that this brand has been sponsoring the German Olympic team for years. The link with sports has become one of Franziskaner's main promotional strategies. Another slogan on the brand internet site reads: '*The sport you choose is your business. The beer you drink afterwards is ours.*' The paragraph following the slogan also mentions the beer's '*fantastic freshness*', a quality which is emphasised, together with the Bavarian origin, by the slogan with which the commercial ends: *Franziskaner Weissbier. Das Frische an Bayern.*

Conclusion

Currently, the Western food system is characterised by the coexistence of global and local foodstuffs. As with other foods, beers tend to occupy positions towards one or other pole of the continuum, global–local. The fact that some beer brands occupy a position which is closer to one rather than the other pole depends on market strategies. These are reflected in advertising policies that target different kinds of consumers. As we have seen, Carlsberg beer addresses young people and insists on the global (and patriarchal) values exemplified by its 'planet'. Conversely, Franziskaner beer fosters identification with locality and tradition.

We believe that the different advertising strategies of these two brands, which stress either globality or locality, rather than opposing and excluding each other, are complementary and create a context from which each may benefit.

Notes

1. The semiotic terminology used in the analysis of this commercial has been taken from Umberto Eco (1978).
2. See internet, http://franziskaner.org.

References

Caldentay, P. and Gómez, A. C. (1996) Productos típicos, territorio y competitividad, *Agricultura y Sociedad*, 80–81: 57–82.
Cazorla, L.M. (2001) Porto Alegre o la otra globalización, *El Pais*, 6 February 2001.
Duboe-Laurence, P. and Berger, C. (1988) *El libro del amante de la cerveza*, J.J. de Olañeta, Barcelona.
Eco, U. (1978) *La estructura ausente*, Lumen, Barcelona.
Flandrin, J.L. and Montanari, M. (eds) (1996) *Histoire de l'Alimentation*, Fayard, Paris.
Marchamalo, J. (1996) *Bocadillos de delfín. Anuncios y vida cotidiana en la España de la Postguerra*, Grijalbo, Barcelona.
Millán, A. (2000) Cultures alimentàries i globalització, *Revista d'Etnologia de Catalunya*, 17: 72–81.
Montanari, M. (1993) *El hambre y la abundancia. Historia y cultura de la alimentación en Europa*, Crítica, Barcelona.
Ramonet, I. (2001) El consenso de Porto Alegre, *El Pais*, 12 February 2001.
Ritzer, G. (1999) *La McDonalización de la sociedad. Un análisis de la racionalización en la vida cotidiana*, Ariel, Barcelona.
Toussaint-Samat, M. (1991) *Historia natural y moral de los alimentos*, Alianza, Madrid.

GLOSSARY

α acids: are found in the resins of hops and provide bitterness when isomerised into iso α acids by boiling. Three main types are found **humulone, co-humulone** and **ad-humulone.**

α amylase: one of the enzymes that converts starch to sugar.

alcohol content: there are numerous ways of identifying the alcohol content in liquids. To have 'proof' that the rum British sailors used to receive at sea was not watered down, gunpowder was immersed in it. This mixture would not burn below 57.15% alcohol by volume (abv.), a ratio of 4:7. This was defined as 100 degrees or 100° 'proof'. An easier and nowadays most frequently used method is to express the alcohol content as a percentage of the volume. Low alcohol beers will range around 2% abv., normal ones around 3–4% abv. The yeast commonly used in brewing beer is destroyed if the alcohol content is higher than that. Strong beers, e.g., the '*Bock*' or '*Doppelbock*' beers from Germany can have as much as 12% abv. These last are produced by using different types of yeast and, also, by partial freezing (Ice *Bock*), so that the resulting fluid has a higher concentration of alcohol. There are further methods for describing the alcohol content of beer. One is to measure, expressed in degrees (°), the concentration of the wort before fermentation has set in; about 1/3 of the wort volume will be turned into alcohol. The total amount of wort (*Stammwürze* in German) produced in a brewery is still used in Germany to determine the amount of tax the brewer has to pay. A rough method for converting these degrees into per cent alcohol is to divide the former by 2.5. Using a general equivalent of these degrees, in the Czech Republic, they refer to ten grades of beer, but it should be noted that the percentage alcohol in beers of the same grade can vary very slightly according to brand.

ales: ales were initially beers brewed without the use of hops but with a variety of herbs and spices for flavouring. They were dominantly malty and sweet in flavour and rich in energy. After the acceptance of hops between 1500–1600 to provide bitterness and flavour, traditional ales became less common and are very rare today. However, the term has been adapted for top fer-menting beers to distinguish them from lagers. The term may also be used for strong beers containing hops and may be used in general labelling to signify a more robust beer than normal.

aleurone: a layer of enzyme-secreting cells surrounding the endosperm of cereal grains.

amylolytic enzyme: a type of enzyme capable of denaturing starch molecules; used in the brewing process to digest starch to fermentable sugars.

Bavarian Purity Law of 1516: in the Middle Ages town magistrates, guilds and other local authorities tried to improve the quality of beer by stipulating which kinds of ingredients and techniques were allowed to brew beer, a common drink in those days which had a low alcohol content and replaced the often polluted drinking water. On 23 April 1516 the Bavarian Count Wilhelm IV decreed that only barley, hops and water were to be used to make beer. He also laid down the prices for the different kinds of beers. This purity law was the first such regulation for a whole country (Bavaria) and has since been adopted by breweries in many countries.

beer: an alcoholic beverage generally brewed from malted grains and commonly flavoured with hops but it can also be made from other starch-containing plants. Generally fermented with the *Saccharomyces cerevisiae* yeast and served with dissolved carbon dioxide to provide carbonation.

beta-endor in: one of the three **endorphins** (see below).

bitter: term used in Britain for a sharp-tasting beer made with hops.

botellón: literally in Spanish this means a large container of liquid, but it is used colloquially in Spain now to refer to a group of teenagers who gather, for example, to drink alcohol.

bottom-fermenting beers: beers produced using a yeast which produces limited yeast head during fermentation. Most of the yeast settles directly to the bottom of the fermenter. These are generally lagers although a number of ale yeasts have now been modified in order to sediment during fermentation for ease of processing.

CAMRA: Campaign for Real Ale in UK.

caramelisation: the act of converting sugar into burnt sugar or caramel.

cask ales: cask ales are generally defined as beers which still contain their brewing yeast. They are often dispensed from a round bellied cask of various sizes from a 9 gallon firkin, an 18 gallon kilderkin and a 36 gallon barrel. The round belly allows the yeast to settle away from the tap so allowing a clear beer to be dispensed. However, after movement one does need to leave the cask for up to 36 hours for the yeast to settle.

catabolisation: the act of breaking down compounds by metabolic processes.

chaptalisation: the addition of extra sugar to the must in order to increase the alcohol content of wine.

contamination: of beer, generally arises from lactic and acetic acid bacteria or from wild yeasts and produces haze and off flavours.

cortical: pertaining to, associated with, consisting of or depending on the cerebral cortex.

cuneiform text: texts in Akkadian, Sumerian and other ancient languages, which were written with wedge-shaped signs (latin: *cuneus*, wedge).

dextrin sugars: intermediate-sized sugars composed of four or more glucose molecules joined together, either as a chain or with a branched arrangement. They are unable to be taken into brewing yeast cells and thus are not fermented.

di-methylsulphide: a cooked vegetable-smelling compound produced from compounds found in malt. This reaction typically occurs during malting or mashing and can result in some beers, particularly lagers, having an aroma of sweetcorrn, cabbage or onion.

emmer: emmer wheat (*Triticum dicoccum*) is a low-yielding, tetraploid wheat. The oldest findings of emmer wheat originate from the Near East about 8,000 BC.

endorphin: a morphine-type (opioid peptide) substance produced in the brain and released in emergency situations like pain and hunger; it causes euphoria.

endosperm: in flowering plants, the nutritive tissue which surrounds the embryo plant. Forms the nutrient reserve in cereal grains.

enzymes: specialised proteins produced by living organisms which accelerate biochemical reactions.

esters: biochemical molecules with solvent and fruity aromas. Different yeasts produce different profiles of esters and so have different effects on beers.

ethanol: the major alcohol produced by yeasts.

fermentation: a series of reactions conducted by certain microorganisms, particularly yeasts, which convert simple sugars, such as glucose, into ethanol and carbon dioxide in the absence of oxygen with the release of energy.

flavonoids: ketone-containing compounds produced by plants which act as antioxidants (important for the protection against cancer) and also have other health-improving effects; they are also called vitamin P or citrin.

flocculation: the association of yeast cells at the end of fermentation to form aggregates which settle leaving clear beer.

glucose: a simple, monosaccharide sugar composed of six carbon atoms with many hydroxyl groups. It is found in all cells and acts as an immediate source of energy when it is digested by cell enzymes in respiration or fermentation reactions.

grist: grist is grain that has been separated from its chaff in preparation for grinding. The mixture of grains prepared for mashing.

gustation, gustatory: relating to the faculty or act of tasting.

gyle: a batch of beer produced in one brewing.

homocysteine concentration: to regulate the plasma level of homocystein, an alpha-aminoacid, a sufficient supply of vitamin B6 and B12 as well as folic acid is important.

hops: flowering cones from the hop plant, *Humulus lupus*, containing lupulin glands with hop resins and hop oils.

humulone: an α-acid (see above).

hydrocarbons: organic compounds that contain only carbon and hydrogen.

keg beer: keg beer is often filtered and/or pasteurised before filling into straight-sided vessels which can be pressurised with gas for dispensing. Yeast is usually absent and the beer can be served soon after delivery.

lager: generally a light-coloured beer produced using specific lager malt, lager hops and lager yeast. Continental lagers are generally low in colour, low in bitterness, spicy in hop character and high in carbonation.

lipoprotein: a compound of proteins and lipids which transports water-insoluble lipids in the blood. Popularly known are the 'good' High Density Lipoproteins (HDL) and the 'bad' Low Density Lipoproteins (LDL).

maillard reaction: the production of brown mellanoidin pigments by the condensation of amine and reducing groups during the brewing process giving beer colour and flavour compounds.

malt: (noun) dried cereal grains which have been germinated for a short period to activate and synthesise enzymes which can then be used to digest starch during mashing.

maltose: a disaccharide sugar composed of two glucose molecules joined together.

maltotriose: a trisaccharide sugar composed of three glucose molecules joined together.

mash bed: an intricate layering of malt husks and particles developed during the running off of wort (see **wort** below) at the end of the **mashing** (see below). Undigested starch grains, precipitated proteins, silicates and other salts are retained by the mash bed leaving clear wort to be collected.

mash tun: a vessel designed to hold the mash. Generally strongly constructed, well insulated and with a means of distributing the malt evenly through the liquor.

mash: (noun) a fermentable, starchy mixture from which alcohol can be produced; the act of converting something starchy into such a pulpy mixture (see **mashing** below).

mashing: the initial step of brewing whereby malt is mixed with hot liquor between 60 and 70°C, and during which starch is digested into simpler sugars.

Maß: also spelled Mass (English 'measure') is a beer mug holding 1 litre of liquid. To say 'I drank four *Maß* at the Oktoberfest', means that the person consumed 4 litres of the extra strong beer brewed for this occasion.

mead: an alcoholic drink made with fermented honey and water.

Mediterranean Diet: a conceptual combination of certain foods supposedly common in the diets of people in southern European countries.

mild: (noun) a British beer with low hop content.

monosaccharide: a sugar such as fructose or glucose, sometimes called a 'simple sugar'.

must: (noun) the unfermented juice being fermented for wine.

nitro-keg beer: a **keg beer** (see above) which has been pressurised with nitrogen.

noradrenaline: similar in chemistry and action to adrenaline, both are also called catecholamine. They are neurotransmitters and hormones produced mainly in the adrenal gland, and they function to prepare the body for 'fight or flight' by raising the blood pressure and causing other physiological changes.

oxalate: a salt or ester of so-called acid oxalate.

palynological: related to the study of fossil spores and pollen.

polyphenols: a class of phenolic substances produced by plants; the **flavonoids** (see above) belong to this class.

polysaccharide: a long-chain carbohydrate made up of many **monosaccharides** (see above).

porter: a dark beer produced using a mixture of pale and roasted malts. Very popular in Europe in the 18th and 19th centuries.

proteins: macromolecules present in all organic cells, composed of linear chains of amino acids and providing structural and enzymatic functions.

psychosis: a term used in psychiatry to describe persons who have mental dysfunctions such as thinking disorders, changes in personality, delusional beliefs or hallucinations.

pub, public house: a place, generally in Britain or Ireland (or aiming to imitate these) or in Australasia, where alcoholic drinks can be bought. Food may also be served, and some have accommodation.

real ale: beer containing yeast that undergoes secondary fermentation and matures in the cask.

saddle quern: the lower stone of a tool or mill for hand grinding, roughly in the form of a saddle.

serotonin: a neurotransmitter and hormone present in many physiological systems of the body, like the bloodstream, the intestinal tract and the brain; in the latter, an excess of serotonin leads, among other things, to impulsiveness and aggression whereas its lack can be responsible for depression.

six o'clock swill: the New Zealand habit of drinking at pubs which closed at 6 P.M.

six-pack: a pack of six cans or six small bottles of beer.

small pack beers: beers packaged into cans or bottles.

sparge: the act of sprinkling to keep moist.

spot tests: simple chemical procedures which uniquely identify a substance.

starch: a macromolecular carbohydrate composed of many glucose molecules joined in a linear chain (amylose) or in a branched chain (amylopectin).

stout: a very dark and strong beer.

'strike' temperature: the temperature of initial liquor mixing with grain in the mash tun, Usually higher than the mash temperature in order to swell the starch grains.

tartrate: potassium bitartrate, also known as potassium hydrogen tartrate. It is a byproduct of winemaking.

top-fermenting beers: beers produced using a yeast which produces a strong yeast head during fermentation. These are generally ale and wheat beers.

toxin: an organic poisonous substance.

Wernicke-Korsakoff Syndrome: also called alcoholic encephalopathy, is a particular stage in malnourished chronic alcoholics who suffer a deficiency of thiamine/vitamin B1 (also called beriberi): its symptoms include amnesia, confabulations, hallucinations and coma; when untreated it leads to death.

wort, malt wort: water and malted barley are mixed in a process called mashing; the liquid derived from that is called wort, it contains sugars which are turned into alcohol during the process of fermentation.

xanthohumol: a prenylated chalcone from hops and beer.

yeast: microscopic fungi which commonly occur on fruits and in many other parts of the environment. Brewing yeast (usually *Saccharomyces cerevisiae*) is adapted to converting simple sugars to ethanol and carbon dioxide by fermentation.

INDEX

Spain, Spanish, Spaniard, 7, 56–57,
  72–77, 81, 83–86, 118–119, 198,
  201–202, 209, 211–216, 218–2119,
  226, 234
sparge, 40, 237
sprout, sprouted, sprouting, 4,
  147–148, 150, 152–153, 159–160,
  175
squirrel monkey, 17
starch, 3, 14, 37–40, 49–51, 55, 57, 60,
  72, 233–234, 236–237
stomach ulcer, 23
stout, 39–40, 90, 93, 213, 237
street, 81–84, 86–87, 93
structure, 22, 30, 57–58, 61, 65, 157,
  226
student, 6, 66, 106, 111–120, 216
stupor, 17, 87
sugar, sugary, 3–5, 8, 13–16, 37–40,
  43–44, 50, 55, 65, 72, 159, 192, 199,
  233–236, 238
Suidae, 13
supermarket, 8, 90, 96–98, 224
symbol, symbolic, symbolically,
  symbolise, symbolism, 1, 6,–8,
  72–74, 85, 93, 96, 107, 112, 128,
  140, 142, 144, 147–148, 151–152,
  155–157, 163, 172, 186, 193, 197,
  210, 215, 219, 223, 225
Syria, 3, 48

T

Tacitus, 55, 64, 66
Tall Bazi, 48–50
tambiko, 163–166
Tanzania, 6, 159, 161, 167
tap, tapped, 18, 53, 90, 104, 136, 200,
  234
tapuy, 198, 199
tartrate, 49, 237

taste, taster, tasting, tasty, 2–6, 9,
  14–16, 39, 53, 55, 61–62, 71, 76,
  81–82, 85–86, 90, 106, 126, 129,
  131, 136, 142, 150–151, 153, 156,
  173, 175–177, 179–180, 216–219,
  226, 229–230, 234–235
tea, 22, 24, 35, 65, 166, 183, 190–192,
  213
technique, 3, 4, 61, 66–68, 134, 153,
  171, 219, 234
technology, technological,
  technologically, 1–2, 5–6, 14, 18,
  22, 47, 50–51, 53, 67–68, 126, 131,
  171, 200, 210, 215–217, 225
teetotaller, 26, 28
temperature, 2, 38–40, 43, 49, 52,
  60–61, 64, 75, 81, 104, 130, 175, 237
thirty years war, 65
toxic, toxicity, toxin, 9, 13, 16, 18, 28,
  30, 238
tradition, traditional, 1–9, 28, 43–45,
  55, 57, 63–66, 68, 74, 76, 77, 85,
  89–91, 93–98, 101, 104, 105–106,
  108, 111–114, 119–120, 136, 138,
  142, 145, 155, 161, 165–167, 171,
  197–198, 200, 213, 215–216, 220,
  226, 228, 230, 231, 233
transnationalisation, 86
triglyceride, 26
tuba, 199, 200
Tupaia glis, 14

U

ulanzi, 159
ulcer, 23, 30
United Nations, 101, 107

V

vessel, 3, 10, 39, 41, 43–44, 47–49, 51,
  53, 57–58, 61, 136, 167, 236
Viking, 64
virility, 120, 156, 201